HUMAN NATURE IN GREGORY OF NYSSA

SUPPLEMENTS TO

VIGILIAE CHRISTIANAE

Formerly Philosophia Patrum

TEXTS AND STUDIES OF EARLY CHRISTIAN LIFE
AND LANGUAGE

EDITORS

J. DEN BOEFT — R. VAN DEN BROEK — W.L. PETERSEN
D.T. RUNIA — J.C.M. VAN WINDEN

VOLUME XLVI

HUMAN NATURE IN GREGORY OF NYSSA

Philosophical Background and Theological Significance

BY

JOHANNES ZACHHUBER

BRILL

LEIDEN · BOSTON · KÖLN

2000

This book is printed on acid-free paper.

Library of Congress Cataloging-in-Publication Data

Zachhuber, Johannes.
   Human nature in Gregory of Nyssa : philosophical background and theological
significance / by Johannes Zachhuber.
   p. cm. — (Supplements to Vigiliae Christianae, ISSN 0920-623X ; v. 46)
Revision of the author's thesis (doctoral)—University of Oxford in Michaelmas, 1997
Includes bibliographical references (p.) and index.
ISBN 9004115307
   1. Gregory, of Nyssa, Saint ca. 335-ca. 394—Contributions in Christian doctrine of
man.   2. Man (Christian theology)—History of doctrines—Early church, ca. 30-600.
I. Title.   II. Series.

BT7001.2.727   1999
233'.5'092—dc21
                                                                99–049289
                                                                CIP

Die Deutsche Bibliothek – CIP-Einheitsaufnahme

Zachhuber, Johannes:
Human nature in Gregory of Nyssa : philosophical background
and theological significance / by Johannes Zachhuber. - Leiden ; Boston ;
Köln : Brill, 1999
   (Supplements to Vigiliae Christianae ; Vol. 46)
   ISBN 90–04–11530–7
[Vigiliae Christianae / Supplements]
   Supplements to Vigiliae Christianae : formerly Philosophia Patrum ;
texts and studies of early Christian life and language. – Leiden ; Boston ;
Köln : Brill.
   Früher Schriftenreihe
   ISSN 0920-623X
   Vol. 46. Zachhuber, Johannes: Human nature in Gregory of Nyssa. –
   1999

ISSN   0920-623X
ISBN   90 04 11530 7

PRINTED IN THE NETHERLANDS

To Patricia

CONTENTS

ACKNOWLEDGEMENTS

The present study is the revised version of a doctoral thesis that was submitted to the University of Oxford in Michaelmas 1997.

Mark Atherton, John Jackson, and Uwe Lang read parts of this study at various stages and offered their criticism on questions of contents and style. As for the latter, many more could be named to whom the present author owes thanks for introducing the non-native speaker to the intricacies of the English language. Jane Anson's contribution towards the perfection of the final manuscript has been of particularly great value. Without her, the book would look very different. It goes without saying that any remaining mistakes are entirely the author's own responsibility.

Regent's Park College provided the combination of academic stimulus and personal support which a college is ideally thought to offer. I wish to mention, in particular, Dr Larry Kreitzer, who was helpful in more than one way.

It goes beyond words to describe the debt this book and its author owe to Dr Mark Edwards and Professor Michael Frede. They accompanied the work and its progress on all its stages and proved inexhaustible sources of critical support and inspiration.

Similarly difficult is the expression of the gratitude which I feel towards my parents. They have rendered me help which it is impossible to calculate, during my time of study and beyond. At the present moment I am particularly aware of how much I owe to their life-long support.

Franziska, Jonathan, Juliane, Immanuel, and Nicholas are to be thanked for the patience with which they have endured the absence of their father on too many occasions. Of all people, they have probably felt most consistently the adverse effects of a project like this.

Finally I wish to thank the one person who has, in a unique way, enriched my life. To her this book is dedicated.

Johannes Zachhuber
Berlin, June 1999

ABBREVIATIONS

Abbreviations of Journal and serial titles normally agree with: S.M. Schwertner (ed.), *International glossary of abbreviations for theology and related subjects*, Berlin/New York ²1992 = *Theologische Realenzyklopädie. Abkürzungsverzeichnis*, Berlin/New York ²1994 (for exceptions see below). Abbreviations used in this book for works by ancient authors are contained in the first part of the bibliography. References to works by modern authors are identifiable in the text by the year of their publication which is, in every case, given alongside the author's name. The full entry appears from the bibliography.

GCS, n.F. *Die griechischen christlichen Schriftsteller der ersten Jahrhunderte. Neue Folge*, Berlin 1995ff.
ET English text
GNO *Gregorii Nysseni Opera*, edd. W. Jaeger et alii, Leiden 1952ff.
JTS *Journal of Theological Studies. New Series*, Oxford 1950ff.
LSJ Liddell, H.G./Scott R., *A Greek-English Lexicon. New edition by H.St. Jones and R. McKenzie*, Oxford 1968
PG *Patrologiae Cursus Completus*, accurante J.-P. Migne, *Series Graeca*, Paris 1857ff.
PGL Lampe, G.W.H., *A Patristic Greek Lexicon*, Oxford 1968
PL *Patrologiae Cursus Completus*, accurante J.-P. Migne, *Series Latina*, Paris 1841ff.
RE *Pauly's Real-Encyklopädie der classischen Alterthumswissenschaft*, ed. Wissowa, Stuttgart 1894ff.

INTRODUCTION

1. *Scope and purpose of the study*

A reader who takes even a cursory glance at the writings of Gregory of Nyssa will probably be struck by the astonishing frequency and regularity of the author's use of *phusis*-terminology. What is more, this terminological predilection, if we may call it this, seems equally present in practically all his extant works and throughout the whole range of theological topics covered. The term 'human nature' alone is used several hundred times, and this figure could be substantially increased if we included such expressions as 'corporeal nature', 'intelligible nature', 'divine nature', and others. It would thus appear self evident that a study is needed of Gregory's use of this terminology, elucidating its meaning and import for his thought. Of this task the present investigation seeks to fulfil one part by exploring the understanding of 'human nature' in Gregory's thought.

What, then, is 'human nature'? A first answer to this question may be found by observing that 'human nature' is often equated by Gregory with 'man' (ἄνθρωπος). This is what he expressly asserts several times,[1] and implicitly this assumption would appear to underlie many more passages employing this phrase. Incidentally, this equivalence seems to hold in modern usage also: 'human nature is frail' could be replaced by 'man is frail' for, I suppose, all practical purposes.

Yet this answer at once generates two further questions: what does Gregory mean by 'man' and, secondly, why does he say 'human nature' instead? To begin with the first question, it would appear that it could be pursued in at least two different directions: one could ask what 'man' is in so far as he is different from other beings, say God or animals, in other words, in so far as he is *human* nature. One would then have to treat of Gregory's anthropology. This is undoubtedly a crucial part of Nyssen's thought. It has, however, found much attention in recent decades[2] and, although many points have, in my view, as yet not been ultimately clarified, it is not the

---

[1] E.g. at *op hom* 16 (PG 44, 185B); cf. *Abl* (GNO III/1, 40,5–9).
[2] E.g. Balthasar (1995), Schoemann (1943), Armstrong (1948), Otis (1958), Ladner (1958), Oesterle (1985), Williams (1993).

intent of the present investigation to pursue this question in detail.

The alternative, then, would be to explore Nyssen's view of man in so far as he is human *nature*. This latter emphasis would, at the same time, appear to touch on my second question, namely why Gregory frequently says 'human nature' rather than 'man' if both phrases are practically equivalent. It would seem that such usage could be indicative of a view envisaging some entity, the 'nature', which is especially responsible for the fact that something is a human being; the term 'man' again would be employed to indicate this entity. This, however, inevitably raises the issue of universal nature: can human nature explain not only why some *individual* can be referred to as 'man', but also why *many* individuals can be given this designation? Is perhaps the fact that there is *one* human nature the reason for the universality of the term? And if so, how is this one item related to the many individuals?

This, then, is the problem which this study is primarily meant to address: is there evidence that Gregory is using *phusis*-terminology aimed at a theory of universal nature? And, if so, what kind of theory is this, and what kind of thing does he believe human nature to be?

The foremost question to be clarified in this connection seems to be whether Gregory's use of *phusis*-terminology in general, and that of 'human nature' in particular, is more than a terminological preference: if *we* hear a person say: 'human nature is frail,' we probably would not normally infer that this person is thereby committing themselves to the assumption that 'nature' stands for anything other than what human beings are. It seems, however, clear that with Gregory this is different: while there are occurrences of *phusis*-terminology that might be understood to be non-committal on the ontological status of 'nature', there are many passages where Gregory's interest in a concept of human *nature* is evident. Indeed, in some passages Gregory's attempt to employ *universal* human nature is, in my view, so obvious as to dispose of any need to argue in principle for the presence of this notion in his thought. This is primarily the case in the context of trinitarian theology, where he draws the well-known (and to some notorious) analogy of three men sharing in human nature to press home the oneness of divine substance or nature (as will be seen both terms can be used equivalently).[3]

---

[3] *Abl* (GNO III/1, 40,5–42,3); *graec* (GNO III/1, 21,2–10).

Yet Gregory's use of such an argument in itself is as yet, I think, no evidence that he aimed at a theory of universal nature. The latter could only be shown by pointing out some effort on his part towards establishing, and some degree of consistency in using, what essentially is a philosophical theory. Otherwise one would have to conclude, and some scholars have reached this very conclusion, that Gregory in those passages is only toying with certain philosophical notions without any serious commitment to them.

It may prove useful to address at this point what appears to be a rather major methodological obstacle presenting itself to the object of the present study. It seems clear that asking for a theory of universal human nature in Gregory means effectively asking for a view which is philosophical in substance. Yet Gregory is not a philosopher. He is often referred to as one of the more philosophically minded among the church fathers,[4] yet unlike, say, Augustine, he never ventured upon a philosophical elaboration except in connection with a theological problem he had to elucidate. Thus, all the crucial passages dealing with human nature are embedded in, and conditioned by, theological discussions which, in Gregory's view, called for a philosophical backup. How, then, should an analysis of such a philosophical concept proceed?

One way would have been to collect all relevant passages, to rearrange them according to the views expressed in them about human nature, and to discuss them in this order. This might have produced a reliable and systematic picture of Gregory's understanding of universal human nature,—provided that he ever held such a systematic view. The latter being a point under investigation in the present study rather than one of its presuppositions, however, there would have been no little danger of reading a systematic answer into Gregory's works instead of finding it there. In general it would appear that, since it is at least possible that Gregory's understanding of human nature in a given text is partially due to the argumentative need in the particular context, it would be unwise to approach the relevant passages other than within their literary and theological context.

There is a further—as it were complementary—problem attached to the systematic approach: as Gregory employs human nature only within certain theological arguments, it regularly appears that this context has to be taken into account in order to ascertain the precise meaning of *phusis*-terminology by means of its argumentative function.

---

[4] Cf., e.g., Dörrie (1983), 884.

For those two reasons, then, it appeared preferable to discard that approach and to choose instead as a principle of systematisation an exposition of the relevant passages within their theological context. Such an approach, to be sure, apparently multiplies the task for, in addition to the elucidation of meaning and relevance of *phusis*-terminology or, strictly speaking, as part of that elucidation, a variety of theological problems also needs to be given consideration. There is, however, no practical alternative to this procedure, and ultimately the results may well justify the effort, as a better understanding of Gregory's use of *phusis*-terminology could also improve our grasp of those theological issues which Gregory illustrates with its help.

This principal decision on methodology, then, conditions the structure of the study: for a number of reasons I decided to start from an elucidation of Gregory's use of universal human nature in trinitarian theology. What was originally meant to be just one chapter grew in the course of my work into the first main part, as it proved necessary to set Gregory's approach in the framework of the Cappadocian solution to the trinitarian controversy. I hope that the insights provided by this elaboration for the entirety of the subject justify its bulk. The second part will then consider whether a systematic use of universal human nature can be proven in Gregory's treatment of the divine economy, that is in the creation, Fall, salvation, and restoration of humankind. In all these cases the conceptual use by Gregory of human nature has been controversial in previous research, which has necessitated a cautious approach.

Answers to the central questions underlying this study will develop in the course of those investigations, and there is no need to anticipate them here. It may, however, be useful to include in this introduction a discussion of a number of more general and controversial points whose decision may be seen to underlie my argument on specific issues later in the book.

2. *Universal human nature in previous research*

Gregory's apparent use of universal human nature has, of course, attracted scholarly attention previous to the present study. Frequently, scholars discussed the relevance of human nature in the context of specific doctrinal fields with which they were engaged. Those discussions, I think, are more properly dealt with in connection with the appropriate doctrinal problem to which they are attached.

In the 1970s, however, two attempts were made, by Balás and Hübner, to approach a more comprehensive treatment of universal human nature in Gregory's thought. Of Balás' research on the topic only a couple of articles have appeared to date.[5] The most recent, published in 1979, contains what appears to be an outline of his project which, in spite of its fragmentary character, may serve as a good starting point for this survey.[6]

Balás finds two views of universal human nature in Gregory's writings which, he thinks, are different, but not mutually exclusive: on the one hand, Gregory uses the idea of nature as a monadic entity that is found equally in all members of the same class (117–9), on the other hand he equates human nature with the totality of human individuals, the *pleroma* of humankind, as Gregory often says (119–21). Previous scholars, Balás observes, have tended either to identify those two views or to regard them as altogether different conceptions, neither of which is, in his view, justified. Rather, he argues, the two are related as, in logical terminology, intension and extension (122–3). Thus, he concludes, while this difference has to be observed, there is no reason to accuse Gregory of inconsistency.

Balás emphatically affirms the theological relevance of universal human nature in Gregory's thought (123). In his view, Gregory employs this concept successfully in a variety of theological subjects and is, among other things, able to use it for theories of universal sin and universal redemption (124–6).

Balás' conclusions on this latter point reaffirm in principle an interpretation of Gregory's theology which had been sharply rejected only a few years earlier by Hübner.[7] In a study on Gregory's understanding of the Body of Christ, Hübner had followed the history of this very interpretation which holds universal human nature to be a central element in Gregory's theology. He argued that it had been originally devised, in the context of soteriology, by liberal German Lutherans, who accused Gregory of maintaining, on the philosophical basis of 'Platonic realism', a 'physical doctrine of salvation' (3–9). Their faulty exegesis of a selection of Gregory's texts together with their interpretation of the philosophical background would then have passed on to a variety of scholars who, without sharing their theological

---

[5] Balás (1969), (1976), (1979).
[6] In the following, page numbers in the text refer to Balás (1979).
[7] Hübner (1974), esp. 2–3, 10–7, 93–4. In the following, page numbers in the text refer to this study.

presuppositions, found the idea of universal human nature as a principle underlying Gregory's theology attractive. Thus, a number of
influential Roman Catholic theologians would argue on its basis for
the inherently social character of Christianity and the Church (17–25),
while others simply relished the idea of universal humanity as a systematic, 'Platonic' core in Gregory's thought.

Hübner's chief aim being to disown the liberal interpretation of
Gregory's soteriology, he decided that, in order to achieve this, he
had to challenge the underlying, 'Platonic' view of universal human
nature allegedly held by Gregory. This, for him, ultimately meant
questioning Gregory's supposed 'Platonism': thus Hübner's result is,
broadly speaking, that there is virtually no evidence for a developed
concept of universal human nature along Platonic lines in Gregory's
writings. There may be cases where Gregory employs universal nature
in theological arguments, but they are to be understood as *ad hoc*
illustrations bearing a rather metaphorical character. This is, in his
view, confirmed by an analysis of their philosophical background,
which reveals borrowings from various, especially Stoic, sources for
practical purposes rather than a conscious adoption of a Platonic
ontological framework.

If Balás and Hübner may thus appear to represent opposite extremes
of the scholarly spectrum, it is interesting also to note where they
are united against previous scholarship. This is first of all the case
with regard to the relevance of Gregory's Platonism for his understanding of universal human nature. While Hübner seems to be openly, and
to a considerable extent, hostile to any notion of Platonism in Gregory's thought, Balás also is reluctant to ascribe too much to this as,
in fact, to any philosophical influence. The latter rather emphasises
biblical and theological precedents of Gregory's views, and otherwise
points to the Aristotelian commentaries as possible sources.[8] Both
studies thus concur, in my view, in indicating the need to be much
more precise in the discernment of philosophical (and non-philosophical) influence behind the thought of the Fathers. Traditionally,
the term 'Platonism' was thought to explain practically everything
which in patristic writings seemed to be alien to the spirit of Scripture.
At the same time, however, it seems to me that Hübner's sweeping
criticism of Gregory's 'Platonism' still betrays the influence of this
very tradition by being equally indiscriminate: the surprised reader

---

[8] Balás (1979), 128–9.

notes how, on a few pages, nearly every scholar who, during the past one hundred years, dared to ascribe to Gregory any sort of Platonic influence receives his share of criticism including, for example, the sober and rather philologically-minded Cherniss.[9]

A further concurrence between the two studies may be seen in the fact that both seem to call for a comprehensive treatment of human nature in Gregory. Hübner, whose primary focus is Gregory's soteriology, nevertheless includes a treatment of Nyssen's use of human nature in his account of creation and in trinitarian theology.[10] Balás, on the other hand, notes that previous studies failed to reach satisfactory results because they limited their scope of investigation to just one doctrinal field.[11] The envisaged results, to be sure, are opposed to each other: Hübner believes he has shown that there is no common core in Gregory's use of human nature in those fields, whereas Balás expresses his conviction that a comprehensive study would yield more positive results.

The present study, then, will attempt to answer the controversial questions by following those lines that were seen to emerge equally from Hübner's and Balás' studies. In other words, it will attempt a comprehensive treatment of human nature in Gregory's thought, whilst also giving much more detailed consideration than has hitherto been given to possible or likely philosophical and non-philosophical sources of Gregory's views.

3. *The problem of Gregory's development*

A methodological problem could be thought to arise from the fact that the passages relevant to the present investigation are to be collected from the entirety of Gregory's writings. Should the study, then, take into account their dates and a possible development of Gregory's thought? In principle, of course, this question has to be answered in the affirmative: where Gregory's views appear to vary considerably between one writing and another while being consistent in each of them, the possibility of a development has to be contemplated. At the same time, however, it would appear that a development of

---

[9] Hübner (1974), 17.
[10] Hübner (1974), 67–94; id. (1971) and (1972) were originally part of his thesis: id. (1974), xi.
[11] Balás (1979), 116.

Gregory's understanding of universal human nature as such is rather unlikely, as there is no evidence that he ever attempted a systematic exposition of this philosophical question. While it is, then, possible or even probable that his views on it vary, the assumption of their 'development' in the strict sense seems difficult to maintain without the evidence of such an attempt. Those variations, however, would most naturally appear to derive from different requirements of the respective argumentative context. Yet, as the context of those passages is regularly one of the doctrinal topics enumerated above, an approach based on the use of human nature for Gregory's doctrinal arguments would again appear the most sensible procedure.

The problem of a development, of course, returns with regard to those topics. Scholars have repeatedly urged that Gregory's theological thinking should be seen as developing,[12] but as yet no comprehensive study on this question is available. The problem is marred by the fact that, while a development should be established on the basis of an accepted chronology, the very chronology of Gregory's works is in many cases uncertain and scholarly assumptions about their dates are often based on a presumed development in his thought, which makes such endeavours sometimes suspiciously unclear.[13]

A detailed investigation into this problem being clearly beyond the scope of this study, I have found, in so far as its subject is concerned, no need, except in one case,[14] to refer to a development in Gregory's thought. Nevertheless I shall, wherever Gregory's views on one and the same doctrinal topic are taken from various writings, include a chronological note elucidating the issue as far as seems possible and necessary. Where his views differ it will be considered whether this must indicate a development or whether the coexistence of several strands in his mind can be maintained.

4. *Gregory's knowledge of philosophical sources*

As this study explores Gregory's use of a philosophical theme it may seem desirable also to say a few words at the outset about the controversial issue of Gregory's readings in pagan, in particular philo-

---

[12] Cf. Daniélou (1966); Mosshammer (1988); Meredith (1995), 56–9; Kees (1995), 199.
[13] Cf. Daniélou (1955), 372 with id. (1963), 160–2 and Balás (1985), 176,53–6.
[14] See pp. 204ff. below.

sophical, literature. I cannot say that I have done much independent research on this particular topic, and thus the following is rather a summary of what previous scholarship has achieved together with some more general considerations which are my own.

It seems almost generally accepted that Gregory can be regarded as one of the more philosophically minded church fathers.[15] It is well known that he devoted a considerable part of his life to the pursuit of the arts, and apparently it was only Basil's rigid intervention, making him Bishop of Nyssa, which eventually determined that the remainder of his life would become inextricably intertwined with the fate of the Nicene church and its theology.[16]

At the same time Gregory was not an archivist who, in the footsteps of Clement and Eusebius, would collect and quote philosophical lore to claim its better parts for the Christian heritage or, in the apologetic tradition, resuscitate the controversies of the philosophical schools to beat pagans with their own weapons. Gregory's use of philosophical writings is of a more subtle kind which makes it difficult, and in many cases perhaps impossible, to determine which of them he read, or is alluding to in any particular passage.[17]

There are two ways which can, and in my view ought to, be followed to ascertain Gregory's philosophical readings. The first of them is, of course, the search for verbal parallels and echoes, which his sources may have left in his works. This search has been pursued in various directions, establishing with certainty Gregory's knowledge of a number of Plato's dialogues[18] and Plotinus' *Enneads*.[19] More difficult, in my view, is the frequent claim that Gregory would have known Stoic writings.[20] These had become very rare by the end of the fourth century, and it is not likely that Gregory of all people would have had access to books which otherwise seem to have all but vanished. This is, of course, not meant to challenge the observation that in some texts Gregory is using what were originally Stoic arguments. Yet, he could have found those arguments in writers

---

[15] *Pace*: Stead (1976), 107.

[16] Cf. esp. Nazianzen's frequently cited *ep* 11 (13,13–14,24 Gallay) scolding Gregory for his perseverance in wordly affairs. For Gregory's early biography cf. Aubineau (1966), 29–82.

[17] Dörrie (1983), 884–5.

[18] Cf. mainly Cherniss (1930).

[19] Cf. Aubineau (1966), Meredith (1991) and Rist (1981), 216–8.

[20] E.g. Gronau (1914), 119; Hübner (1974), 146–55. Jaeger (1914, 68) had been more careful.

who, like Philo or Galen,[21] were influenced by Stoic thought without
belonging to that school or, indeed, in Neoplatonists who, like Plotinus,
felt free to use Stoic material without committing themselves to Stoic
doctrines.[22] The difference with regard to Gregory might seem minute
but, as the 'stoicism' of those Neoplatonists is now seen less as eclec-
ticism and more as an integration of that material by means of its
reinterpretation, Gregory's use of it may equally appear in a different
light if it could be shown that his use of Stoic arguments mirrors
their Neoplatonic interpretation rather than the original concerns of
the Stoics themselves.

Be this as it may, it seems to me that the search for verbal and
other parallels between Gregory's writings and philosophical literature
should, quite generally, be accompanied by a subsidiary consideration
about the likelihood of his knowing one or the other writing. This
can, as in the Stoics' case, lead to the conclusion that in spite of
parallels a direct knowledge is rather unlikely; it can also, however,
lead to the opposite conclusion, namely that despite the want of literary traces in Gregory's writings, his knowledge of a particular work
is quite likely.

This, I should suggest, is the case with writings which at that time
would be seen to form the basic knowledge of any educated person.
For philosophical texts this elementary reading can be established
on the basis of our information about the standard curriculum: this
would start with the study of Porphyry's *Isagoge* and continue with
Aristotle's *Organon* accompanied by the respective commentaries.[23]
For the extent to which these books were considered to be universally known we have a telling example in a remark by Jerome, who
comments on the fact that a certain person had criticised his treatise *Against Jovinian* as follows:

> You inform me that this home-grown dialectician (. . .) has read nei-
> ther the *Categories* of Aristotle nor his *On Interpretation* nor his *Analytics*
> nor the *Topics* of Cicero. (. . .) How foolish I have been to suppose
> that without philosophy there can be no knowledge of these subjects.
> (. . .) In vain have I perused the commentaries of Alexander; to no

---

[21] About Gregory's knowledge of Philo cf. Daniélou (1967); id. (1953, 247) asserts
Nyssen's acquaintance with Galen.
[22] Cf. Porphyry, *vit Plot* 14,4–6 and Rist (1967, 173–7) for Plotinus' use of Stoic
material.
[23] Lloyd (1990), 4–6.

purpose has a skilled teacher used the *Isagoge* of Porphyry to instruct me in logic . . .[24]

It is true that Jerome at times boasts of readings which in fact he did not have,[25] yet in the present case all the details suggest that he is referring here to an actual experience.[26] He must therefore be writing about his own elementary, philosophical training, which would thus appear to have coincided with what we know from the Neoplatonic curriculum. I should thus suggest that, in a similar way, Gregory's knowledge of these books ought to be taken for granted. There is, of course, no certainty as to whether Gregory, like Jerome, read Alexander's commentaries, or rather those by Porphyry[27] or Iamblichus[28] or, perhaps, all of them.

One might object that, since in Gregory's case the precise amount of his formal education is uncertain, such inferences should be drawn only with caution. However, that it is *uncertain* does not mean that it is non-existent. It seems to me that scholarship has frequently overstated the case by all but asserting that Gregory had no external tuition whatever and was educated largely at home.[29] This view is, as far as I see, entirely based on the following passage from one of Gregory's letters to Libanius:

> As far as your (sc. the Greek) wisdom is concerned, of which those who are able to judge say that it streams from you as from a source so that all, who to any degree partake of reason, receive a share of it—for this is what I heard the admirable Basil, your pupil and my teacher, say to everybody—you may know that I have nothing excellent to tell about my teachers: I was together with my brother only for a short time and was polished by his divine tongue only to such an extent that I could discern the ignorance of those uninitiated into rhetorics.[30]

---

[24] Jerome, *ep* 50,1,2–3 (388,13–389,6 Hilberg), ET: Fremantle (1893), 80.

[25] Kelly (1975), 16.

[26] Kelly (1975), 16,39. Kelly argues convincingly that this must have taken place at Antioch, not Rome, if only because Jerome's Greek would not have allowed him such reading prior to his lengthy stay in the East.

[27] Cf. Courcelle (1967). Dörrie's claim that Gregory of all philosophers did *not* use Porphyry (1983, 887–8) seems to me to be without foundation.

[28] Cf. Heine (1995, 29–49) for parallels between Gregory's and Iamblichus' exegesis.

[29] Aubineau (1966), 44–5.

[30] *Ep* 13,4 (GNO VIII/2, 45,19–28).

While this text seems to state that Gregory enjoyed little training, it ought to be seen in its context: Libanius had apparently complimented Gregory on his style, and Gregory now seeks to return this compliment. He might have felt that the most appropriate way to do this would be if, as Libanius' pupil, he could say that whatever he is, he is through his teacher. Yet he cannot say this since Libanius was not his teacher. Thus Gregory devises the somewhat twisted argument that he got it all from Libanius via Basil, which is a somewhat awkward, but for Gregory very typical, way of returning a compliment:

> If, then, on the one side we never had a teacher, which I deem to have been our case, and if on the other it is improper to suppose that the opinion which you entertain of us is other than the true one— nay, you are correct in your statement, and we are not quite contemptible in our judgment,—give me leave to presume to attribute to you the cause of such proficiency as we may have attained. For if Basil was the author of our oratory, and if his wealth came from your treasures, then what we possess is yours, even though we received it through others.[31]

Once this rhetorical purpose has been recognised, it seems evident that Gregory's statement should not be pressed as saying that Basil was his only teacher, let alone that he was something of an autodidact. Thus we are left with the aforesaid uncertainty about Gregory's education. Yet this is largely a biographical uncertainty: it would appear from his writings that Gregory's education was certainly above average. Whether Basil or any other Neocaesarean rhetorician was tutoring him at a specific time is, I think, ultimately of secondary importance for this question. I would, however, contend that a person, who is proven to have read Plato and even Plotinus, should be credited with the knowledge of what would be regarded as standard introductions into philosophy. In the following, therefore, I shall assume that Gregory was in principle acquainted with those writings.

Otherwise, I shall freely adduce parallels from late ancient philosophers without committing myself to the assumption that Gregory must have read any particular book. Quite generally, I believe that he may have read more than is sometimes thought, but much further research would be required before a more thorough assessment of this question can be ventured upon.

---

[31] *Ep* 13,5–6 (GNO VIII/2, 46,3–10), ET: Moore/Wilson (1893), 533.

5. *Human nature and related expression—a note on terminology*

As I have said, the primary task of this study is the investigation of Gregory's use of *phusis*-terminology. Consequently, it would appear that its chief purpose is to focus on passages which contain phrases like ἡ ἀνθρωπίνη φύσις, ἡ φύσις τῶν ἀνθρώπων, ἡ ἡμετέρα φύσις and so forth. There are, however, a number of expressions which, it appears, are often or always used as equivalents by Gregory. Among these expressions are the following: τὸ ἀνθρώπινον ('the human item'), ἡ ἀνθρωπότης ('humankind'), ὁ ἄνθρωπος ('man'). Texts containing those cannot, therefore, be excluded from the present investigation. Of course, it will have to be considered in each single case whether and to what extent the equivalence holds and what understanding of human nature the use of those parallel phrases suggests.

The same applies for *ousia*-terminology, which is used chiefly in the trinitarian context. It seems clear that the Nicene dogma conditioned the use of the word οὐσία, since the struggle for the acceptance of its key-phrase, ὁμοούσιος, was ultimately a struggle for the appropriate interpretation of *ousia*-terminology in trinitarian theology. It seems equally obvious that Gregory's (and, of course, not only his) analogy between universal human nature and the Trinitarian Godhead was drawn to precisely that end, and it is thus not surprising that in many passages in that context Gregory employs *ousia* and *phusis* interchangeably. I shall therefore feel entitled to approach Gregory's use of human nature in the trinitarian context on the background of the controversy about the *homoousion*.

PART ONE

HUMAN NATURE IN TRINITARIAN DOCTRINE

INTRODUCTION

Not only in Gregory's, but in all the Cappadocians' writings universal human nature is employed as an analogy for the Trinity. The idea is that the way 'man' is one and many at the same time provides an analogy for the intratrinitarian relations. As Basil once puts it:

> For each of us partakes of being (εἶναι) through the common formula of being (τῆς οὐσίας λόγῳ), but he is one or the other through the properties (ἰδιώμασιν) attached to him. So also there (sc. in the Godhead) the formula of being is the same, like goodness, divinity and what else one may conceive of: but the *hupostasis* is seen in the properties of fatherhood or sonship or the sanctifying power.[1]

At face value, what we have here is a conceptual and terminological means to distinguish between identity and differentiation within the Godhead. And indeed, the context of this quotation is one of Basil's attempts to explain his celebrated differentiation of *ousia* and *hupostasis*. At the same time, however, in so far as the underlying concept of *ousia* is concerned, the use of this analogy seems to condition a specific understanding of the Nicene Creed, in particular of its key phrase, ὁμοούσιος, the one word which was at the heart of the controversy about its acceptance or rejection: in so far as they share the same formula of being (λόγος τῆς οὐσίας) men are *homoousioi*.[2] This interpretation of Nicaea, it appears, is novel with the Cappadocians, and it will be necessary to determine how precisely they conceived of human and divine *ousia* so that they could draw this analogy. As it is, however, clear that their working out of a trinitarian theology did not happen in a vacuum but was part of attempts to solve theological controversies of more than half a century, any analysis of their concepts has to take into account this historical background.

It has often been thought that the most conspicuous feature of the Cappadocian approach, as expressed by Basil in the above passage, is its lack of the notion of unity in the Trinity or, at least, the utter weakness of this unity: three men *are*, after all, three and not

---

[1] Basil, *ep* 214,4,9–15 (vol. III, 205 Courtonne).
[2] So expressly (Basil), *ep* 38,2,25–6 (vol. I, 82 Courtonne).

one! We have to distinguish here between two questions: it is one thing
to ask whether *we* finally decide that this analogy cannot sufficiently
account for divine unity, it is quite another matter whether this would
have seemed the same for the Cappadocians themselves and for their
contemporaries. Only the latter question is relevant if a genetic
account of their teaching is to be given. Now, this latter question
has regularly been answered in the affirmative too, and this answer
has then been used for an explanation of the background and character of the Cappadocians' adherence to the Nicene *homoousion*. This
explanation assumes that by means of the human analogy with its
weak notion of unity the Cappadocians achieved a *rapprochement*
between the majority of Eastern bishops, who could not accept the
original doctrine of Nicaea for fear of 'Sabellianism' (i.e. neglect of
the separate existence of the Persons), and the Creed of Nicaea into
which the word *homoousios* had indeed been inserted to lay particular
stress upon the unity of the Godhead.

It is the chief intention of the first chapter of the present part of
this study to demonstrate that this theory cannot be upheld. As a
matter of fact, a great part of its presuppositions has already been
shaken by recent research so that it may be sufficient to refer sum-
marily to the results of those studies. This is particularly the case
with the interpretation of the Nicene Creed underlying that view. It
will, furthermore, be shown that criticism of the Nicene Creed in
the 350s and 60s was directed not so much against the notion of
identity allegedly conveyed by the word *homoousios* as against the
notion of co-ordination which the *homoousion* was said to imply. It
will, then, appear that Athanasius' and Apollinarius' 'derivative' understanding of the term was naturally apt to reconcile the more moderate opponents of Nicaea. In contrast to this, it will finally emerge,
the Cappadocian teaching does not appear conciliatory at all as their
basic interest will be shown to be the complete co-ordination of the
divine Persons; their phrasing regularly alludes to Aristotle's *Categories*
(cf. the 'formula of being' in the above quotation) with its well-known
tenet that there is not a more or a less in a substance (*cat* 5 [3^b33–4^a9]).
The second chapter will therefore have to venture upon a new explanation of their doctrine based on a thorough examination of their
actual utterances.

A word perhaps needs to be said about terminology. I shall frequently use expressions like 'Cappadocian theology'. Now, it has
sometimes been argued that there is no such thing as a 'Cappadocian

theology'.[3] I certainly do not wish to return to the traditional view that made no distinctions between the three theologians who are normally subsumed under this designation. Nevertheless, as for their trinitarian teaching I should contend that the broad consensus which traditional scholarship has detected in them is warranted by their respective statements on that subject.[4] The main focus is, of course, on the special contribution made by Gregory of Nyssa. As it is, however, vital for my argument to approach the Cappadocian solution as developing in the framework of the trinitarian controversy of the latter half of the fourth century, I shall consider the decisive statements indicating this development (largely from Basil's pen) as expressing a common 'Cappadocian' doctrine unless there are grounds for believing the opposite. That this is not an arbitrary decision will, I hope, emerge from the argument in the second chapter, in particular from its analysis of Gregory's position in the *Contra Eunomium*.

---

[3] Cf. for this view Holl (1904) whose argument has dominated much of German scholarship on this issue since. Hübner, esp. (1972), 464 and now Drecoll (1996), 326 expressly acknowledge this debt.

[4] For Basil and Gregory of Nyssa, see pp. 56ff.; for Nazianzen, cf. his *or* 29,13,14–22 (204 Gallay/Jourjon); *or* 40,41–3 (292–300 Moreschini/Gallay).

CHAPTER ONE

HOMOOUSIOS AND THE ANALOGY OF HUMAN NATURE IN THE 350S AND EARLY 360S

1.1   *A controversial starting point and its presuppositions*

While I shall start this chapter from some more general considerations about the trinitarian controversy in the latter half of the fourth century, it will not be, nor can it, my aim to provide an overview here of such a large and much researched period of doctrinal history.[1] I shall rather confine myself to the problem of how the Nicene watchword, the celebrated *homoousion*, was understood and interpreted as it is for its elucidation that universal human nature became relevant for the Cappadocians.

For a long time it was held almost unanimously that the term *homoousios* indicates originally and truly a monistic (monarchian) understanding of the Trinity.[2] In this sense it was supposed to have been used by some theologians, notably Greek speaking Westerners, to render Tertullian's formula 'una substantia'. Its insertion into the Nicene Creed was consequently explained by the allegedly strong Western influence on the course of that synod.[3] It is the merit of recent research, notably by C. Stead,[4] to have shown that this view of the events at Nicaea can hardly be squared with our historical knowledge of that council. There is no need to rehearse again the evidence accumulated against that theory. Suffice it to say that there is no

---

[1] Cf. on this time in general: Gwatkin (1900), 146–278; Schwartz (1935); Ritter (1965), 19–131; Meredith (1972); Grillmeier (1975), 249ff.; Dinsen (1976), 101–84; Kopecek (1979); Hanson (1988), 417ff.; Brennecke (1984); (1988); Drecoll (1996). All general accounts of Church or doctrinal history contain, of course, extended sections on this period.

[2] Zahn (1867), 8–32; Gwatkin (1900), 46–7; Harnack (1894) vol. IV, 1ff.; Bethune-Baker (1901), 11–30; Kelly (1972), 254 (for the Nicene Creed, 'at anyrate implicitly'); Dinsen (1976), 1–2; different: Prestige (1936), 197–209; Kraft (1954/55); Ricken (1969), 333–41.

[3] The classical account of this view is to be found in Harnack (1894) vol. IV, 50–9. Ulrich (1994) demonstrates now that and how the Nicene Creed was received in the West from the 350s onwards.

[4] Stead (1977), 223–66. Accepted by Hanson (1988), 198–202.

evidence linking the term *homoousios* to the debate between pluralistic and monarchian theology at Nicaea nor in its immediate wake.[5]

A corollary of this reshuffle, which to my knowledge has not yet
been universally recognised, is that with the collapse of the traditional explanation of *homoousios* in the Nicene Creed the character
of the controversy about the acceptance of the Nicene Creed and,
in particular, the *homoousion* is in need of reconsideration as well.
The traditional view of Zahn and Harnack had, if anything, the
advantage of providing a convenient explanation for the fact that
only in the Cappadocians' interpretation did the formula of Nicaea
eventually win the day. Zahn had argued that this 'neo-Nicene' theology was characterised by a generic reinterpretation of the Nicene
homoousion, effectively a reversal of its original, unitary meaning.[6]
Thus, Nicaea would have succeeded only in an understanding directly
opposed to the intention of its originators: rather than advocating a
monadic, strongly monotheistic doctrine, neo-Nicenism allowed for
the development of a pluralistic quasi-Origenistic trinitarian theology of precisely the kind the historical Council of Nicaea had wished
to exclude. The father of later orthodoxy would have been Basil of
Ancyra rather than anybody else.[7] Accepting this theory, it would
indeed be difficult not to see in this development with Harnack 'the
most cruel satire'.[8]

Now, this theory has (outside Germany, at least) never held sway
in the way Zahn's interpretation of Nicaea itself did. Bethune-Baker
argued[9] that the theory of a neo-Nicene orthodoxy would not hold
at all, but that Meletius and the Cappadocians ought to be understood
to have followed firmly the Athanasian lead. Others, like Prestige,[10]
agreed, but one could certainly not say that either view enjoyed universal acceptance at any time.

Be this as it may, at that stage both advocates and critics of the
neo-Nicene theory were in agreement in so far as the interpretation

---

[5] Abramowski (1982), esp. 254ff. n. 59. Cf. also Williams (1983) for the conceptual background of the early debate between Arius and his opponents.

[6] Zahn (1867), 87.

[7] Harnack (1894) vol. IV, 100; cf. Gwatkin (1900), 246–7.

[8] Harnack, loc. cit.

[9] Bethune-Baker (1901).

[10] Prestige (1936), 232, 242; similar: Lebon (1953), 681ff.; Ritter (1965), 282–91.
Hanson (1988), 696–99, 734–7 seems to argue for a *via media* criticising both positions.

of the original, Nicene *homoousion* was concerned. Neither doubted that in the thought and language of Athanasius *homoousios* conveyed a unitary emphasis. Thus, with the acceptance of the latter theory crumbling, both views can be said to have lost their force. Ensuing questions may be subsumed under the following headings:

1. As there doubtless was a controversy in the 350s and 360s about the acceptance of Nicaea and the *homoousion*, what was its theological substance? Why was the *homoousion* rejected or insisted on?
2. Was there a difference between the way Athanasius and the Cappadocians defended the *homoousion*? If so, how could it best be described?
3. What was the role played by original non-Nicenes, like homoiousians and homoians, in this process? Is there evidence that the interpretation of Nicaea was at any point tactically devised to facilitate their integration into the Nicene party? In particular, can their influence be detected in the thought of the Cappadocians?
4. What was the relevance of the analogy of human nature in this development?

To my knowledge, the first full-scale study to start from this new *status quaestionis* has been J.N. Steenson's thesis on Basil of Ancyra. Steenson's argument may be summarised as follows: the debate of the 350s and 360s merely *resulted* in the emergence of Nicene orthodoxy. The existence of a Nicene party for the early 350s has to be critically questioned. It would therefore be wrong to understand 'homoiousians' like Basil of Ancyra as reacting against 'Nicenism' if understood as denoting the views of a clearly defined theological camp. Steenson wants rather to have it that the interaction of Athanasius and Basil of Ancyra created something like Nicene orthodoxy in the first place, a process which, in his view, is perfectly legitimate as the homoiousians served to integrate the Origenist-Eusebian tradition into accepted orthodoxy. This, then, could both explain and justify the influence of both Athanasius and Basil of Ancyra on the Cappadocians: to make the Ancyran one of the fathers of 'neo-Nicene' orthodoxy would thus in no way be a cruel satire, but a sober evaluation of historical facts. Cappadocian theology would be the result of the intended *rapprochement* between Athanasius and the homoiousians.

In my judgment, Steenson has made a most valuable point in demonstrating that the theological opposition that generations of

scholars have seen between Athanasius and the homoiousians must
be questioned. I shall disagree, however, with Steenson's conclusion
regarding the Cappadocian position. Without denying that the Cappadocians drew on traditional patterns for their teaching on the trinitarian issue, I shall emphasise the novelty of their central tenet, the
co-ordination of the divine Persons. This tenet certainly cannot be
derived from either of the two parties Steenson wants to make the
Cappadocians' ancestors, but is clearly contrary to their intentions.

If, then, the identification of the *homoousion* with a unitary theology
has proved groundless for Nicaea itself, it can no longer be simply
presupposed that it was so during that time in which more and more
attention was focused on the term. It really requires a thorough re-
examination of what was being said about the *homoousion* to make
out the underlying assumptions of this debate.

This task, as far as I can see, has not yet been systematically
undertaken, and it is certainly beyond the scope of this study to follow it in every detail. In the following, I shall explore part of it by
concentrating on four people or groups of people who have all been
said to have influenced the Cappadocians' position: the homoiousians, Athanasius, Apollinarius and Meletius.

1.2   *The homoiousian rejection of the* homoousion

The name 'homoiousian' has often been given indiscriminately to
two groups of people, without making clear how far they actually
coincide: it is on the one hand the designation of an ecclesiastical
party led by Basil of Ancryra; on the other hand the name is often
used to mark out that majority of Eastern theologians who in the
course of the trinitarian controversy were neither clearly Arian nor
strictly Nicene (i.e. Athanasian). It seems, however, desirable that these
two notions should not be confused: it becomes more and more clear
that the theological landscape of those years was much more com-
plex than traditional scholarship wished to believe (partially mislead,
no doubt, by the simplifications of Athanasius), and it serves the
proper understanding of neither the 'real' homoiousians nor the many
others if they are counted together simply on the grounds of concur-
ring with neither Athanasius nor Arius.

In the following, 'homoiousian' and related terms are employed solely to designate members of the aforesaid party. This party must have existed from c. 358 into the latter half of the 360s, although their political relevance appears to have terminated effectively with the homoian triumph at Constantinople in 360.[11] We know something about their theological views mainly from two documents preserved by Epiphanius.[12] From those documents it seems clear that these bishops are theologically conservative, belonging to what one may call the Origenist-Eusebian tradition, and that they wish to follow a *via media* between the 'extremes' of Marcellus' and Arius' doctrines.

The exact number of their adherents is naturally difficult to pin down, but something can be (and has been) done on the basis of the signatures attached to several of their documents.[13] It seems clear, then, from such indicators that there is no justification on this basis to be gained for the claim that this party represents a majority of Eastern bishops.[14] It is clear from the main documents that they object to Nicaea, in particular to the *homoousion* on various grounds. It has often been assumed that, because of their apparent obsession with the theology of Marcellus (the predecessor, after all, of their leader on the Ancyran see!), their rejection of the Nicene Creed was due to its Marcellan overtones, but Steenson has convincingly questioned this assumption. The following analysis of those passages that refer to the *homoousion*, while correcting some of his contentions, will confirm his main conclusion.

1.2.1   Homoousios *in the Ancyran synodical letter (358)*

The letter written from what appears to be the founding synod of the party (Ancyra, 358) expressly condemns the *homoousion* in its nineteenth anathema.[15] This text is often claimed as evidence that the rejection of the *homoousion* was due to its Sabellian, that is Marcellan, implications:

---

[11] Cf. Steenson (1983), 51–5.

[12] *Haer* 73,2–11 (vol. III, 268,30–284,9 Holl/Dummer); 73,12–22 (vol. III, 284,12–295,32 Holl/Dummer).

[13] Cf. Steenson (1983), 55–63.

[14] But cf., e.g., Gwatkin (1900), 165: 'The council of Ancyra might be understood to speak for the East in general.'

[15] Epiphanius, *haer* 73,11,10 (vol. III, 284,4–5 Holl/Dummer). Cf. for this passage: Steenson (1985). I wish to indicate my debt to Steenson's analysis of the nineteenth anathema although my eventual interpretation differs from his. On the synod in general see: Steenson (1983), 126–208; Hanson (1988), 350–7.

And if someone, calling the Father Father of the Son *qua* power and
ousia, calls the Son ὁμοούσιος or ταὐτοούσιος with the Father, be he
condemned.[16]

Here *homoousios* is rejected alongside with the term ταὐτοούσιος. The
latter, it is assumed, is self explanatory: the authors of the declara-
tion wished to identify the confessors of the *homoousion* with such
monarchians as claimed that Father and Son were numerically one.[17]
However, is this interpretation warranted? What the writers may
have in mind is made clear by an earlier passage in the same writing which appears to expound what 'the same' means. There it is
claimed that

> it is obvious that what is like can never be the same (ταὐτόν) as that
> to which it is likened. (Of this) we have evidence in the (biblical word
> of his) having been 'made in the likeness of men' (Phil 2,7): the son
> of God became man, but not in all regards *the same* as man, and being
> 'in the likeness of sinful flesh' he was in those passions which cause
> sin in the flesh, of hunger, we say, and thirst, and the other, but not
> in the *sameness* of sinful flesh.[18]

From this passage it appears that the homoiousians were prepared
to accept that all human beings are the same, the relationship between
Father and Son being, however, different from that between men.
The analogy they would accept is rather that between Christ *qua*
man and other human beings. If we allow (with Steenson)[19] an interpretation of the nineteenth anathema on the background of this passage, it will appear rather unlikely that ὁμοούσιος and ταὐτοούσιος
there refer to the Marcellan doctrine of a monadic unity of one
prosopon of the Godhead. If all men are conceded to be 'the same',
the issue cannot have been one of 'monadic' vs. 'generic' unity.

It is furthermore interesting that the rejection of *homoousios* seems
to be connected with a rejection of human nature as an analogy for
the Trinity. This analogy is thus unlikely to have reduced those theologians' misgivings towards the Nicene Creed.

---

[16] Epiphanius, *haer* 73,11,10 (vol. III, 284,4–5 Holl/Dummer).
[17] Cf. e.g. Gwatkin (1900), 166; Dinsen (1976), 138–9; Hanson (1988), 356.
Epiphanius, of course, claims that the Nicene *homoousion* would be equidistant to
both the Arian ἑτεροούσιος and the Sabellian ταὐτοούσιος (*haer* 65,8,1 [vol. III,
11,7–11 Holl/Dummer]; 76,7,8 [vol. III, 348,12–4 Holl/Dummer]). But he should
perhaps not be thought to be the most empathic interpreter of homoiousian doctrine.
[18] Epiphanius, *haer* 73,8,8 (vol. III, 279,7–13 Holl/Dummer).
[19] Steenson (1983), 201–3, (1985), 269–70.

It is less easy to see what notion precisely the homoiousians wish to avoid here. Steenson assumes that we encounter here a 'materialistic' understanding of the *homoousion*.[20] He cites a passage from Sozomen[21] to the effect that, according to the homoiousians, material substances were *homoousios*, intelligible ones, *homoiousios*. The absence of sexual generation would thus forbid one to apply the *homoousion* both to the man Jesus, born from a virgin, and to the eternal Son of God.

There is indeed a sentence in the synodical that seems to favour this interpretation.[22] Nevertheless, I cannot say that I find it particularly convincing. It appears that Sozomen's statement has not much to say about the logic of the present argument: Christ *qua* man is unlikely to be thought of as an intelligible substance; thus, the rejection of the *homoousion* in this case, at least, cannot easily be deduced from the aforesaid principle. Moreover, there is no analogy between the way the Son was begotten and Christ was begotten to be detected here; indeed, such an analogy would surely have spoiled the argument, as Christ was supposed to have been begotten *not* by man. Thus I regard the issue of sexual generation as misleading inasmuch as the point of the present analogy is concerned. It seems to me that the actual relevance of the argument is much less complicated, and at the same time perfectly in line with the tendency of the synodical in general. I should assume the author's assumption about human beings to be that 'being man' means the same for each of them *except* for Christ *qua* man, and that it is biblical to use the term 'likeness' for the latter relationship. Whether this sameness is ultimately due to the procreative process or anything else is, I believe, of secondary importance for this particular argument. At the same time it is, however, clear that the main thrust of the argument in the epistle as a whole is directed at establishing a limited but decisive difference between Father and Son in so far as they are God. I take it therefore that the rejection of 'the same' implies exactly that the meaning of 'being God' with the two Persons does not have an analogy in human beings generally, but in the 'likeness' of Christ's and our humanity: Father and Son are thus not *homoousios* because they are not the same *qua* God in the way men are the same *qua*

---

[20] Steenson (1983), 204–5.
[21] *Hist eccl* III 18,3 (132,14–8 Bidez/Hansen).
[22] Ap. Epiphanius, *haer* 73,9,2 (vol. III, 279,20–3 Holl/Dummer).

man. Why not? The answer, I think, must be: if they were, there
were two separate, co-ordinate first principles (ἀρχαί). To avoid this,
a limited, but decisive subordinationism must be maintained which
makes the Father *qua* source ontologically prior to the Son.

1.2.2   *The* Sirmian Epistle

Unfortunately, the most elaborate treatment of the term *homoousios*
from this time we do not possess any more. The epistle about its
use and its ambiguities prepared by Basil of Ancyra for the court
bishops Ursacius and Valens in 359, the so-called *Sirmian Epistle*, is
not extant. All we have is indirect information about it, the most
reliable, it appears, from the pen of Hilary of Poitiers.[23] In his *De
Synodis*[24] Hilary gives an account of that document as far as the rejection of the *homoousion* is concerned. He lists the following three points:

1. The word *homoousios* might suggest the existence of a *substantia
   prior* which has subsequently been divided into two. This would
   have two consequences: Firstly, the common substance would be
   a third thing beside the two divine Persons. Secondly, Father and
   Son would in fact be collaterals.[25] Hilary adds that this is a sec-
   ular (*profanus*) sense of the word which ought to be generally
   rejected by the Church.
2. The synod that condemned Paul of Samosata at Antioch in 268
   had also rejected the word *homoousios* as part of Paul's Sabellian
   theology. Here *homoousios* is indeed linked to Sabellianism, but we
   cannot be sure that Hilary's report is correct.[26]
3. At Nicaea the word had been chosen only to condemn Arius;
   with this situation overcome there would no longer be any reason
   to continue to use it.

---

[23] I consider the superiority of Hilarys' report over against Athanasius as established by Brennecke (1984ᵃ) 276–84; *pace*: Prestige (1936), 201–9. Cf. for the following also Brennecke (1988); F. Dinsen (1976), 140–2.

[24] *Syn* 81 (PL 10, 534A–C).

[25] Cf. *syn* 68 (PL 10, 525B–526A).

[26] The question is intricate, as it is intertwined with the problem of the reliabil-
ity of this claim. Many scholars (e.g. Abramowski [1982], 255, n. 59; Brennecke
[1984ᵃ], followed by Hübner [1989], 284, n. 13) now doubt that the Antiochene
synod of 268 did at all condemn the *homoousion*. In this case one may find it impossible to ascertain in what sense precisely the homoiousians connected the term to
that event (cf. Stead [1994], 395–6). To be sure, Paul was at that time often seen
as a second Sabellius and a forerunner of Marcellus and Photinus (cf. e.g. Epiphanius,
haer 65,1–2 [vol. III, 3,9–5,6 Holl/Dummer]) and it would thus seem natural to

For the present investigation the first argument is of major importance. It is often said that we encounter here a possible 'materialistic' misunderstanding of the *homoousion*,[27] but again I cannot see why
this should be the case. It rather appears to me that this reason fits
in perfectly well with the argument cited above from the Ancyran
document. In both cases the rationale of the criticism of the term
homoousios is that to employ the term would require a complete co-
ordination of the divine Persons. In the former instance this was, as
has been seen, the upshot of the rejection of 'sameness', in the present passage the idea is similarly that *homoousios* describes a relationship of such a kind as to make its unity possible only by positing
the common substance beside or beyond the two Persons.[28] The suggestion that Father and Son might in fact be siblings makes the decisive point particularly distinct: the derivation of the Son from the
Father, so vital for maintaining the monarchy within the Trinity,
seemed endangered by the *homoousion*. Again it is clear that a comparison with human nature would not have served to ease this fear.[29]

Why would *homoousios* be understood that way? It is well known
that the quest for the word's original meaning is an intricate one.[30]
The following remarks are not meant to address this problem.
Whatever the 'original' implications of *homoousios* had been, forbid-
ding Arius and his friend to sign the Nicene Creed in 325, the situation around 360 was different as by that time the term had become
a theological watchword and there would have been some reflection

---

assume that the homoiousian bishops wished to use his name in that connotation.
However, if the term was in whatever sense involved in Paul's condemnation, the
question of its meaning becomes more relevant. I should follow Brennecke's argument in that Hilary's report deserves more credit than Athanasius' and thus conclude that Paul would have used rather than rejected the *homoousion*. However, this
does not exclude the possibility that it conveyed the notion of a co-ordination of
Father and Son: Paul, it appears, taught some kind of adoptianism (cf. Eusebius,
hist eccl VII 30,11), and such a 'divisive' christology could easily follow from a trinitarian theology employing ὁμοούσιος in that sense.

[27] So, e.g., Dinsen (1976), 140. But cf. the perceptive analysis of this argument
by Williams (1983), 66ff. The insistence of the *priority* of the common item would
indicate that the argument is of Platonic origin: in Justin (*dial* 5,5–6), who is,
to my knowledge, the first Christian to employ it, the argument is used to reject
the view that souls are ingenerate. Could this echo a 'middle-Platonic' debate on
psychology?

[28] Cf. also for this logic Origen, *hom in Num* 12,1 (95,3–13 Baehrens), a passage
discussed by Stead (1977), 249–50.

[29] Cf. also Stead (1977), loc. cit.

[30] Cf. esp. Dinsen (1976); Stead (1977), 190–222; Abramowski (1982), 254,
n. 59.

as to whether and why it was to be accepted or rejected with regard
to the Deity.

For the present findings, then, I would advance the following explanation. The use of the word *homoousios* for the intratrinitarian relation would be seen as implying that there is a single *ousia* of the
Godhead. I would suggest that the problem of *homoousios* in the present text and elsewhere is to a considerable extent a problem of how
ousia could be employed appropriately in trinitarian doctrine. It appears that *homoousios* could always be paired with terms like ὁμογενής[31]
or ὁμοφυής[32] indicating that the single *ousia* is not only a *phusis*, but
also, in a certain sense, a genus. This has little to do with the notorious 'generic' interpretation of *ousia*.[33] However, a long tradition
among philosophers of various schools required that member of a
genus should be ontologically co-ordinate. This principle was first
asserted by Aristotle, who attributed it to the academics and accepted
it for himself too.[34] The claim in the *Categories* that there is no possibility of a more or a less within an *ousia*[35] could be understood to
be based on essentially the same tenet. Critics of the Aristotelian
concept, notably Plotinus, would therefore preferably point to the
contradiction between a genus '*ousia*' and the apparent differences
in rank between its members.[36]

In this framework it would be perfectly sensible to call men
homoousioi, as there is one *ousia*, the species 'man', with regard to
which they are all on the same plane. But this was, assuredly, not
the way the homoiousians wished to conceive of the relation between
the members of the Trinity, as has been seen.

Inextricably intertwined with this was the problem, raised by the
homoousion, of what kind of entity the divine *ousia* would be. The
homoiousians apparently took for granted a Platonic approach assuming that the common *ousia* must be a separate entity ontologically
prior to the items partaking of it (*substantia prior*). Not surprisingly,
they find this concept unsuitable in trinitarian theology. The quest

---

[31] Cf. Athanasius, *sent Dion* 10,5 (53,21–54,1 Opitz); *syn* 48,2 (272,22–5 Opitz).
[32] Cf. Athanasius, *syn* 53,3 (276,28–9).
[33] On this cf. Loofs (1922) and Stead (1977), 247.
[34] Cf. Aristotle, *EN* I 6 (1096ª17–9) for the attribution of this doctrine to the academics, *met* B 3 (999ª6–10) and, esp., *pol* Γ 1 (1275ª34–8) for Aristotle's acceptance of it.
[35] Aristotle, *cat* 5 (3ᵇ33–4ª9).
[36] Plotinus, *Enn* VI 1,2.

for an orthodox definition of the *homoousion* thus generated a need for a more refined application of the tools of philosophy. We shall see presently how this need was answered.

In summary, the homoiousian rejection of the *homoousion* was largely due to its alleged connotation of co-ordination: in this sense, it was supposed to be aporetic with regard to the Godhead. A corollary of this implication was the argument that the common *ousia* had to be introduced as a separate entity to guarantee the community of the *homoousioi*. Men, it was noticed incidentally, would be *homoousioi* in this sense, but as such they would *not* provide for an analogy for the Trinity that would make the Nicene watchword any more acceptable.

1.3   *The witness of Athanasius*

There is perhaps no other issue pertaining to the present investigation that has been as thoroughly researched as Athanasius' use and understanding of the *homoousion*.[37] I take it as an established fact, then, that Athanasius made the term part of his trinitarian thinking only from c. 356 onwards.[38] The introduction of the word into his terminology coincides with his decision to regard the Nicene Creed as the crucial and sufficient formula of faith; this makes it likely that both developments were linked. Indeed, it appears that *homoousios* is used by him almost exclusively where he has to defend and justify it as part of the Nicene Creed.[39] The theology expressed by the term, on the other hand, does not seem to differ from what Athanasius had previously held;[40] he employs *homoousios* mainly to describe an asymmetric relationship based on generation. It may thus appear that the term was interpreted to fit his thinking rather than *vice versa*.[41]

For the present enquiry Athanasius' teaching is interesting for two

---

[37] Harnack (1894) vol. IV, 26–38; Loofs (1950) vol. I, 186–90; Lebon (1952); Stead (1961); (1974); (1977), 260–6; (1994), 418–22; Meijering (1975), 19–30; Hanson (1988), 417–58; cf. Widdicombe (1994), 145–254.

[38] Taking this with Hanson (1988, 419) and Abramowski (1982, 259) as the date of the *decr Nicaen*. Stead ([1994], 418, following Schwartz [1904], 401 and Opitz, note ad *decr Nicaen* 2,2) prefers a slightly earlier date (c. 350), but a precise decision is not relevant for the present purpose. The only occurrence of ὁμοούσιος in Athanasius' writings which is with certainty to be dated earlier is at *c Arian* I 9,2 (117,36 Tetz).

[39] Stead (1977), 260.

[40] Stead (1994), 419, *pace* e.g. Lietzmann (1950) vol. I, 222–3.

[41] Stead (1977), 260–1.

reasons: first, he confirms the rejection found above of the trinitarian use of the term *homoousios* on the grounds of the alleged need to
introduce a *substantia prior*; it is telling to see his defence against this
charge. Secondly, he seems to illustrate *homoousios* in a few passages
with the human analogy.

In his writing *De Synodis Arimini et Seleuciae* (written in c. 359–61)[42]
he cites at one point the following criticism of the Nicene position:

> They say, as you write, that one must not call the Son *homoousios* with
> the Father since he who says *homoousios* implies the existence of three:
> an antecedent substance and the two *homoousioi* that are generated out
> of it. From this they conclude that, if the Son be *homoousios* with the
> Father, a substance will necessarily be antecedent to them from which
> they both were generated. Thus they will not be Father and Son, but
> mutually collaterals.[43]

This criticism is apparently identical with the above first argument
of the homoiousians in their Sirmian epistle. It is interesting that
Athanasius himself calls this the interpretation of the Greeks which
again corresponds to what Hilary writes (who calls this understanding 'profanus'), although to my mind it is not clear whether Athanasius
found this remark in the text he is dealing with here or whether he
recalls this characterisation from elsewhere.

Athanasius' reply is telling. He does not altogether disavow this
interpretation although he denounces it as a Greek interpretation
which would not be relevant for Christians. He does, however, argue
that in such a triad of a *substantia prior* and its two derivatives any
of the latter would also be *homoousios* with the former since otherwise
they would have to be ἑτεροούσιος.[44] That is, he claims the *homoousion*
for beings that are not equal, but related *qua* derivation without
unequivocally rejecting the 'Greek' use of the term.

It is crucial to see that Athanasius does not by any means wish
to concede the co-ordination of Father and Son, which he rather
agrees to find absurd.[45] Instead, his attempt is directed at establishing

---

[42] So: Hanson (1988), 421. Different, e.g., Opitz in his edition (231): between the
death of Constantius and the 362 synod at Alexandria.
[43] *Syn* 51,3 (274,35–275,4 Opitz). A similar argument appeared at *c Arian* I 14,1
(123,31–3 Tetz). Cf. again Williams (1983), 66 who cites other occurrences of this
argument and Widdicombe (1994), 172–5.
[44] *Syn* 51,4–5 (275,5–11 Opitz).
[45] This also is the upshot of the related argument at *c Arian* I 14 (see n. 47
above).

a specific interpretation of the *homoousion*. The present passage might thus support the view that Athanasius' endorsement of the *homoousion* was bound up with a conscious reinterpretation of the term, for there is presupposed here an understanding of *homoousioi* as collaterals (which might, for example, be human beings) that is obviously a current non-theological use of the term, while it is agreed to be aporetic with regard to the Godhead.

We have to keep this in mind in approaching those passages where Athanasius himself seems to allow human nature to stand as an illustration of divine consubstantiality. The most famous of these passages is to be found in his second letter to Serapion.[46] There the argument, which is intended to show the unsoundness (τὸ σαθρόν) of the Arian heresy, starts from the following premise:

> If we are similar to others, we also share identity with them and are *homoousioi*: as men, then, we are similar and share identity, and we are to each other *homoousioi*.[47]

From this Athanasius proceeds via a similar statement about angels to the claim that, while there is no similarity to be found between the Son and creatures, Son and Father are similar and thus *homoousios*.[48]

It seems to me that what Athanasius has in mind here is not that human nature as such is a suitable analogy for the intratrinitarian relations. Rather he presupposes the 'Greek' use of the *homoousion* in order to bring home his particular—and distinct—understanding of the relationship between Father and Son. What he claims appears to be the following: human beings share certain similarities (being mortal, corruptible, changeable, from non-being),[49] and they are the same and *homoousioi*; similarly Father and Son will be the same and *homoousioi* as they too share certain (important) properties. That men are *homoousioi* is thus granted, and it is the similarities that are compared in order to secure the same predicate for the Godhead.

To find here the trinitarian use of *homoousios* applied to the relationship between men *qua* man would be to press Athanasius' argument too far. There is no indication in the text that he is at all

---

[46] *Serap* II 3 (PG 26, 612B–613A).

[47] *Serap* II 3 (PG 26, 612B): Ὧν ἐσμεν ὅμοιοι, καὶ τὴν ταυτότητα ἔχομεν τούτων, καὶ ὁμοούσιοί ἐσμεν· ἄνθρωποι γοῦν ὅμοιοι καὶ ταυτότητα ἔχομεν, ὁμοούσιοί ἐσμεν ἀλλήλων.

[48] Ibid.

[49] Ibid.

interested in whatever particular characteristic this sort of relationship might possess to make it a proper analogy for the Trinity. In
fact, the upshot of Athanasius' argument turns out to be his well-
worn alternative that the Son has to be *homoousios* with either the
creation or with the Father; the similarities between the Son and
the latter are then cited to account for their being *homoousioi*.[50]

Rather, this text should be seen to confirm the aforesaid suggestion that Athanasius could presuppose the use of *homoousios* with
regard to men. This seems to support the above interpretation of
the homoiousian synodical epistle, which we found had rejected the
homoousion in precisely that sense. Nor is it difficult to maintain that,
as men are collaterals, the present case is one illustration of the
'Greek' use of the *homoousion* with which we have seen Athanasius
deal elsewhere.

The same conclusion has to be drawn from a related text from
De Synodis. There[51] Athanasius argues that it is not enough to say
'similar' as similarity would refer to accidents while substances are
'the same':

> A man is called similar to (another) man not in so far as his *ousia*, but
> in so far as his form and shape are concerned: for *qua ousia* they are
> connatural (ὁμοφυεῖς).[52]

Again, I would argue that it would be wrong to see Athanasius here
employ the unity of man as an analogy for that of the Godhead.
What he eventually wants to say is that likeness-terminology is less
suitable in trinitarian theology than the use of *homoousios*. To this
end he again presupposes the fact that men are referred to as ὁμοφυεῖς
(note the apparent equivalence with *homoousios*) when we talk about
their substance; therefore, he concludes, the word has to be employed
for the substantial relationship between Father and Son as well.

From this brief survey three facts have, I hope, emerged:

(i) Athanasius knows that *homoousios* is employed for collaterals. He
calls this a 'Greek' use of the term and finds it impossible to
apply the word in this sense to the Trinity.
(ii) He insists that this use is not applicable to trinitarian theology
where the word properly describes a derivative relationship based
on generation.

---

[50] Ibid. 612C ff.
[51] *Syn* 53 (276,21ff. Opitz).
[52] *Syn* 53,3 (276,26–8 Opitz).

(iii) He finds it natural nevertheless to employ this 'Greek' use without making it a direct analogy for the intratrinitarian relations. It should perhaps be pointed out that he nowhere indicates in what sense he believes men to be *homoousioi*, i.e. how he conceives of their common substance.

It appears, then, that on (i) Basil of Ancyra and Athanasius are agreed. They also concur, in principle, on the derivative nature of the intratrinitarian relationship. Their disagreement is largely about whether or not *homoousios* can take on a meaning to match this relationship. Only Athanasius claims that there is a special meaning denoting a derivative relationship ('out of the substance') which *homoousios* assumes in the trinitarian context. Thus there emerges a limited convergence between the two positions that could have resulted in something like a *rapprochement*.[53] It does not appear, however, that the use of human nature as an analogy for the trinitarian unity would have furthered this development.

1.4 *Apollinarius' answer to Basil*

We encounter a position very similar to that of Athanasius in c. 362 in Apollinarius of Laodicea's first letter to Basil.[54] For two reasons the writing has to be dealt with here: first, the Athanasian claim that *homoousios* can be used for a derivative relationship receives here an intrinsically philosophical foundation. Secondly, it is here that for the first time humanity is made an analogy for the Trinity.

In a preceding letter to Apollinarius (*ep* 361) Basil had enquired about the word *homoousios*, expressing concerns seemingly very much in line with what we have found so far:

> Furthermore be so kind as to inform us in more detail about the *homoousion* itself (. . .) which meaning it has and how one may soundly employ it of things in which neither a common overlying genus is seen, nor a pre-existent material substratum, nor a division of the first into the second.[55]

---

[53] The closeness of these two positions is one of the central claims of Steenson's thesis (1983, 15–6).
[54] (Basil), *ep* 362. About its genuineness, which I here presuppose, see fundamentally Prestige (1956) and de Riedmatten (1956); for the date cf.: Hauschild (1973) vol. III, 252, n. 682; 253, n. 690.
[55] Basil, *ep* 361,15–22 (vol. III, 221 Courtonne = 202,3–8 de Riedmatten).

Nevertheless I hope to show that one would be altogether mistaken in assuming that Basil's own position even at this early point in his career was basically identical with the views of, for example, the homoiousians (see below pp. 49–55). For the moment, however, it is more important to see that one could think it was, and that this is apparently what Apollinarius did. For Apollinarius' explanation of the meaning of *ousia* in trinitarian theology seems to be specially designed as a means of reconciling the mainstream Eastern opposition to the use of *homoousios* with this term.

Apollinarius describes how he understands the relationship between Father and Son as follows:

> We call one *ousia* not only that which is numerically one, as you say, and that which is in one (individual) circumscription, but also, specifically, two or more men who are united *qua* genus: thus two or more can be the same *qua ousia*, as all men are Adam and (thus) one, and the son of David is David being the same as him; in this respect you rightly say that the Son is *qua ousia* what the Father is. For in no other way could there be a Son of God, given that the Father is confessed to be the one and only God, but in some way like the one Adam is the primogenitor of men and the one David the originator of the royal dynasty. In this way, then, both (the idea of) one antecedent genus and (that of) one underlying matter in Father and Son can be removed from our conceptions, when we apply the prodigenital property to the Supreme Principle and the clans derived from a primogenitor to the Only-begotten Offspring of the one Principle. For to a certain extent they resemble each other: there is neither one antecedent substance of Adam, who was formed by God, and us, who were born of humans, but he himself is the principle (ἀρχή) of humanity, nor matter common to him and us, but he himself is the origin of all men.[56]

To begin with, it is interesting that as an answer to a question concerning the *homoousion* Apollinarius embarks on an exposition of how *ousia* can be understood. This confirms to some extent the above argument that the controversy about the *homoousion* was essentially a debate about the appropriate use of substance-terminology with regard to the Christian understanding of God. The express purpose of the explanation forwarded here is to propose a definition of *ousia* that avoids the introduction into the Godhead of something additional to the divine Persons. This was, as we have seen, one of the standard objections to the Nicene watchword (the 'Greek' use) explicitly put

---

[56] (Basil), *ep* 362,4–23 (vol. III, 222–3 Courtonne = 203,4–19 de Riedmatten).

forward by Basil. To this end substance is defined here in terms of descent. This concept understands 'genus' as a class of things that share their derivation from the same being, which is thus both, the first element of the class and the genus itself. This comes out quite clearly in Apollinarius' examples: Adam is for him both the individual first human being and also 'man',[57] for to say: 'we are all Adam,' is tantamount to saying: 'we are all men.' The same point can be made about the descendants of David: the family embraces all of them including the king himself, but the latter is also the originating principle of the class.

But it appears that, implicitly, the Apollinarian doctrine steers clear also of the co-ordination of divine beings that was seen to be implied by the word *homoousios*. For it is obvious that genus is here not understood as a class of things which have the same *logos* or definition as was the case in the Aristotelian *Categories*. In the latter view, as I noted above, a genus would not allow for any prior or posterior among its members. This would, however, be different if the first member itself was the genus. Apollinarius' genus would so allow for, even require, a derivation of the Son from the Father, thus identifying the latter with the *ousia* in the first place while giving the former a share in it.

1.4.1 *Philosophical background*

I should point out that Apollinarius' suggestion is not simply an arbitrary re-definition of traditional terminology. Rather, he could claim to be in accordance with Neoplatonic philosophers. Plotinus himself had criticised Aristotle's doctrine of categories on the grounds that substance (οὐσία) could not be a genus in the Aristotelian sense as it contains items that are ontologically prior and posterior (*Enn* VI 1,2); substance does constitute a *category*, he argues, but in the sense in which the Heraclids constitute a 'genus', i.e. a family, on account of their derivation from one person (ibid. 3). This suggestion of Plotinus was subsequently taken up by Porphyry who gives the example of the Heraclids in his *Isagoge* as one illustration of how to understand 'genus'.[58] One might object that the parallel is limited; after

---

[57] Apollinarius probably would have known about the Hebrew meaning of Adam; cf. Origen, *c Celsum* IV 40 (vol. I, 313,17–8 Koetschau).

[58] *Isagoge* (1,18–2,10 Busse).

all, the Neoplatonists would not say that all the Heraclids are Heracles. Yet, the Heraclids are for them an illustration of *ousia*, that is a means of explaining why many things on various ontological planes can all be thus called.

If, then, *ousia* is conceded to be a derivative quasi-genus[59] rather than an Aristotelian one, things which are related *qua* descent can be called *homoousios* as well as, or, perhaps, with even more justification than, those that share the same *logos*.

This, then, appears to be the philosophical background of Apollinarius' theory. His view thus coincides with the one we encountered in Athanasius, but while the latter was normally content to express it by means of the traditional physical metaphors (sun–ray; source–river),[60] Apollinarius gives it a more philosophical framework. This coincidence need not surprise us as the co-operation of both theologians in the 350s is well known.[61] Indeed it would seem not impossible that Apollinarius was the theological mastermind behind Athanasius' decision (after the year 350!) to adopt the phrase *homoousios*. However, to pursue this question would require an independent investigation.

It is nevertheless probably not too much to say that the background of the present interpretation of the *homoousion* was an attempt to allow such theologians the acceptance of the *homoousion* as would take exception to the 'Aristotelian' understanding, i.e. the ontological co-ordination of the Persons (= the 'Greek' understanding of the *homoousion*). The mediatory theology with which the Cappadocians have often been credited could thus with more justification be ascribed to Athanasius and Apollinarius.[62]

---

[59] On this term cf.: Lloyd (1955), (1990), 76–8.

[60] Cf. for sun–ray: *syn* 51,7 (275, 19 Opitz), for source–river: *sent Dion* 24 (64, 3–25 Opitz); but see also *c Arian* III 20 (PG 26, 365A).

[61] Direct information is scarce, but cf. Leontius of Byzantium (ap. Lietzmann [1904], 279) who reports that Apollinarius could boast scores of epistles from Athanasius and Serapion; upon those letters, Leontius writes, Timotheus' *Church History* was based. Both Apollinarius himself (Apollinarius, *ad Diocaes* [255,21–4 Lietzmann]) and Epiphanius (*haer* 77,2,1 [vol. III, 416,31–417,2 Holl/Dummer]) emphasise his connection with the Alexandrian pope. According to one episode, reported by Sozomen (*hist eccl* VI 25,12 [272,3–6 Bidez/Hansen]), George of Laodicea excommunicated Apollinarius in 346 because of his hospitality towards Athanasius; this, the historian writes, 'terminated in the strictest friendship'.

[62] Cf. Meredith' judgment that 'this fusion of two images, far from being a derivation from the path of so-called 'Nicene and Athanasian' orthodoxy, can be regarded as a not unsuccessful attempt to join together, if not to blend completely, the two principal models that must lie at the back of most Trinitarian thinking. It includes the real oneness and the real difference in a composite formula' (1972, 240).

1.4.2 *Apollinarius' application of human nature*

Perhaps even more important for the present investigation is the fact that here, for the first time, we find human nature consciously employed as an analogy for substantial unity within the Trinity. Why did Apollinarius choose this analogy?

It has at times been thought that he offers here a 'generic' explanation of the *homoousion* in order to pacify the Origenist opponents of Nicenism and that thus the present text documents a position halfway between Athanasius and the Cappadocians.[63] However, of all explanations this seems perhaps the least convincing one: to begin with, the term 'generic' has to be challenged as being not precise enough; the present analogy has, it appears, much less to do with the Cappadocian 'generic' understanding of the *homoousion* than with Athanasius' non-generic view.[64] Secondly, since neither the controversy as a whole nor, indeed, Basil's preceding letter indicate that the unitary meaning of *homoousios* was feared, it is difficult to prove that this alleged charge conditioned Apollinarius' choice of an analogy. Furthermore, and this is probably the strongest argument, Apollinarius' 'generic' analogy is in a sense nothing but an expansion of the Father–Son analogy, which is in many ways the most natural and most biblical of all analogies. If the present analogy is inappropriately 'generic', then one can hardly defend the latter, and *vice versa*. At the same time it seems clear that the relationship between these two analogies bears witness to the closeness of Apollinarius' and Athanasius' positions. In brief: there is no indication in the present document that would justify the assumption of Apollinarius as going beyond the Athanasian position towards an un-Nicene interpretation of the *homoousion*.

A more likely explanation appears to be that Apollinarius offers humanity as an analogy because he could presuppose the acceptance of it as an *ousia*; we have had indications that several authors believed men to be *homoousioi*, which would seem to imply that humanity was taken to be an *ousia*.[65] Apollinarius may thus have found that to offer his interpretation of this *ousia* as a quasi-genus was the best possible evidence for a derivative meaning of the *homoousion*. A further advantage

---

[63] Harnack (1894) vol. IV, 84–5, n. 3.
[64] See also: Stead (1977), 247.
[65] Cf. Didymus *in Ps* 54,4 (*fr* 527, vol. II, 9,15 Mühlenberg) for the use of ὁμοούσιος for 'fellow-men'; see also: Prestige (1936), 199.

of this analogy (as we shall see in due course: pp. 55–57 below) is that it allows the discussion of logical questions related to the trinitarian doctrine as, for example, the precise meaning of divine predicates. However, as Apollinarius does not give a reason himself, all this remains speculative; why eventually he chose to offer this analogy to Basil we have no means of ascertaining.

An inevitably ensuing question regards the relationship of Apollinarius' use of the analogy of human nature to that of the Cappadocians: is the theory developed in the present letter the origin of the later Cappadocian use of this analogy? I shall argue that in a sense it is indeed, but in a negative one: the Cappadocian teaching, it seems to me, must be understood as developing an alternative answer to the same question with similar means.

1.5   Confession of the homoousion by Meletius and his followers at Antioch in 363

In 363 we find for the first time original non-Nicenes confessing the Nicene Creed including the *homoousion*. This occurred at a synod at Antioch which had been convened by Meletius, the formerly homoian bishop of the city.[66] From what we learn in Socrates[67] it appears that those bishops came together on the occasion of Jovian's accession[68] in order to compose and present to the new emperor their own credal formula. The relevant section of their letter runs, according to Socrates, as follows:

> . . . we submit to Your Reverence that we accept and hold to the creed of the holy Council of Nicaea which was assembled a long time ago. And when we mention the word in it which appears 'strange'[69] to some, the *homoousion*, it has received a sound interpretation among the

---

[66] About Meletius' career cf. McCarthy Spoerl (1993) who eventually adopts Schwartz' conclusion (1935, 126) 'that Meletius is one of the least clear of fourth-century ecclesiastical figures' (123). On the synod and its epistle I have written more extensively in my paper 'The Antiochene Synod of AD 363 and the Beginnings of Neo-Nicenism' in *ZAC* forthcoming.

[67] *Hist eccl* III 25,6–18 (225,27–227,11 Hansen) Sozomen's account at *hist eccl* VI 4,6–11 (241,4–242,8 Bidez/Hansen) largely corresponds. Socrates' remark that the decision of those bishops reveals their opportunism is obviously his interpretation which he may have taken over from Sabinus: Brennecke (1988), 174; cf. Hauschild (1970), 110.

[68] The precise date of the synod is unknown: Brennecke (1988), 173–4, n. 97.

[69] Reading <ξένον> from Sozomen, *hist eccl* VI 4,9 (with Hansen).

fathers, signifying that the Son was begotten from the *ousia* of the Father and that he is like the Father in *ousia*; it does not mean that any passion occurred in the ineffable generation, nor was the word *ousia* taken by the fathers in a certain Greek use, but to refute the "from non-existence" which Arius impiously dared to apply to Christ, and which the anomoians, who are around today shamelessly parade in an even more desperate and daring manner to the injury of the church's peace.[70]

In this case, it will be noted, the *homoousion* is accepted, but with two caveats. It must not be understood as implying any notion of passion, and it must not be understood according to a certain 'Greek' use. It is rather the derivative interpretation of the term that is endorsed (ἐκ τῆς οὐσίας τοῦ Πατρός), which is then illustrated by the addition of 'like according to substance'.

As for the precise meaning of those statements, the text in itself hardly provides for more than a haphazard guess, but on the basis of our previous findings it does not appear particularly daring to assert that the authors wish to ally themselves with the Athanasian position:[71] they accept, although with some diffidence, the derivative meaning of the *homoousion*, while they are also aware of the normal ('Greek') meaning of the term referring to collaterals. As for the latter, I take it that the 'Greek' use is identical with what we saw both Athanasius and Hilary call by that name. Incidentally, the present text provides a good example against the assumption that whoever employs 'likeness'-terminology with regard to the Trinity must be counted as a 'homoiousian': it is clear that Meletius, who would have been responsible for the formulation, was at no point affiliated with that party.

The term neo-Nicene, then, can here be applied only in a political sense for the fact that we have an early example of Nicene 'converts'.[72] The theology they adopt is the mediatory interpretation of the Nicene Creed endorsed by Athanasius in the latter half of the 350s, that is, an interpretation seeking to avoid doctrinal ramifications by redefining

---

[70] Socrates, *hist eccl* III 25,13–15 (226,17–27 Hanson); ET: Hansen (1988, 581, with changes).

[71] Thus Bethune-Baker's conclusion on *this* point remains authoritative: 'We have, accordingly, here both ἐκ τῆς οὐσίας and ὅμοιος κατ' οὐσίαν: that is to say, ὁμοούσιος is accepted precisely in the terms which Athanasius declared to be an exact equivalent' (1901, 36).

[72] Drecoll wishes to take account of this fact by calling this group 'right-wing homoiousians', not 'neo Nicenes' (1996, 17).

the *homoousion* to fit the derivative relationship between Father and Son in the Godhead.

A further point should be noted. In comparison it appears that, while the homoiousians (as reported by Hilary) had argued that with the disappearance of the Arian heresy the *homoousion* had lost its only justification, conversely the present document argues that with the rise of the anomoian heresy Arianism had reared its head again, which would make the reappraisal of the Nicene formula necessary. This points to a link between the emergence of neo-Nicenism and Eunomius' theology, a link which, as we shall presently see, is of vital importance for the understanding of the Cappadocian teaching.

I should conclude from what has been discussed so far that doctrinal opposition to the term *homoousios* in the late 350s and early 360s was often expressed on the grounds not of its Sabellian implications, but of its alleged tendency to co-ordinate beings ordained under this term. This co-ordination was feared, it was found, because, first, it makes Father and Son siblings, thus endangering the monarchy and, secondly, because it makes the introduction of an antecedent common substance seemingly inevitable. As an answer, apparently, we have seen Athanasius and especially Apollinarius develop an understanding of *homoousios* based on a derivative use of *ousia*, a view that would appear to steer clear of both those aporiae at once.

The last discussed text has also made it clear that the emergence of neo-Arianism caused a renewed interest in the Nicene formula including the *homoousion*: this is not surprising; if *homoousios* was thought to convey the strictest notion of co-ordination, then its relevance was bound to grow in the light of a new and extreme kind of subordinationism.

CHAPTER TWO

THE CAPPADOCIAN TEACHING

Basil, I believe, was bound to be left unimpressed by Apollinarius' missionary attempt.[1] The latter, it appears, had misconceived of the theological position behind Basil's letter, a misunderstanding which, indeed, Apollinarius shares with many scholars since. For in spite of certain similarities Basil's position was, I believe, fundamentally different from that of those whose resentment towards the *homoousion* has so far been analysed.[2] To be sure, Basil is uncertain as to how to avoid apparent pitfalls of the *homoousion*, and he regards 'undeviatingly similar in substance' as a better expression of his belief.

This belief, however, as Basil himself sketches it, starts from the *equality* of Father and Son *qua* divinity. Indeed, I shall show in some detail that precisely the 'Aristotelian' model of completely co-ordinated members of a species was at the core of Basil's trinitarian thinking from the very beginning. It is difficult to overestimate the importance and the novelty of this decision: the derivation of the Son from the Father had always been taken for granted as the foundation of a proper understanding of the Son's deity. In that respect, Origen, Athanasius, Apollinarius, and Basil of Ancyra have more in common than any of them has, in this particular question, with Basil of Caesarea. What, then, led the last-named to adopt this view? I would suggest that this was the impact of the neo-Arian theology of Eunomius positing the alternative of substantial dissimilarity *or* equality. This alternative, I suggest, Basil felt he could not eschew, and consequently chose the latter view, a view which Eunomius himself had meant to be a *reductio ad absurdum* of any position other than his own. Prior to the analysis of Basil's teaching it is therefore necessary to elucidate Eunomius' position as far as it is relevant for the present investigation.

---

[1] *Pace* Hanson (1988, 696) I do not think that Apollinarius ought to be credited with having led Basil towards the *homoousion*.

[2] For Basil as an early homoiousian cf. now Drecoll (1996, title!), but even Steenson (1983), whose helpful clarifications about the term 'homoiousian' have not found as much attention as they deserve, takes it that Basil's theology must be deduced from that of the 'homoiousians' (289–337).

2.1 *The teaching of Eunomius*

Quite generally, it seems to me, the importance of the anomoian heresy for the emergence of neo-Nicenism has been underestimated.[3] Many texts from that time, however, make it clear that this movement was considered a substantial threat to Christianity. All major theologians from that generation and beyond, theologians indeed from various and rival camps, wrote against Eunomius: Apollinarius of Laodicea, Didymus the Blind, Diodore of Tarsus, Theodore of Mopsuestia, Theodoret of Cyrus, and Sophronius, not to mention Basil and the two Gregories.[4]

The essence of Eunomius' teaching[5] was, to put it briefly, that the only adequate way of thinking about God required that he was an unbegotten substance, simple and eternal.[6] According to Eunomius this understanding excluded any substantial relationship between God (the 'Unbegotten')[7] and the Son (the 'Offspring').[8] He goes out of his way to assert that any such assumption resulted in equally absurd consequences. It is for this reason that he earned the notorious nickname 'anomoian': the Son, he taught, is 'substantially' unlike the Father. However, this negative statement is only half the story; Eunomius urges that the Son is similar in his activity: 'like in will and energy, but unlike in being (εἶναι)', in this form (as reported by Basil of Ancyra)[9] the formula has, I think, some claim to represent the core of Eunomius' teaching.

What is the relevance of this teaching? It appears that Eunomius confronted his contemporaries with a simple alternative: 'either you accept (as I do) substantial dissimilarity between Father and Son or else you will have to accept their complete equality.' To say *homoiousios* would thus be tantamount to saying *homoousios* or ταὐτοούσιος in the sense in which we saw it rejected by the homoiousians.[10]

---

[3] For this judgment cf.: Brennecke (1989), 249–53. Steenson (1983, esp. 104–25), on the other hand, wants to make neo-Arianism the background of the entire trinitarian debate of the 350s including Athanasius' and the homoiousian contribution.

[4] Cf. Vaggione (1987), xiii.

[5] For a general account of Eunomius' life and thought see: Abramowski (1966); Meredith (1972), 39–52; Kopecek (1979), vol. II.

[6] Cf. e.g. *apol* 7 (40 Vaggione).

[7] For 'unbegotten' cf. *apol* 8 (40–2 Vaggione).

[8] *Apol* 9–11 (42–6 Vaggione); for 'offspring' cf. esp. 12,6–12 (48 Vaggione).

[9] Ap. Epiphanius, *haer* 73,13,2 (vol. III, 285,30–286,3 Holl/Dummer); for the manifesto's authorship cf. Steenson (1983), 212–14. Hanson (1988, 365–6) would leave the question undecided.

[10] So also: Kopecek (1979), vol. II, 317–20; Williams (1983), 70.

His argument starts from the simple and uncomposite character of divine substance. In such a substance, then, there is no room for any difference in rank or time, as this would require that either of those is a genuine part of the substance, which for Eunomius is absurd:

> But if it neither is nor ever could be lawful to conceive of these (sc. attributes like shape, mass, and size) or anything like them as being joined to the substance of God, what further argument is there which will permit the likening of the begotten to the unbegotten substance? Neither the likening nor the association of the substance has left any room for a pre-eminence or a distinction but has manifestly yielded an equivalence (ἰσότης) and along with that equivalence has shown that the thing likened or compared is itself unbegotten. But after all, there is no one so ignorant or so zealous for impiety as to say that the Son is *equal* (ἴσον) to the Father! (Reference follows to John 14,28)[11]

This contention must have struck at the heart of the attempts by many Eastern theologians of the time to develop a framework for the proper description of the unique relationship between Father and Son. As we have seen, those attempts were aimed at avoiding the complete co-ordination of the Trinitarian Persons for which the *homoousion* was supposed to stand. Eunomius equally rejects such co-ordination, indeed he considers it absurd. However, he goes on to argue[12] that, as God *qua* substance is absolutely simple, any term indicating his substance must indicate it entirely; it is therefore impossible to say that the Son and the Father have only certain properties in common while other properties maintain their difference. According to Eunomius this would mean to introduce the notion of composition into the Deity which again would be blasphemous.

In this context mention has to be made of a further view held by Eunomius that was to become influential.[13] Eunomius could not easily deny that Scripture uses the same names for both Father and Son. To account for this fact he argued again that due to God's simplicity all names that refer to him must have exactly the same meaning, i.e. 'unbegotten'. However, if this is conceded, those same names when used for the Son must either indicate 'unbegotten' too or else must be used for the Son in a different sense. As the former view is obviously wrong, the only possible explanation would be that,

---

[11] Eunomius, *apol* 11,4–10 (46 Vaggione); ET: Vaggione (1987), 47. Cf. Kopecek (1979), vol. II, 319–20.

[12] *Apol* 19 (56–8 Vaggione).

[13] Loc. cit.

in spite of common names the underlying substances are dissimilar.

It is the merit of Eunomius to have brought into the open here a simmering logical problem of early Christian theology: Scripture ascribes many names, notably 'God', but also, for example, 'light' equally to the Father and the Son. However, what is the meaning of such predication? For anybody approaching this question from the background of Aristotle's *Categories* (*cat* 1 [1ª1–12]) there seem to be two possible explanations: such predication can either be unequivocal or equivocal. In the former case the community of names would be indicative of community of being (in Aristotle's language those things would be 'synonymous'), whereas in the latter case it would not (those things, then, would be 'homonymous'). The examples given by Aristotle are that both man and cow are 'animal' synonymously, while a (living) animal and a painting are referred to as 'animal' homonymously. The latter example is, I think, of some importance here. It is often argued that what Aristotle had in mind were puns: two things are only incidentally given the same name. An English example for this would be 'ball', which means both a sphere and a dance. However, it is not clear that this is what the text means and, whatever Aristotle himself may have thought, his late ancient commentators certainly understood him in a different way.[14] They suggested he had spoken of an animal and the painting of an *animal*; while the latter item might be called 'animal' as well, it is nevertheless clear that it *is* something completely different from the animal being. Such an interpretation of homonymity makes Aristotle's distinction obviously quite relevant for philosophical thought: if, for example, one believes in the existence of Platonic forms as paradigmatic entities subsisting outside the sensible realm, such a form (of man, for example) might be called 'man' as well as the particular rational animal: nevertheless the two would be 'homonyms'. Or else, if the Bible calls men 'gods' (Ps 82,6) this does, of course, not mean that those men *were* god in the same sense as the one God, although, on the other hand, this name is not randomly given to them.

The means to distinguish between those kinds of predication was, according to the *Categories* (1 [1ª1–12]), the application of the formula of being (λόγος τῆς οὐσίας). If it is the same in both cases, we have a case of synonymity, otherwise it is homonymity. Thus, for example, we can call both Paul and Peter 'man'; substituting 'rational

---

[14] For a lengthy discussion cf.: Simplicius, *in Cat* (31,22–33,21 Kalbfleisch).

mortal animal' for 'man' the statement remains true. If, however, we call both the apostle of the gentiles and a statue 'Paul,' it is clear that an explanatory account of both items would reveal that their essences are entirely different. For it was not by chance that the definition was referred to as λόγος τῆς οὐσίας: such an account was indeed thought to indicate a thing's essence or being.[15]

The derivative relationship discussed above (ἀφ' ἑνός or πρὸς ἕν)[16] was a matter of debate: many commentators counted them as kinds of homonym, as Aristotle himself had done, but some apparently thought they would not coincide with either of those alternatives.[17] At any event, it appears that at times it must have been difficult to maintain an exact distinction between 'homonymous' items and such things as constitute a derivative genus. If, for example, the form of man is thought of less as a paradigm and more as the cause of the individuals' existence, then they would probably constitute a quasi-genus rather than be 'homonyms'. Equally, one may wonder, whether the created light is really 'homonymous' with the uncreated light, or whether the common name does not rather indicate that one is the origin of the other.

For upholders of the derivation theology described above the consequences were severe: they had to deny the latter claim, but to maintain that the derivative relationship holds good within the Trinity only. They then had to explain that the same word, for example 'light' meant one thing, when used for the Father, another, when used for the Son, and again quite another, when used for created beings. Quite generally, it appears that the problem broached here turned out to be an enormously difficult one. Without pursuing this question here, I would suggest that it was at this point that the *ousia-energeia* distinction became relevant: a product of the *ousia* would be in a derivative relationship to its cause, while a product of the *energeia* would not.[18] Eunomius himself suggested that God's own *ousia* would always remain unproductive;[19] he introduced a strict separation between God's substance and his energy, and only for the latter

---

[15] About the meaning of οὐσία in this phrase cf. Ammonius, *in Cat* (20,26–21,2 Busse).

[16] The commentators make a difference between the two (Simplicius, loc. cit.)

[17] Simplicius, loc. cit.; cf.: *paraphr Themist* 18 (136,30–137,12 Minio Paluello); Philoponus, *in Cat* (16,21–17,19 Busse) who all count them as homonyms.

[18] Very helpful for this problem is the discussion in Steenson (1983), 166–95.

[19] Cf. M. Barnes (1985).

did he permit the name 'Father'.[20] This, he insisted, would be the only biblical, non-Greek way of understanding God's transcendence. The Unbegotten and the Son would thus be 'homonyms' with regard to whatever predication. To this Eunomian doctrine Gregory of Nyssa bears witness as he comments on one particular passage from Eunomius' *Second Apology* as follows:

> To say that the most honorouable names are applied to the weakest things, though not having by nature an equal apportionment of dignity, secretely paves the way, as it were, for the blasphemy to follow, that he may teach his disciples this; that although the Only-begotten is called God, and Wisdom, and Power, and Light, and the Truth, and the Judge, and the King, and God over all, and the great God, and the Prince of peace, and the Father of the world to come, and so forth, His honour is limited to the name. He does not, in fact, partake of that dignity which the meaning of those names indicates.[21]

What must have annoyed his opponents was again the way Eunomius stressed the exclusiveness of the alternative. They were, in the great majority, not at all willing to concede that names were used unequivocally for the divine Persons as this again would have amounted to the introduction of equality *qua* substance.

In summary, then, it appears to have been Eunomius' chief goal to disown the kind of derivation theory which, in one form or another, had by then been held by most Eastern theologians with regard to the Trinity. His argument was that dissimilarity in substance was the only possible alternative to the introduction of complete co-ordination of the Persons which he held to be incompatible with Christian monotheism and logically absurd. Leaving aside here the question of how compelling this logic was, I should contend that it was quite successful; certainly not in the sense that a majority felt convinced by the anomoian theology, but in so far as the emergence of the latter marked, quite generally, the decline of the traditional derivation theology.

---

[20] Cf. his *reductiones ad absurdum* of Basil's claim that 'Unbegotten' and 'Father' have the same meaning: *apol apol*, ap. Gregory of Nyssa, *Eun* I 577 (GNO I, 192,20–193,1); ibid. 600 (GNO I, 199,4–10).

[21] *Eun* II 329–332 (GNO I, 322,6ff.); ET: Moore/Wilson (1893), 283.

2.2 *The Cappadocian reaction*

For this the Cappadocian position, as it was first developed by Basil and later adopted by the two Gregories, offers primary evidence. The influence exercised by Eunomius on them consisted, briefly, in the following: (1) Eunomius' alternative of either dissimilar or equal was effectively accepted; the latter position, rejected by previous theologians and considered absurd by Eunomius himself, is adopted; (2) names used for both, Father and Son, mean the same in both cases (Father and Son are 'synonyms'); (3) a plurality of names does not contradict the notion of divine simplicity as names are generally applied to things by conception (ἐπινοίᾳ).[22] I shall concentrate on the first two points; they mark the relevance of the use of human nature as an analogy for trinitarian unity.

This description outlines a concept that developed during the 360s and 70s. Nevertheless, it appears that it is, in principle, present in Basil's early statements on the subject already, the earliest example being his letter to Apollinarius. Could this letter, which seems to react to the 359/360 synod at Constantinople,[23] already be influenced by Eunomius' teaching? We know that Basil had his first encounter with Eunomius at that synod, a somewhat mysterious event as far as our sources are concerned, which may well be due to the fact that Basil did not particularly shine there.[24] Furthermore, it appears likely that it was at this synod that Eunomius originally presented his *Apology*, that is the writing Basil would later set out to rebut.[25] Thus, there is nothing unlikely in the assumption that the letter to Apollinarius, although not alluding to Eunomius or the anomoian cause in general, shows the traces of the impression made by Eunomius upon Basil.

---

[22] Basil, *adv Eun* I 5–8 (PG 26, 520C–525D); the bulk of Nyssen's *Eun* II is devoted to this argument.

[23] Cf. *ep* 361,8–11 (vol. III, 221 Courtonne = 202,7–9 de Riedmatten): ἐπεὶ οὖν οἱ πάντα φύροντες καὶ λόγων καὶ ζητημάτων τὴν οἰκουμένην ἐμπλήσαντες, τὸ τῆς οὐσίας ὄνομα ὡς ἀλλότριον τῶν θείων λογίων, ἐξέβαλον, . . .

[24] Cf. Gregory of Nyssa, *Eun* I 78–88 (GNO I, 49,9ff.); Philostorgius, *hist eccl* IV 12 (64,3–5 Bidez/Winckelmann). *Pace* Drecoll (1996, 3–4) it seems clear from the passage in *Eun* that both, Gregory and Eunomius presuppose Basil's presence at the council in question.

[25] The date of the *Apology* has been much debated (cf. the brief account in: Roeder [1993], 43–56). Most scholars now seem to agree that the work ought to be connected to one of the Constantinopolitan synods of 359 and 360 (Wickham [1969]; Vaggione [1987], 8; Kopecek [1979] II, 305–7; Roeder [1993], loc. cit.); a precise decision does not appear necessary for the present purpose.

As I suggested earlier, this epistle has often been misunderstood as a document testifying to Basil's early alliance with his Ancyran namesake. As the assumption that Basil in his early days was a homoiousian is still regarded by much of scholarly literature as an established fact, it may be worthwhile to subject it to somewhat closer scrutiny at the present place.

Excursus: Was Basil ever a homoiousian?

Answering this question we should first of all recall the above (p. 26) considerations about the term 'homoiousian'. In their light I shall regard as evidence for Basil's homoiousianism only indications that (1) he was personally attached to the homoiousian party or (ideally, of course, *and*) (2) that his theology coincides with that of extant documents of this party. As (2) is addressed more generally by the present chapter I confine myself here to (1).

It is often said that Basil attended the 360 synod at Constantinople as part of the homoiousian camp. This claim is based on Philostorgius (*hist eccl* IV 12), but there are indications that the latter depends for his information on Eunomius.[26] The fact of Basil's presence at the synod should not be doubted in itself, but, as neither of the two authors gives any details of Basil's alliance with those homoiousian bishops, only cautious conclusions are to be drawn from it. Moreover, it should be allowed that these two anomoians had as little interest in differentiating between their opponents as, *vice versa*, Athanasius had: the mere fact, then, that both Basils opposed the anomoian cause could have accounted for their being regarded as allies.

Allowing even that Philostorgius' report is basically accurate, it would still be the most likely assumption that Basil's support was solicited by Eustathius; his deference for the latter, however, resulting from his asceticism rather than from doctrinal teaching, it appears again difficult to infer anything about Basil's homoiousianism from this fact.

These considerations may not seem to weaken considerably the

---

[26] The fact that Philostorgius introduces Basil as 'Βασίλειος ἕτερος' points to Eunomius' remark (ap. Gregory of Nyssa, *Eun* I 27 [GNO I, 30,13–9]) that Basil of Ancyra troubled him 'by means of a namesake'; for Philostorgius' dependence on Eunomius' account of the events at Constantinople (ap. Gregory, *Eun* I 78–86 [GNO I, 49,13–52,4]) cf. Gummerus (1900), 147, n. 1.

case for Basil's early homoiousianism. They gain their force, however, from that evidence which can be adduced *against* an affiliation of Basil with the homoiousian party. This evidence consists, to put it briefly, in his early and apparently wholehearted commitment to the neo-Nicene party headed by Meletius. Now, Basil's connections with those neo-Nicenes are so obvious that they are indeed difficult to ignore. That, nevertheless, they have not prevented scholars from assuming a homoiousian Basil is partially due to the fact that those Meletians have often been thought to be break-away homoiousians themselves. However, as far as I can see they all have a homoian background;[27] there are no traces linking them personally to the homoiousian party. On the contrary, it seems clear that there was considerable hostility between these two camps from the very beginning. This is not surprising: many of those Meletian bishops held sees on which they had replaced deposed homoiousians in 360. This meant that, beyond doctrinal differences, there were substantial institutional rivalries current between them, which could not easily be settled. The best known of such cases is that of Eustathius of Sebaste and Meletius; we learn from Basil's letters that Basil himself almost forfeited the trust of both sides as he attempted to maintain his ties with both of them.

Keeping this in mind, the fact of Basil's alliance with those break-away homoians can only be explained by either assuming a complete lack of conscience on his part or by rejecting his homoiousian past. Consider, for example, how he writes to Athanasius of Ancyra around the year 365 (*ep* 25) and on the latter in *Epistle 29*. This would have been the person who had replaced Basil of Ancyra only a few years ago! Possibly the latter had died in the meantime (we do not hear from him after 363); nevertheless, Basil's attitude would testify to the most abhorrent opportunism. Such a characteristic cannot, of course, be ruled out; however, how likely is it? After all, the party Basil joined now, and to which he was to be faithful until his death, was not powerful at all. On the contrary, it was at odds with the emperor Valens throughout his reign, and Basil would not live to see it triumphant. I should therefore conclude that Basil's decision to join the neo-Nicene party of Meletius weighs strongly against a formal homoiousian past.

This is not to deny, of course, Basil's personal links to leading homoiousians. Looking for homoiousians among the many people

---

[27] Brennecke (1989), 245–8.

whom Basil addresses or mentions in his letters does not, however, yield many results: it appears that the only person who was both homoiousian *and* affiliated with Basil for a long time, is Eustathius of Sebaste. However, their connection seems to have been conditioned by their common devotion to monasticism in the first place (cf. *ep* 223,3). Indeed, it seems to me that Basil's extended description of the vicissitudes of their friendship in *Epistle 223* makes *more* sense under the presupposition that they never belonged to the same ecclesiastical party. For, granted even that Basil here is quite diplomatic with the truth it would be difficult to account for his claim of *continuity* in faith[28] had there been such a clear-cut border-crossing as the change of party affiliation. It is much easier, I believe, to understand the history and break-up of their friendship under the assumption that its substance was always the common ascetic ideal while doctrinal concurrence was presumed—until, finally, it was discovered to be missing.

Via Eustathius, Basil may have met other homoiousians as, for example, Silvanus of Tarsus.[29] Although Basil speaks highly of him (*ep* 69; 244,3), it seems difficult to ascertain the precise nature of their relationship.

From *Epistle 223*[30] it might appear that the homoiousians attempted to solicit Basil's support for the synod at Lampsacus (365), and some have thought that Basil must have attended it. But it is, to my mind, not clear that this is a correct interpretation of the relevant passage. What Basil writes is that he was called to a place called Eusinoé,[31] where something like a preparatory meeting for that synod must have been held and that *there* they talked about doctrinal matters. He does *not* say that he attended the synod at Lampsacus, nor does he intimate the precise character of his involvement with that preparatory meeting. His phrasing (προσεκαλέσασθέ με) seems most naturally to suggest that he did not attend it as a member or a sympathiser of the party, but that, for whatever reason, his advice was sought. Incidentally it may be noted that at the synod of Lampsacus it was

---

[28] *Ep* 223,3,30ff. (vol. III, 12 Courtonne).
[29] Assuming for the sake of the argument that the v.l. in *ep* 223,5,5 is genuine (*pace* Courtonne, vol. III, 14).
[30] *Ep* 223,5,5–7 (vol. III, 14 Courtonne).
[31] Perhaps to be identified with Εὐσήνη, a place situated between Amisos and the mouth of the Halys (cf. Zgusta [1984], 176–7); this would have been near Basil's monastery.

decided to send a delegation, including Eustathius of Sebaste, to Italy, which then confessed the Nicene Creed to Pope Liberius:[32] if Basil ever had hopes to win the homoiousians over to the Nicene side, this would have appeared most justified at that time.

From all these considerations I should conclude that there is no conclusive evidence that Basil ever joined the homoiousian party; it appears most likely that he never did.

What, then, is the homoiousianism of the *Epistle 361?* It is true, Basil there expresses certain reservations towards the *homoousion*, and those reservations are in line with the arguments we encountered with several theologians, including homoiousians. Moreover, he suggests the phrase ἀπαραλλάκτως ὅμοιος κατ' οὐσίαν as an alternative formulation.[33] There, however, the similarities end. Basil's brief sketch of his own position makes it, to my mind, abundantly clear that his approach to the trinitarian question is anything rather than a further development of the homoiousian view:[34]

> For we hold that whatever the substance of the Father is by hypothesis assumed to be, this must needs be altogether assumed of the Son's substance as well; so that, if one calls the Father's substance 'intelligible, eternal, unbegotten light', he will call the substance of the Son also 'intelligible, eternal, begotten light'.[35]

Contrary to both the homoiousian and Apollinarius' view, according to these lines it is not his generation from the Father that accounts for the Son's divinity in the first place, but the community of *logoi*: whatever can be said of the Father *qua* substance holds equally good for the Son too. This is the principle of synonymity from the *Categories!* In the light of what has so far been found, this finding is quite surprising and of some significance. If Basil knows what he is doing, then the meaning must be that *equality* has replaced derivation as the principle of community in the Trinity. And indeed, a little later,

---

[32] Sozomen, *hist eccl* VI 10–2 (249,3–254,14 Bidez/Hansen).

[33] But phrases containing 'likeness' were used and even explicitly endorsed by Athanasius himself, cf: *c Arian* I 20. 21. 26; III 26 and *syn* 41,3–4 (267,3–11 Opitz).

[34] This point has also been established by Meredith (1972, 240–52): 'The obvious differences between the beliefs stated or implied in this programme (sc. the 358 homoiousian manifesto) and the system of the Cappadocians are so great as to dispose of any suspicion that there was any great influence exercised by the Homoeusian party upon the neoNicenes' (op. cit., 247).

[35] Basil, *ep* 361,24–9 (vol. III, 221 Courtonne = 202,20–4 de Riedmatten).

Basil expressly asserts (perhaps an allusion to *Categories* 5 [3ᵇ33–4ᵃ9])
that there is not more or less between light and light.[36] That is, Basil
chooses precisely that understanding of divine unity that had so far
been consequently rejected: the co-ordination of the Persons.

However, if this is his theological intent, then his enquiring after
the meaning of *homoousios* is at least likely to indicate more than a
'political' interest: for it had been precisely this corollary of the Nicene
term, that, as we have seen, had so far conditioned its rejection.
Basil would have known about this, and so he sensed a convergence
of his own and the Nicene theology. To be sure, difficulties remained,
and these difficulties account for the letter to Apollinarius. They do
not, however, obliterate the basic theological agreement. Those
difficulties concern mainly the unsolved problem of the status of the
ousia in such a Trinity. One can see that this problem was bound
to gain an even more prominent place in Cappadocian thinking than
it had hitherto occupied: they could no more argue that the Father
qua being the *arche* was quasi-identical with the *ousia*; what, then, was
the latter's character? This question must have troubled Basil and
his followers; could there be any answer to this dilemma that was
not aporetic? One consequence of this seems to be that they never
felt passionate towards the *homoousion* (as, for example, Victorinus at
the same time did), but (like Athanasius)[37] mainly employed it where
they had to defend it as part of the Nicene Creed. Otherwise, they
preferred to talk about Father and Son being the same in substance
(κατ' οὐσίαν) rather than being one substance.

In spite of this, however, they accepted the *homoousion* since, *by
means of its connotation of co-ordination*, it eventually best expressed their
genuine understanding of the Trinity; and I should contend that this
theological position is witnessed by the present document already.

But why did Basil opt for this co-ordinate model in the first place?
Prima facie several reasons seem possible: Basil could have drawn on
particular local traditions that are no longer known to us; he could
have arrived at this position following theological considerations of
his own, attempting to untie the conceptual knot that was at the
root of the trinitarian controversy. One reason, which has often been
said to have been at the heart of Basil's decision to adopt the *homoousion*, the political need to unite all the anti-Arians in the light of the

---

[36] *Ep* 361,31–5 (vol. III, 221 Courtonne = 202,25–8 de Riedmatten).
[37] Cf Stead (1977), 260.

new anomoian threat should, I think, be discarded: as we have seen, the sheer absurdity of co-ordinating the Persons had been a major reason for rejecting Nicaea and the *homoousion*. In comparison, the other two explanations may well contain elements of truth.[38] However, in the light of what has been found so far and, in particular, considering the hitherto almost universal rejection of Basil's view, it seems to me that the influence of Eunomius' polemic should be regarded as crucial: Basil would have accepted that, in order to avoid Eunomius' blasphemous conclusions, one had to opt for equality among the divine Persons.

2.2.1 *The Cappadocian application of human nature*

In this sense, I shall now show, the Cappadocians adopted humanity as an analogy for the Trinity. Previous scholarship has often argued that the introduction of this analogy was due to its weaker sense of unity which would have facilitated the adoption of the *homoousion* by its more moderate opponents. However, it is not obvious that there is much evidence to support this view: those homoiousian opponents, as we have seen, would reject the *homoousion* alongside the analogy of humanity. Quite generally, the initial survey has, I hope, shown that *homoousios* was primarily rejected not because of its Sabellian tendencies, but because of the very same notion of co-ordination that apparently made it attractive for Basil in the first place. Again, Apollinarius' interpretation of human nature as a substance derived from its first instantiation might have pleased the homoiousians, but we have seen that this is not how Basil wanted the *homoousion* to be understood. Indeed, we shall presently see in some detail that, where human nature is employed as an analogy for the Godhead by the Cappadocians, its use was consciously different from the Apollinarian interpretation in *Epistle 362* and in line with the sketchy description Basil gives of his own position in the same place.

Perhaps it is again the needs of the Eunomian controversy which offer the best explanation for the fact that and the wa in which this analogy was drawn. I have argued above that one of the relevant issues brought into the open by Eunomius was the application of names to the Trinitarian Persons: in what sense do we call both,

---

[38] As for the first one, it may be recalled that Basil twice claims that an otherwise unknown Hermogenes, bishop of Caesarea, had written the Nicene Creed: *ep* 81,24–5 [vol. I, 183 Courtonne]; 244,9,9–12 (vol. III, 82 Courtonne).

Father and Son, for example, God? Eunomius himself had given one
answer that seemed unacceptable to most of his contemporaries.
However, in order to formulate a solution that would not only avoid
Eunomius' theory, but would also account for the implications of
their orthodoxy, his opponents had to employ the appropriate kind
of analogy. It is obvious that the very vivid physical imagery of sun
and ray, or source and river, which had been so dear to the entire
tradition, could not fulfil this purpose, whereas humanity could;
human nature would thus have suggested itself in this situation as
an analogy primarily because it could illustrate how predication in
the Godhead was to be understood. It would thus have gained its
relevance as a *logical* analogy in the first place. In a sense this analogy was all but new: given the biblical language the comparison of
Father and Son to human parent and offspring would appear to be
the most natural one. Nevertheless, it is clear that it is one thing to
argue that the relationship between Father and Son in the Godhead
resembles that of a human parent to his offspring, quite another to
compare the former relationship to that of two men *qua* man.[39] The
latter analogy appears to have been introduced not primarily to give
the unity or the plurality in the Godhead a particularly strong emphasis, but rather in order to press home the unequivocal use of 'substantial' predicates for all divine Persons; that is, against both the
contentions of Eunomius and the tacit presupposition of most of the
tradition it was maintained that such names mean the same with
both Father and Son the way they do with human beings.

At the same time, of course, this analogy could also demonstrate
how the Persons were different from each other; this is the relevance
of the *ousia-hupostasis* distinction which was popularised by the Cappadocians. I will not here go into a thorough debate of the origin of
that distinction.[40] As is well known, our probably earliest reference
to it is found in Victorinus in c. 358;[41] but he claims that it is employed
by the Greeks. It would thus appear that the Cappadocians did not
invent it. Moreover, Basil does not seem to have known it at all
when he wrote his *Adversus Eunomium*, i.e. in the early 360s.[42]

---

[39] Cf. Stead (1977), 265: '. . . we entirely mistake the point of the Father-Son
analogy if we treat it as equivalent to that of two men *simpliciter*.'
[40] Cf. Abramowski (1979).
[41] *C Arium* 2,4,51 (*CSEL* 83,1,178).
[42] Cf. now Drecoll (1996), 101–2.

Nevertheless, it is one thing to use *hupostasis* for the Trinitarian Person,[43] quite another, to give it the particular definition it received in the Cappadocians' writings. Whether anybody else ventured upon such a definition prior to them, we do not know. Thus I cannot see why we should not credit them with originality in this particular question.

2.2.2   *The Antiochene background*

Upholders of the traditional view might argue that in Basil himself it often appears crucial that the danger of Sabellianism should be warded off.[44] Indeed, he regularly urges that the term *hupostasis* has to be employed in order to exclude ambiguity in that respect.[45] He also seems to intimate that the Nicene *homoousion* could be misunderstood as furthering the Sabellian error.[46] Thus he writes at one point:

> Consider, admirable friend, that the forgers of the truth, who have introduced the Arian schism into the sound faith of the fathers, could not adduce another reason for not adopting the pious dogma of the fathers than the notion of consubstantiality (ὁμοούσιος). This they interpreted perversely and in order to slander the faith saying that the Son was called by us *homoousios* in *hupostasis*.[47]

What do we have to make of this statement? As we have seen there is no evidence that the rejection of the *homoousion* was at any point specially due to its allegedly Sabellian implications. On the other hand, it seems difficult simply to write off this statement as it comes from an important first-hand witness of those events.

It seems to me that the most natural interpretation of these lines, as of similar texts from Basil's pen, is that they represent a feared or real problem of Basil's own trinitarian teaching. If it was his own theory that Basil felt he had to defend against such an interpretation, this line of defence is not surprising. Once the complete co-ordination

---

[43] This, of course, had been done by many authors since Origen (cf. e.g. *in Ioh* II 75 [65,15–7 Preuschen]).

[44] Cf., e.g., *ep* 125,1,16–50 (vol. II, 31–2 Courtonne). Incidentally, it may be noted that the initially discussed theory of a 'Sabellian' interpretation of the term ὁμοούσιος had Basil as its chief witness (Zahn [1867], 10).

[45] *Ep* 214,3 (vol. II, 204–5 Courtonne); 236,6,22–8 (vol. III, 54 Courtonne); 258,3,34–40 (vol. III, 103 Courtonne).

[46] Cf. again *ep* 214, 3; in *ep* 52,3,1–6 on the other hand he argues that ὁμοούσιος would, conversely, rule out the danger of Sabellianism (vol. I, 135–6 Courtonne).

[47] *Ep* 214,3,1–7 (vol. III, 204 Courtonne).

of the Persons had been maintained, it was easily argued (and we have evidence that this did indeed occur)[48] that this would necessarily result in either tritheism or Sabellianism: in the former case the three Persons would be independent principles, in the latter, simply aspects of one divine being. However, these two arguments are but two sides of one coin: both derive their legitimacy from the central Cappadocian tenet of equality within the Trinity. It is interesting to compare here a statement of the 'Sabellian' Marcellus from his letter to Pope Julius:

> That the divinity of Father and Son is indivisible, we have learned from the divine Scriptures. For if one separates the Son, that is the Logos, from the almighty God, he will necessarily either conceive of there being two gods, which is thought to be alien to the divine teaching, or confess that the Logos is not God, which again appears to be alien to the correct faith as the evangelist says, 'and the word was God'.[49]

It appears that this statement provides for an interesting parallel to Basil's argument. To be sure, their interests are opposed to each other: while Basil argues that Nicaea without 'three *hupostaseis*' would be Sabellian, Marcellus argues that the assumption of a subsisting Logos would either be Arian or ditheistic. Nevertheless, behind this *prima facie* contradiction there is an important agreement: both reject the possibility of a derivative divine *ousia* which we have seen at the heart of those theological attempts that were analysed in the previous section.

If one can thus draw a line from Basil back to Marcellus, it is perhaps not entirely surprising that the closest precedent to the Cappadocian trinitarian position is to be found in a fragment ascribed to Eustathius of Antioch.[50] There are problems of authenticity attached to this fragment, but even if it is not Eustathius', it certainly is 'Eustathian', i.e. it represents the teaching of his minority church at

---

[48] Cf. the line of argument of the pneumatomachoi reported in Nyssen's *Eust* (GNO III/1, 5,3–14).

[49] *Fr* 129 (215,25–30 Klostermann/Hansen).

[50] Lorenz (1980). The fragment from an as yet unpublished part of Peter of Callinicus' books *Against Damian* had previously been edited in parts by Martin (in J.-B. Pitra's *Analecta Sacra* IV, Paris 1883, 212 [442]). Its proper understanding had furthermore been marred by a mistaken translation by Cowper (1861, 60), cf. Wickham (1990, 348). Hübner (1971, 208f.) denied the authenticity of the fragments and ascribed them to Gregory of Nyssa, but his case has been settled by Lorenz' publication (op. cit., 122–4). See further pp. 108–9 below.

Antioch. About Eustathius' own trinitarian teaching we do not have much information except that he was one of the champions at Nicaea; a number of fragments from anti-Arian works are extant. It is a matter of debate among scholars how 'Marcellan' his theology was.[51] I take it, however, that, while he must have spoken of one *hupostasis*,[52] apparently identifying *ousia* and *hupostasis*, he nevertheless conceived of a personal Logos.[53] Whether one believes that he himself employed for this the term *prosopon* depends partly on the authenticity of the aforesaid fragment; his followers, at any rate, must have used it.

That this doctrine was suspected of Sabellianism is well known, but it was also called tritheistic. The former charge is indeed frequently levelled against Eustathius' followers by Basil himself.[54] This fact has, I suppose, prevented scholars from noticing rather striking similarities between the two positions. Those similarities come out, however, quite distinctly from the aforesaid fragment. There Eustathius defends his position against the charge of tritheism, which, it appears, Photinus had directed at it. What was the substance of this charge? Lorenz, who first published the entire fragment together with a discussion of its authorship and theology, suggests that in comparison with the radically unitary theology of Photinus, Eustathius' doctrine of Trinitarian Persons was, as it were, 'comparatively' tritheistic.[55] However, from the argument developed by Eustathius it appears that his opponent's case must have rested on the assumption that a distinction between Persons on the same ontological plane *ipso facto* amounts to tritheism: Photinus simply seems to have applied the logic of his former mentor, Marcellus.

In his answer, Eustathius defends precisely that tenet. He argues that the name 'God' is not indicative of a Person, but of nature so that, as there is one divine nature, there is also one God, not three. Note the striking difference to the argumentative pattern for example in Apollinarius: the latter would argue that there is only one God because the Father is God in the first place, as we are all men

---

[51] That his doctrine was strongly unitary is asserted by Sellers (1928, 88–99) following Loofs (1924, 296ff.). Different, however, Sellers (1940, 122–3); Spanneut (1967, 21); Lorenz (1980, 114–6; 1982, 545); Hanson (1988), 208–17.

[52] Otherwise one cannot explain the outbreak of the Antiochene schism; cf.: Athanasius, *tom ad Ant* 6 (PG 26, 801C–804A). See also Eustathius' *fr* 38 Spanneut.

[53] Cf. Socrates, *hist eccl* I 23,8 (70,10–4 Hansen).

[54] *Ep* 263,5,2–11 (vol. III, 125 Courtonne); 214,3–4 (vol. II, 204–6 Courtonne).

[55] Lorenz (1980), 117.

in so far as we are all Adam.[56] Neither is it by chance that Eustathius' arguments prefigure those to be adduced by Gregory of Nyssa in his defence against tritheism. The latter, as we shall see, made intensive use of Eustathius' writing in his *Ad Graecos*. That Eustathius cites 'common nature' as the element of unity seems to coincide with the dangerous 'Greek use' of the *homoousion*, rejected by both Athanasius and the Meletians, which was said to imply the existence of something further beyond the Persons.

Now, the term *homoousios* is not used in the fragment, nor is the analogy of human nature expressly drawn. Nevertheless it seems to me that both are implied. That the Eustathian community was Nicene we should not doubt, and as such they would have used the *homoousion* in the tradition of their former bishop.

Be this as it may, the fact that for his doctrine of equality in the Trinity Basil was largely indebted to the Eustathian tradition helps explain his insistence on 'three *hupostaseis*'. That Basil in an almost obstinate way urges that it is not sufficient to say 'three *prosopa*' we have already seen. This has at times been explained by a certain ambiguity of the latter term, which would allegedly leave a loophole for a denial of the real subsistence of the persons.[57] However, it is not clear that this is the case. We have evidence that the term *prosopon* was employed alongside *hupostasis* by the Cappadocians themselves, in particular by the two Gregories;[58] it is, to my mind, not obvious that this indicates a conceptual shift away from Basil's doctrine.[59] It is, on the other hand, easily argued that due to his theological affiliations with the Eustathian view Basil had to distance himself from Eustathius' followers if he wanted to remain a credible ally for Meletius, who was becoming more and more a central figure in the Eastern church. It appears, then, that the emphasis placed on the *ousia-hupostasis* distinction is Basil's way of balancing these two interests.

---

[56] Apollinarius, *KMP* 18: ὥστε εἴ τις ἔροιτο Πῶς εἷς θεός, εἴπερ ἐκ θεοῦ θεὸς εἴη ὁ υἱός; ἐροῦμεν ὅτι Τῷ τῆς ἀρχῆς λόγῳ, καθ' ὃν μία ἀρχὴ ὁ πατήρ. (...) 19 καὶ πάλιν ἐὰν εἴπωσιν οἱ ἀσεβεῖς Πῶς οὐκ ἂν εἶεν τρεῖς θεοὶ τρία πρόσωπα, εἰ μίαν ἔχοιεν τὴν θεότητα; ἐροῦμεν Ἐπειδὴ ὁ θεὸς ἀρχὴ καὶ πατήρ ἐστιν τοῦ υἱοῦ, καὶ οὗτος εἰκών ἐστι καὶ γέννημα τοῦ πατρὸς καὶ οὐκ ἀδελφὸς αὐτοῦ, ... (173,17–26 Lietzmann).

[57] Cf. Andresen (1961), 30–2 following Basil's own statements, cf. n. 45 above.

[58] Cf. Gregory of Nyssa, *graec* (GNO III/1, 33,3–4); Nazianzen says in his oration to the Constantinopolitan Council of 381 that the debate about one or three ὑποστάσεις was a mere quarrel about words (*or* 42,16,26–30 [84 Bernardi]). Cf. also the, certainly not Sabellian!, homoiousians ap. Epiphanius, *haer* 73,16,1 (vol. III, 288,20–3 Holl/Dummer).

[59] *Pace* Holl (1904), 177 (for Nazianzen).

While I should thus maintain, that the analogy of human nature was primarily drawn to uphold the tenet of co-ordination within the Trinity, it appears that the *ousia-hupostasis* distinction was emphasised in order to maintain alliance with the majority of Eastern theologians and eschew an outright identification with the small Eustathian minority in Antioch.

What precisely is the understanding of human nature in this analogy? To find out we now have to look more closely at those passages where it is indeed used.

2.3   *The writing* On the Difference of *ousia* and *hupostasis*

This is first of all the case in the writing *On the Difference of* ousia *and* hupostasis, which is most conveniently found in the editions of Basil's letters (*ep* 38). As it contains the most ample treatment of human nature as an analogy for the Trinity, it is important to discuss its doctrine here. Its authorship is debated as only part of the manuscript tradition ascribes the treatise to Basil, while other manuscripts witness a claim to Gregory of Nyssa's authorship.[60] The latter is now often thought to be the real author.[61] However, no unambiguous evidence has been adduced in his favour so far.

For the present purpose, however, a decision on this question is not vital. For, contrary to the arguments of some scholars,[62] it does not appear that there is a clear-cut distinction to be made between Basil's and Gregory's approaches to the *ousia-hupostasis* distinction and the understanding of the *homoousion*.

Those claims have been based on a number of passages in Basil's *Contra Eunomium*.[63] There Basil, arguing against certain Eunomian contentions, refers to the human *ousia* as to the material substratum (ὑλικὸν ὑποκείμενον) and seems to say that this *ousia* accounts for men's being *homoousioi*. To this effect, apparently, he also cites Job 33,6 ('From clay have you been formed . . .'). Elsewhere in the same

---

[60] Cf. Fedwick (1978) for a discussion of this question; Fedwick concludes that a decision cannot be reached on the basis of external evidence.

[61] For this position cf. Cavallin (1944), 71–81; Hübner (1972); Fedwick (1978); recently, however, their argument has been criticised as insufficient by Hauschild (1973, vol. I, 182–9), while Hammerstaedt (1991) and now Drecoll (1996, 297–331) wish to demonstrate Basil's authorship.

[62] Mainly Hübner (1972), passim, esp. 474; cf. Holl (1904), 208–220, esp. 220; Balás (1976).

[63] Basil, *adv Eun* I 15 (PG 29, 548B); II 4 (577C).

writing he goes as far as to imply the consubstantiality not only of
men, but of all creatures.[64] Some scholars have taken these statements as evidence that Basil, unlike Gregory, was crucially influenced
by stoicism.[65]

Now, it would perhaps seem not very surprising that Basil should
have been attracted by that Stoic doctrine at first sight. For it must
by now be clear that the Cappadocians faced no easy task defend-
ing their understanding of the *homoousion*. The full force of all the
arguments traditionally rehearsed against the Nicene watchword was
bound to be directed at them. While for their tenet of equality they
could venture on a theological justification (as we shall actually see
them do), the omnipresent corollary of that notion, the problem of
a separate *ousia*, must have caused them great concern. From this,
it might have appeared, the Stoic notion of *ousia* offered a way out.
For it clearly allows for co-ordination and yet is not an entity to be
hypostatically separated from the individuals.

Still it seems clear that Basil never really embraced this view. As
a matter of fact, he makes it quite clear, in the *Contra Eunomium* and
elsewhere, that *ousia* in the Stoic sense cannot be an analogy for the
Trinitarian Godhead.[66] This in itself suggests taking the aforementioned passages as *ad hominem* arguments which, like those presented
by Athanasius in his *De Synodis* (see pp. 33–4 above), start from the
presupposition that men are permitted to be consubstantial in order
to draw certain analogies from their relationship to that of the
Trinitarian Persons. If we consider furthermore that from Basil's epistle to Apollinarius, which was written at about the same time as the
Contra Eunomium, we know that at that time he was as yet uncertain
as to how the term *homoousios* could be reasonably applied to the
Godhead, the conditional character of those passages appears even
more clearly. The mere fact that there is no trace of this line of
argumentation in Basil's later works should forbid us to take them
as establishing his essential doctrine.

That, on the other hand, the doctrine espoused in the *Epistle 38*
corresponds with much of what Basil would write later in his career
is easily demonstrated and has, in fact, been done elsewhere,[67] while

---

[64] *Adv Eun* II 19 (PG 29, 613C).
[65] Cf. Balás (1976), 279; Hübner (1972), 474–82. See also pp. 101–103 below.
[66] Cf. *adv Eun* I 19 (PG 29, 556A–B).
[67] Cf. mainly Hauschild (1973) vol. I, 186, n. 185; 187–8, n. 199.

its concurrence with Gregory's teaching is to be shown later in the present chapter. I shall therefore treat the *Epistle 38* as documenting the Cappadocian teaching on this problem.

The present analysis is in principle limited to that part of the letter, in which the author expounds his understanding of *ousia* and *hupostasis* with regard to humanity.[68] Where statements elsewhere in the epistle bear on this matter they will, of course, have to be taken into account, but the entirety of the epistle will not be subjected to close scrutiny.

The argument in this part of the epistle unfolds in two steps: it starts from a distinction between universal and proper names and their respective indication to proceed to a consideration concerning *ousia* and *hupostasis* as *principles* of universality and particularity. I will try to reconstruct this argument and evaluate its significance for the trinitarian teaching. Afterwards, I shall attempt to elucidate its philosophical background.

2.3.1 *A semantic theory*

The author starts from a distinction between two kinds of noun (2,1–19): all nouns can, according to this theory, be divided into those that are predicated of more than one thing (πρᾶγμα) and those that can be predicated of one thing only. Thus, although they both refer to the same things, they indicate them in different ways: whereas the former kind points out their nature (φύσις) without making the individual existence unequivocal, the latter kind determines the individual.

To understand precisely how the author conceives of this distinction, we have to look somewhat more closely at the text. Let us begin with universal names. The author says of them that

1. they can be said of numerically different things (2,1–3);
2. that by means of such a name the common nature (κοινὴ φύσις) is pointed out or indicated (2,4);
3. that the word does not mark out an individual (2,4–6);
4. that its meaning extends equally over all those who are ordained under it (2,8–9);
5. that it indicates by means of such properties as are common to all the things belonging to the nature (2,12–7).

---

[68] *Ep* 38,2,1–3,12 (vol. I, 81–3 Courtonne). In the following, references in the text will be to section and line of Courtonne's edition.

Of proper names, on the other hand, we learn that

1. in their signification a circumscription is seen of one thing marking out its difference from those to which it is generically related (2,12–6);
2. they are needed to provide for a subdivision (ὑποδιαστολή) of the things signified by the universal term (2,8–11);
3. they indicate or point out one thing (3,6–8).

From this it appears, in the first place, that the author's view on the signification of names is characterised by the analogical treatment of proper and universal terms. Both are said to indicate or point out: the proper name a thing, the universal name a *phusis*; both have a signification also: the proper name of the circumscription of one individual, the universal of properties common to all the members of the class. I shall argue that a specific understanding of the semantics of proper names provides for the paradigm of the author's more general theory. For this reason, I shall start by exploring this aspect of his theory to proceed with the consequences this will have for his view on universal *phusis*.

To begin with it seems clear that the author assigns to the proper name a deictic or referential function:

> For he who says 'Paul' shows that the *phusis* subsists in the thing *indicated by the name* (ἐν τῷ δηλουμένῳ ὑπὸ τοῦ ὀνόματος πράγματι: 3,6–8).

The use of the proper name is thus supposed to include reference to an object, more precisely to one *pragma*. The latter term must, in my view, be here used for what Aristotle called πρώτη οὐσία in his *Categories*, i.e. one concrete, individual thing. It would appear, then, that the relation between the proper name and such a thing is thought of as unequivocal: employing the proper name is in any case sufficient for identifying the object in question.

At the same time it would seem evident that the semantic function of the proper name cannot be reduced, according to this theory, to its reference. The author quite clearly holds that proper names have a signification which would appear to consist in the unequivocal notion of one particular thing's character:

> For no more does such a word (sc. a proper name) refer to what is common in the *phusis*, but it separates from the comprehensive meaning and, where there are certain circumscribed things, it conveys a notion of those by means of the names. (2,16–9)

Proper names, according to these lines, convey the notion (*emphasis*) of individual things. This same notion is earlier said to be the

> circumscription of one particular thing (πρᾶγμα) which has, in so far as it is particular, nothing in common with the other members of the class (πρὸς τὸ ὁμογενές). (2,14–5)

It would seem cogent, then, to conclude that the Cappadocian author ascribes to proper names apart from their referential function in relation to concrete objects (πράγματα) the signification of a notion comprising properties which are particular to this thing and, therefore, capable of sufficiently identifying it.

It must be left open for the moment whether this notion again corresponds to some sort of item. This would not be impossible as there is a clear difference between the contents of this concept and the individual that is said to be pointed out by the proper name. The latter comprises all its particular properties plus the more universal ones, i.e. those that are characteristic of its species and genus; the notion conveyed by the proper name, however, should contain only those properties that are particular with this individual. There could thus conceivably be an entity corresponding to this notion, namely the individual component of the thing. The latter would, then, appear as compound of universal and particular elements.

Now the author's treatment of universal names is to be submitted to somewhat closer scrutiny. I think that his approach causes him to assign to those names a dual function also: they signify a set of properties characteristic of all the individual items to which the name can be applied while at the same time fulfilling a deictic function. As for the former, this would seem not particularly surprising. That the use of a word like 'man' should be connected with the notion of such properties as all human beings have in common might appear natural to most. Still, it is remarkable that the author is rather circumspect about this function of the universal name. In the passage cited above (2,16–7) the universal term is said—by implication—to 'refer to what is common in the *phusis*', while a little earlier the author had asserted, again implicitly, that 'in what is signified (sc. by the universal term) the community of the nature is seen' (2,12–3). Both texts are to be read, I should suggest, as saying that the term 'man' signifies what is common to all human beings.

In any case, it would appear that thinking of a referential function of this term causes us considerably more difficulties. At the same time it seems indubitable that the universally accepted view in antiquity would have required this assumption: 'names are significant of things' (πραγμάτων ἐστί σημαντικὰ τὰ ὀνόματα), Basil writes in one of his letters,[69] and substantially the same statement is to be found in Simplicius' magisterial commentary on the *Categories*.[70] To this corresponds, in the *Epistle 38*, the author's insistence that the universal term 'shows' (δείκνυμι: 2,4) or 'indicates' (δηλοῦν: 3,4–5) the *phusis*.

What kind of thing, then, could be the object of reference of a universal term? We have no reason to believe that ancient authors found the answer to this question less puzzling than we do. Various answers have been given or hinted at. As for the Cappadocians, as for Gregory in particular, I should suggest that the thing the universal name 'man' is supposed to point out or indicate is humanity in its entirety. I should further suggest that the term *phusis* in Gregory's writings is often employed in this sense and that this is the case in the present writing, too. Thus, the *phusis* that is said in the *Epistle 38* to be pointed out by the universal name would be all mankind.

Why should this be so? I must admit for a start that the evidence that can be gathered for this interpretation from within the *Epistle 38* is not in itself altogether conclusive. I should contend, however, that viewed against other texts from the Cappadocians' works and beyond, it can be confirmed to a reasonable extent.

To begin with, the observation that *phusis* in Gregory can stand for the entirety of men, angels, rational creatures etc. has been made by various scholars;[71] incidentally, this is a usage that goes back at least to Plato.[72] One of the most celebrated instances of this is a line from Gregory's *De hominis opificio*:

> When the word says that God made man it points out on account of the indefiniteness of its (sc. 'man's') signification the entire human item (ἅπαν τὸ ἀνθρώπινον). For the name 'Adam' is not used here for the creature as the history says in the following; but the name given to the created man is not the individual (ὁ τὶς) but the universal one (ὁ καθόλου).

Cherniss, Balás, and Hübner all agree that what Gregory here has in mind, the 'entire human item' or human nature, as he will write

---

[69] Basil, *ep* 210,4,25 (vol. II, 194 Courtonne).
[70] Simplicius, *in Cat* (10,22 Kalbfleisch).
[71] Cherniss (1930), 33; Hübner (1974), 83–7; Balás (1979), 119–21.
[72] Cf. Plato, *rep* II, 359 c.

later in the same passage, is the whole of humankind. That this still allows for a variety of interpretations concerning this passage and its context is clear; those will, at a later point (pp. 155ff. below), be subject to inquiry. For the moment it is crucial to note the striking similarity between this passage and one statement from the *Epistle 38* (3,2–6):

> For he who says 'man' produces in the ear a somewhat scattered notion on account of the indefiniteness of its signification so that the nature (φύσις) is indicated from the name, but the subsisting thing (πρᾶγμα), which is specifically indicated by the name, is not signified.

The parallel formulation ('on account of the indefiniteness of signification') has been noted by Hübner, who takes it as evidence in favour of Gregorian authorship of the *Epistle 38*.[73] This it need not be, but it would seem difficult to deny a common conceptual background. In the *De hominis opificio* 16 the indefiniteness of the term's signification was cited to support the author's point that the whole of humanity was the object of God's creation as reported in Gen 1,27. What is it the author of the *Epistle 38* wishes to point out by his statement? The crucial difficulty about its interpretation appears to be this: the author first says that the term indicates the *phusis*, then that it indicates specifically a thing, but does not signify it. From this it would appear, in the first place, that the author here makes a distinction between indication (δηλοῦν) and signification (σημαίνειν). What he may have in mind is that in calling something 'man' we do refer to one thing without, however, making the object of our speech unequivocal. Gregory, at one place, gives a very vivid description of this kind of situation:

> When we address any one, we do not call him by the name of his nature (sc. call him 'man'), in order that no confusion may result from the community of the name, as would happen if everyone of those who hear it were to think that he himself was the person addressed, because the call is made not by the proper appellation but by the common name of their nature.[74]

The idea clearly is that using the universal name we may wish to refer to one individual, but we do not do so, since a multitude of objects answer to the same designation. In certain situations this

---

[73] Hübner (1972), 486–8.
[74] *Abl* (GNO III/1, 40,10–5); ET: Moore/Wilson (1893), 332.

problem may be negligible because it is obvious from accompanying circumstances which object is being referred to. In the middle of the desert the phrase 'a man' may seem reasonably precise; this, however, would not seem to impinge on the principal issue.

Gregory's example, I think, explains two problems of the above statement from the *Epistle 38*. First, it helps understand what the author means by saying that the term 'man' indicates an individual *pragma* but that it does not signify it. It is clear that the indication of the term 'man' cannot, in principle, be different from individual men: calling something 'man' we do not mean to say that we have just spotted a particular set of properties or, for that matter, an enmattered form. What we wish to point out is one individual thing whose identity, however, we are not able to make unequivocal by using this name.

Thus, secondly, it provides us with a clue as to the 'indefinite' meaning the Cappadocian author ascribes to the universal term: the name 'man' is indefinite in so far as it points out the individual in a way that does not allow for its unequivocal identification.

It would seem now that one possible explanation for this 'indefiniteness of signification' is that the force of the name is really directed at the entirety of humankind. This would appear, without much doubt, to be the view of Gregory in the aforementioned passage from *De hominis opificio* 16. In the above statement of the *Epistle 38* this interpretation finds supported from the author's use of the term 'scattered' or 'dispersed' (ἐσκεδασμένη) for the notion produced by the universal term. This probably means that the name directs our thoughts to a multiplicity of objects.[75] Thus, if an object is referred to as 'man', the person hearing this designation thinks of the 'nature' in the first place; he does not primarily think of that individual, but of the whole class. This, then, would account for the indefiniteness or lack of precision in the universal term.

Consequently, the *phusis* that the universal term 'man' was said to indicate would be the totality of human individuals. Its relation to the individual *pragma* is, then, probably that of a whole to its parts. In what sense this can be a sensible understanding of universal nature and what ancient parallels there are for such a view remains to be seen.

---

[75] Cf. ὄχις ἐσκεδασμένη (Xenophon, *Cynegeticus* V 26); according to LSJ (s.v. σκεδάννυμι) this means: 'vision not confined to one object'.

There are other observations within the first part of the *Epistle 38* that would seem to support this interpretation. From one passage (2,16–9) it appears that the author ascribes a comprehensive meaning (περιληπτικὴ σημασία) to the universal name. Now, comprehensive name (περιληπτικὸν ὄνομα) is a technical term of the grammarians meaning a collective noun[76] (examples are people, crowd etc.). Speaking of a comprehensive meaning with regard to the universal makes it, to my mind, likely that the two classes (universal and comprehensive names) are treated as equivalent here. This interpretation, it seems, is reinforced by the way the relevant statement relates the signification of universal and proper names: the proper name is thought to separate or cut off (χωρίζειν) the notion of an individual from that of a whole which the universal name conveys. The use of χωρίζειν suggests, I think, a conception of the individual as a part of the nature, which would fit excellently with the collective meaning the universal term was argued to have.

It may be noted additionally that a very similar position is encountered in Boethius. In his commentary on *De Interpretatione* 7 he writes that

> ... upon hearing 'man' the mind turns to the many whom he knows to be contained (*contineri*) in humankind.[77]

Boethius, who would have had the bulk of his information from Porphyry's lost commentary on the same work,[78] here appears to endorse precisely the extensive meaning of the universal which, it has been argued, we find in the *Epistle 38*. Elsewhere, in his writing *On Division*, where again to all appearance he depends heavily on Porphyry, he argues that the species man is a whole composed of parts, the individuals:

> We call parts of man also Cato, Virgil and Cicero who, while being particulars, combine to compose the whole man (*totus homo*).[79]

From all this I would conclude

---

[76] Dionysius Thrax, *ars gramm* 12,15 (40,4–41,1 Uhlig).

[77] *In de Int* II 7 (137,16–8 Meiser).

[78] Cf. Boethius, *in de Int* II 1 (7,5–9 Meiser). This is confirmed by the extensive parallels between his and Ammonius' commentaries; cf. on this question: Blank (1995), 3–4.

[79] Boethius, *div* (PL 64, 877D = Porphyry, *fr* 169f., 53–6 Smith). Cf. *fr* 169f., 605–8.634–7 Smith.

(i) that the Cappadocian author of the *Epistle 38* thinks of universal names as referring to something he calls *phusis*;

(ii) that the specific character of this deictic function is revealed by his mention of the 'indefinite' way in which those names refer to individuals;

(iii) that the reason for this 'indefiniteness' is the indication by the term of the whole of humankind;

(iv) that, finally, humankind as the totality of its individuals is universal *phusis* as employed by the author.

2.3.2   *The* ousia-hupostasis *distinction*

So far we have found the Cappadocian author focussing on the juxtaposition of universal and particular, which he understands in terms of a whole and its parts. This, it was argued, was the essence of his distinction between *phusis* and *pragma*. Their difference and, consequently, that of the respective names consisted in the indication of one or many individuals.

At the same time it has emerged that the Cappadocian author knew of a further meaning of those names. To both, proper and universal names he assigned the signification of a set of properties. In the case of the universal term these were the characteristics all individuals of the class have in common; proper names would produce the notion of such properties as belong to only one individual. With regard to those notions the individual *pragma* could be said to be a composite of universal and particular properties both of which would be part of the concrete thing. As yet it has not been possible, though, to decide whether or not those sets of properties correspond, in the author's view, to some sort of item, which in this case would be the particular or universal complement of the individual thing.

In what follows (2,19–3,12) this issue is considerably enlarged upon. It is remarkable that in this context the author for the first time introduces *ousia*-terminology:

> If now of two or more who are (man) in the same way, like Paul and Silas and Timothy an account of the *ousia* of men is sought, one will not give one account of the *ousia* of Peter, another one of Silas and again another one of Timothy; but by whatever terms the *ousia* of Paul is shown, these same will fit the others as well. And those are *homoousioi* to each other, who are described by the same formula of being (λόγος τῆς οὐσίας). (2,19–26)

This is a crucial passage; since it is quite dense each phrase has to be given its own weight:

κατὰ τὸ αὐτὸ ὄντων: this I take to mean that the two or more individuals are man in precisely the same sense. This is what the author implies by the mention of the formula of being (see below). Compare for this Aristotle's explanation of synonyms (*cat* 1 [1ᵃ10–2]):

> For if one is to give an account (λόγος) of each (sc. man and ox)—what being an animal is for them (τί ἐστιν αὐτῶν ἑκατέρῳ τὸ ζῴῳ εἶναι)—one will give the same account.[80]

It is obvious that man and a statue would not be 'in the same way'; note, however, that Adam and the rest of mankind would, according to Apollinarius' theory, not be κατὰ τὸ αὐτό either.

περὶ τῆς οὐσίας . . .—ἐφαρμόσουσι: what is said now is that in such a case each account, which one could give of the *ousia* of one of them, would fit the *ousia* of the others as well. An account of the *ousia* can, I think, only mean: an account that reveals what it means for them to be man.

λόγος τῆς οὐσίας: The phrasing is Aristotelian; at the end of the present passage it is used again. Aristotle had employed the phrase right at the outset of his *Categories* (1ᵃ1–2). For his ancient commentators[81] it was a matter of fact that Aristotle had been writing there about one possible kind of relation between two things. According to them, each thing could be indicated by both a name and a formula.[82] Two things could therefore correspond in both, name and formula, or in one of them only, or in none.[83] The 'formula of being' would thus be something like a definition. To the question: 'Why did Aristotle employ this odd phrase instead of ὅρος,' they would respond that, as neither supreme genera nor individuals could properly speaking be defined (*per genus et differentiam*, that is), the phrase 'formula of being' as the more comprehensive one is employed,

---

[80] ET: Ackrill (1963), 3, with slight changes.

[81] In the following I refer to writings some of which have been written centuries after the *ep* 38 was composed, and thus cannot have been known to its author. It is, however, generally accepted that those later writers reproduced rather faithfully a commentary tradition going back to the first three centuries AD. It is therefore legitimate to illuminate a fourth-century writer with the help of a sixth-century commentator.

[82] Simplicius, *in Cat* (22,15–9 Kalbfleisch).

[83] Simplicius, *in Cat* (22,23–33 Kalbfleisch).

embracing both ὅρος and ὑπογραφή.[84] The origin of that distinction
is Stoic: according to the Stoics we can discern an exact definition
from something like a rough outline of an item that would suffice
for everyday purposes.[85] In this view there would obviously be both,
horos and *hupographe* of many items, but of some there would only be
a *hupographe* as they could, for whatever reason, not be defined. In
this latter sense, then, the distinction was applied to the Aristotelian
text. Thus we read in Porphyry:[86]

> For the definition (ὅρος) is a formula of being inasmuch as it indicates
> the substance (οὐσία) and the circumscription (ὑπογραφή), inasmuch as
> it signifies the property which is around the substance (περὶ τὴν οὐσίαν).

Nevertheless, it does at times appear that the term λόγος τῆς οὐσίας
was not wholeheartedly embraced for individuals. Thus Porphyry
argues in his *Isagoge* that only specific and generic, not individual
differentiae are contained in the λόγος τῆς οὐσίας.[87] This restricted
use of the phrase was, I believe, due to the meaning it carried regarding *ousia*: if it was thought objectionable that individuals of one species
differ *qua* substance, then their account would not describe an *ousia*.

This latter understanding, I suggest, is presupposed by the author
of *Epistle 38*, for the introduction of the phrase λόγος τῆς οὐσίας here
makes sense only if we assume that the *perigraphe* (περιγραφή) of the
individual item is not a λόγος τῆς οὐσίας, as otherwise the author
could not say that the *logos* is the same with all men. Moreover, one
will hardly err in the assumption, that it is in particular the word
ousia that makes the phrase attractive to the theological author. After
all, he defines the Nicene watchword *homoousios* with the help of the
λόγος τῆς οὐσίας (see below), which obviously indicates that community of substance, as indicated by the common account, is the cri-
terion for consubstantiality.

On the other hand, however, his phrasing also points to his awareness of the comprehensive meaning of the phrase λόγος τῆς οὐσίας:
he writes that those men are 'circumscribed' (ὑπογραφόμενοι) by the

---

[84] Simplicius, *in Cat* (29,16–24 Kalbfleisch); cf. also Porphyry, ap. Simplicius, *in Cat* (30,5–15 Kalbfleisch = *fr* 51F Smith).
[85] Cf. Galen, *def med* 1 (vol. XIX, 349 Kühne = SVF II, 75,26–9); Antipater of Tarsus, ap. Diogenes Laertius VII 57 (= SVF III, 247,27–31).
[86] Loc. cit. (n. 84 above).
[87] Cf. also his *Isagoge* (9,14–6 Busse) where he asserts that only specific differentiae and not the so-called inseparable accidents (i.e. the individual properties) are contained in the λόγος τῆς οὐσίας.

same *logos*. Nowhere indeed does he indicate a particular interest in a formal definition of the *ousia*, and as for the Godhead more than a circumscription could hardly be ventured upon anyway.

The meaning of ousia

It has at times been thought that the meaning of *ousia* in this context is that of the Aristotelian second substance (δευτέρα οὐσία).[88] However, such an interpretation has to be qualified. For in the phrase λόγος τῆς οὐσίας the term does not signify the first category, but means 'being' which, in theory, occurs in all the categories.[89] To be sure, in the context of the *Categories* 'man' as a species would be a second substance (*cat* 2ᵃ14–7). Thus it would be the case that men, having their formula of being in common, are also a second substance. But red and green, for example, would *qua* colour also share the same 'formula of being' although they are qualities. On the other hand, however, it appears that the author deliberately employs examples from the first category as he wishes to maintain that there is no possibility of a more or a less among beings that share the same *ousia*. This, however, is, according to Aristotle, a property of substances (*cat* 5 [3ᵇ33–4ᵃ9]).

To understand this ambiguity one has to see that *ousia* in the phrase 'formula of being' had in the interpretative tradition been partially assimilated to the *eidos* of Aristotle's *Metaphysics*. This is in a sense not surprising, as the latter seems to fulfil a somewhat similar function, but it means, of course, a limitation of its meaning: in the context of *Metaphysics* an account of an *eidos* would certainly not point out the being of a quality! Thus, it is understandable that a fourth-century author, who was not restricted by the rigid requirements of commenting on the text of the *Categories*, would find it natural to think of the *ousia* indicated by the formula of being as of the essence (εἶδος) of a substantial thing. This, I think, is what the Cappadocian author does.

In the light of our previous findings it is perhaps worthwhile to add a few remarks about the relationship between *ousia* and *phusis* here. This has been a long-debated question with some scholars, notably Bethune-Baker and Prestige,[90] arguing in favour of a general

---

[88] Hübner (1972), 469–70.
[89] Cf. Aristotle's own explanation at *cat* 1 (1ᵃ4–6) and Ammonius' commentary, Ammonius, *in Cat* (20,23–21,2 Busse).
[90] Bethune-Baker (1901), 49–59; Prestige (1936), 234–5.

distinction between the two terms and many others, like Meredith,[91] denying it. There can be but little doubt that in many cases it would be impossible, to maintain a difference in the Cappadocians' use of those terms.[92] However, confining myself to the present writing I should argue in favour of a slight, but noticeable differentiation here.

Let me begin with a formal observation. It has already been noted that in the initial exposition of the semantic theory the word *phusis* is employed throughout: this would be surprising if it were exchangeable with *ousia*, given that the author had announced in the proem his intention of clarifying the difference between *ousia* and *hupostasis*. It could be explained if the point the author wants to make (*phusis* as indicated by the universal name, being the totality of individuals) requires *phusis*, not *ousia*, to stand as the appropriate term.

But even later in the epistle the author repeatedly says that the universal term indicates the *phusis*, he nowhere says that it indicates the *ousia*. He does, however, say that the account (λόγος) points out the *ousia*. It would, further, be difficult to maintain that in the passage analysed above—or, indeed, anywhere else in the epistle—*ousia* means the totality of all men, while this was exactly what we had found to be the meaning of *phusis*. Indeed, if the preceding analysis of *ousia* is accepted, the term cannot indicate the whole of mankind in the extensive sense. It rather indicates the item which is responsible for each individual's being man, his essence. As such an item—once its existence is conceded—it can, I think, be thought of as universal without much difficulty: it would be an item of such a kind that it is both one in all members of the species *and* whole in each of them. As will be shown below, both Stoics and Peripatetics (not to mention Platonists) held views that could account for the present theory. Its universality, it is true, is not emphasised in the present epistle, but elsewhere it is clearly asserted (cf. pp. 99–100 below).

I should, then, conclude that the way *ousia* and *phusis* are used in the *Epistle 38* points to a difference in their meaning: *phusis* stands for the multitude of actual human individuals including their respective individual properties. *Ousia*, on the other hand, is the name of that item which causes something to be man; as such it is not identical with either one individual man or with their totality.

---

[91] Meredith (1972), 244–5; 252–4.
[92] See at pp. 96; 100 below.

It may be remarked here that this distinction between *ousia* and *phusis* is not carried through in either Basil's or Gregory's works on the terminological level. It will be seen later in this study that Gregory can employ both terms for both notions. On the conceptual level, however, this distinction is, I should contend, of vital importance for Gregory's thought. What is distinguished as *ousia* and *phusis* in the *Epistle 38* is recurrent as a duality of complementary concepts in the entirety of Gregory's utterances on universal nature. As he often concentrates on one or the other element it is crucial to see that in the present place their interaction is clearly displayed. It thus becomes clear—and this is the primary relevance of the present observation— that and how the two notions are both different and closely related, even complementary to each other. The latter fact may in turn explain why Gregory often treats the terms as equivalent.

καί εἰσιν ἀλλήλοις . . .—ὑπογραφόμενοι: with this sentence we get to the heart of the author's theological interest. He defines the Nicene *homoousion* within the philosophical framework that has been analysed so far. Those, who can be given the same formula of being, are *homoousioi*. This interpretation of the *homoousion* has often been thought to be characterised mainly by its weak notion of unity. However, this is not the only, nor probably even the most intricate, problem with regard to this concept. It has on the other hand become clear, I hope, that, in the light of the recent vicissitudes of the Nicene watchword, the assumption of its present interpretation as a compromise is all but impossible: on the contrary, given the strong reservations precisely against the alleged connotation of co-ordination in the *homoousion* the emphasis here on this very tenet (that individuals are men 'in the same way') appears to be the exact opposite of any attempted compromise solution.

The result of the present analysis with regard to the author's use of *ousia* is confirmed by his respective statements about *hupostasis*. Again, I should contend that its meaning does not simply equal that of the individual *pragma*, but, as in the case of *phusis* and *ousia*, differs from the former in so far as it indicates that item which is specially responsible for the thing's individuality. It is in this sense that I understand the author's remark that the word *hupostasis* indicates 'what is individually predicated' (τὸ ἰδίως λεγόμενον: 3,1). Again, I think, it would be wrong to assume that the phrasing ('is predicated') necessarily suggests that the author has expressions in mind. That things (πράγματα) are predicated of each other is Aristotelian usage[93] and was thus passed on to those ancients who would have read and studied his works. Even if this background was not present to the Cappadocian author, the present passage would most naturally be understood as implying that, corresponding to the predication, there is an individual element in each thing which accounts for its being what it is *qua* individual as its *ousia* accounts for what it is *qua* species. Just as the latter is pointed out by the formula of being, the former is indicated by an individual account (ὁ ἑκάστου γνωριστικὸς λόγος: 2,28–9) containing the individual properties. In this sense, I think, the author refers to the *hupostasis* as the 'conflux of the properties which are around each individual' (6,4–6).

Besides marking out the individual existence thus accounting for a thing's unequivocal identification, however, *hupostasis* has a further function: it makes the individual an individual by giving it its own existence or subsistence. In fact, this seems to be why, in the author's view, the name *hupostasis* is given to this item. He writes (3,4–8) that it is the individual thing (πρᾶγμα) that subsists and that the nature subsists in those things, which is perhaps not surprising given the meaning *phusis* was found to have. He then goes on as follows (3,8–12):

> This, then, is *hupostasis*. It is not the indefinite notion of *ousia*, which finds no stability (στάσις) on account of the community of what is signified. It is that notion which sets before the mind a circumscription in one thing (πρᾶγμα) of what is common and uncircumscribed by means of such properties as are seen with it (ἐπιφαίνομαι).[94]

This passage appears to say that by means of the *hupostasis* we gain a concrete idea of one individual thing including both its individual *and* its specific properties. Of those, however, the former are contained in the notion of *hupostasis* as it were directly, the latter indirectly. That is to say that by giving an explanatory account of one individual we nevertheless think of that individual as of a man. Indeed, one could hardly think of Socrates or Paul except as men. Why, then, do we need both universal and individual names and accounts? It seems to me that as an answer to this difficulty the Cappadocian author understands *hupostasis* as by nature individualising the *ousia* (to which it is thus tied) while, conversely, the latter

---

[93] Cf. e.g. *cat* 2 (1ª20).
[94] Here: 'appear on the surface' cf. LSJ, s.v. (e.g. of the Platonic idea in its images).

subsists only in particular *hupostaseis*. Thus, this latter notion provides at the same time for a connection between *ousia* and *hupostasis* which is important; both are interdependent. While the *hupostasis* cannot even be thought of without the *ousia*, the latter could not exist except through the former.

Pressing the formulation one could argue that in the present passage the author refers to *hupostasis* as to a concept. However, this would mean to mistake his thinking: he assumes, I believe, that the concept (ἔννοια) expressed by the explanatory account corresponds to an item, which he terms *hupostasis*. This being so, it is not difficult to see how he can substitute concept, account and *hupostasis* for each other: in his view they are equivalent.

A more serious criticism was directed by Prestige against the theology of the *Epistle 38* on account of the present passage. He argued that by identifying *hupostasis* with the individual element the author (he believes it to be Basil) jeopardised its concrete character:

> In the working out, by the Cappadocians, of the exact senses to be attached to terms of theological definition, Basil (. . .) had dallied dangerously with a tendency to identify hypostasis with idioma. (. . .) As Basil was inclined to define the term, it covered only such abstract elements in an *ousia* as were left over when the physis or abstract *ousia* had been substracted. But as his successors, and indeed his contemporary theologians, employed it, it meant the concrete whole, objectively presented—*ousia* plus individuality, not individuality as distinguished from *ousia*.[95]

To appreciate the relevance and justification of this criticism it may be worthwhile to view it against the *Epistle 38*'s entire theory of which I therefore first give a brief résumé.

The author had started from a juxtaposition of two kinds of name, universal and proper names. Of these, it was found, the former indicated a nature by signifying their common properties, the latter referred to an individual thing while signifying its individual characteristics. Nature (φύσις) was understood to mean the multitude of individuals that can be given the same specific name.

In a second step the author introduced *ousia* and *hupostasis* as such items which, while not being identical with individuals or their classes, are causes for things' being part of a nature or one particular individual respectively. This latter pair of items would be pointed out

---

[95] Prestige (1936), 275–6.

by means of a definitional account bringing out the contents of the names' signification. The two, it was found, are interdependent: the notion of *hupostasis* always presupposes that of *ousia*, while the latter is in need of *hupostasis* for its existence or subsistence in individuals.

The conceptual framework behind the present theory is thus quite complicated. We ultimately have four entities: the individual thing (πρᾶγμα), a class or species of such individuals (φύσις), the specific essence (οὐσία), the principle of individuation (ὑπόστασις). They appear to be related as follows: the individual thing is a compound of *ousia* and *hupostasis*. This is why a given person can be called both 'man' and, say, 'Peter'. It is also clear that *ousia* and *hupostasis* occur only in this combination. *Phusis* is the whole of which those individuals are parts. Both its identity and unity, it appears, are safe-guarded by the underlying unity of *ousia* which is one in many. *Ousia*, then, is one in the entire nature, yet whole in each individual. It can, however, never subsist on its own. *Hupostasis*, finally, is unique with each person thus accounting for their individuality.

By way of evaluation it should perhaps be said that the theory developed in these lines is remarkably subtle, certainly more so than scholarship at large has so far recognised: its author can claim to have explained why each Trinitarian Person can be called 'God', yet there is one God, not three gods; he can account for the fact that the three Persons subsist separately, but are still united and one *qua* nature and substance. Not least, he has achieved all this on the basis of his tenet of their co-ordination, not on the traditional deriv-ative model.

The main problem of this theory is perhaps that its four con-stituent elements are somewhat difficult to balance. A trinitarian doc-trine along these lines which primarily focuses on what is called here *ousia* and *hupostasis* can be seen as giving rise to Prestige's criticism: while, certainly, the Cappadocian author does not regard *ousia* or *hupostasis* as 'abstract' notions, the fact remains that they are not sim-ply identical with the individual *pragma* and its class thus apparently introducing into the Godhead further items beyond the three Persons. What is more, *ousia* and *hupostasis* are clearly two different things. It is true, they cannot occur without one another, but they are nev-ertheless distinct. This, however, confirms in the end the frequent suspicion associated with the 'Greek use' of the *homoousion*: the need, that is, to introduce the *ousia* as a further item beyond the *hupostaseis*.

One might wonder, then, whether a theory solely on the basis of our author's distinction of *phusis* and thing might not have fared better? Such a view, it might appear, could steer clear of both the above *aporiae* and of a criticism concerning the applicability of such an analogy to the Godhead. Such criticism, that is, as might be directed at the notion of divine Persons as effectively composite.

However, it does not appear that a simple change of emphasis could ultimately salvage the present theory. The concept of *ousia* is needed, I think, both for the preservation of real unity in the *phusis* and for maintaining the presence of the universal within each individual. Removing it would leave the analogy open to the charge of tritheism. It appears, then, that the best one could do for this view is to try and balance all four of its constituent elements while stressing the inadequacy of each trinitarian analogy.

2.3.3 *Philosophical background*

It is noteworthy that this theory is expounded here without any direct[96] reference to the doctrinal problem the author had set out to solve; both the topic and its discussion are purely philosophical. One can therefore hardly avoid asking for the philosophical background of this theory. Indeed, we may expect that such an elucidation contributes decisively to our grasp of the author's intention. Doing so, however, requires a caveat: what we are attempting to elucidate is the philosophical background of the human analogy as it is presented by the *Epistle 38*; this does not automatically mean that this is also the philosophical background of the author's trinitarian theology. Although he writes that one would rightly apply the difference between *ousia* and *hupostasis* in men to the Godhead (3,30–3) the latter doctrine might require some qualifications. The following concentrates entirely on the philosophical background of the analogy.

In previous research various answers have been given to this question: Platonic,[97] Aristotelian[98] and Stoic[99] doctrines have been suggested to stand behind the epistle's view. In no case, however, has a precise elucidation of it been ventured upon. Those who emphasised the Platonism of the present theory, Lebon and Ritter, did not,

---

[96] The passage defining the *homoousion* refers indirectly to the theological background of the debate.
[97] E.g. Lebon (1953), 641–57; Ritter (1965), 286–91.
[98] Holl (1904), 131; Hübner (1972), 469–70.
[99] Grillmeier (1975), 267–77.

as far as I see, attempt to demonstrate the influence of any one particular Platonic writing upon the *Epistle 38*; what they intended was
rather to disown an unquestioned 'nominalism' in its interpretation.
In this they certainly succeeded. Moreover, in a time as heavily
steeped in Platonism as was the fourth century, *some* sort of Platonism
is detectable with practically every writer. If the claim of a Platonic
background of the present theory extends beyond such general assumptions, it has to be qualified. It is sometimes taken for granted, for
example, that *the* Platonic approach to the problem of universals is
represented by Plato's theory of ideas as we find it in his middle-
period dialogues. In this view, the idea or form would be an independently subsisting entity in which individuals participate. Such a
view cannot underlie the *Epistle 38* as the *ousia* there has its being
immanent in the individuals. Nor should it be called 'Platonic' without qualification either, since it appears that all late ancient philosophers, being Platonists, rejected such a view, assuming that Plato
himself had not really held it in the first place. My suggestion would
be to describe as 'Platonic' such an understanding of universals that
gives them ontological priority over against particular being. It will
be shown later that Gregory of Nyssa's understanding of universal
nature can be called Platonic in this sense (p. 154 below). For the
present topic, however, the theory of the *Epistle 38*, such a qualification
seems problematic. The author does not ponder questions of ontological priority or posteriority here; indeed, they would be adverse
to his intention. I should therefore suggest leaving aside the question of the author's Platonism here.

An attempt to elucidate the present theory against a Stoic background has been presented by Grillmeier. He compares the juxtaposition of universal and particular in the *Epistle 38* to the Stoic
assumption of universal and particular qualities which, being added
to the unqualified *ousia*, contribute jointly to an individual's being.
Grillmeier's analysis is, I believe, correct and helpful up to a point.
There are many elements in the exposition presented in the *Epistle
38* which need the Stoic background to be explained; we shall
presently see in some detail where this is the case. Grillmeier seems
to be mistaken, however, in thinking that the background of our
author's understanding of *ousia* is Stoic. The Stoic *ousia* was conceived of as an unqualified substratum; it was regularly paralleled
with matter (ὕλη):[100] this certainly is not the view of the *Epistle 38*.

---

[100] Cf., e.g., SVF II, 126,30–42.

Rather, *ousia* would somehow correspond to the universal quality of the Stoics, but this cannot explain the name given to it here.

Hübner, finally, has argued for an Aristotelian background of the epistle's theory. He pointed, quite rightly, to parallels in the *Categories* and *De Interpretatione*, although he felt he had to express doubts as to whether the author could have known these writings.[101] It will presently become apparent that, according to my own research, Hübner's conclusions about the epistle's Aristotelian background are fully justified. His analysis is marred, however, by what I judge to be rather substantial misinterpretations of this Aristotelian background as well as of its relevance for the Cappadocian author's theory. Questionable presuppositions of his reading are the identification of the second substance in *Categories* with the *eidos* of the central books of *Metaphysics*,[102] also the interpretation of the former as an abstract essence and, at the same time, apparently a nominalistic universal.[103] Consequently, in his view, the *Epistle 38* witnesses the unlikely theory of three Trinitarian Persons, who are three individuals with *ousia* as a mere concept abstracted from their common properties. Needless to say, such an interpretation falls short of the rather complicated theory we found the Cappadocian author reaching out for.

In the following I will argue that this theory owes most to a particular, late ancient interpretation of Aristotle's philosophy. This interpretation itself, however, can only be understood on the basis of its development, which has to take into account several strands, some of them non-Aristotelian.

Let me begin with the grammatical theory employed by the author of the epistle. It seems clear that this theory is not his own invention. Rather, we find its precedents in grammatical textbooks. All ancient grammarians knew of this distinction between universal and proper names, but apparently it was in particular Apollonius Dyscolus who introduced it as the crucial division of nouns.[104] Those grammarians, it appears, owed this theory to the Stoics.[105] The latter had not only distinguished between name (= proper name; ὄνομα) and appellative (προσηγορία), but had employed this distinction for their own ontology; thus, the universal name would indicate a universal quality (κοινὴ ποιότης) and the proper name, a particular one (ἰδικὴ

---

[101] Hübner (1972), 469–70 with nn. 39–40.
[102] Op. cit., 471.
[103] Ibid.
[104] Apollonius, *nom* (48,30–41 Schneider).
[105] Cf. for the following: Frede (1987b).

ποιότης), both of which would be added to the material substratum (ὕλη, οὐσία) to make up a thing.[106] To call something 'Socrates' would thus point out in the thing referred to the presence of a particular quality corresponding to that name (provided that the predication is true, of course), while the name 'man' would indicate the respective universal quality. Neither name would thus indicate the compound thing as such, although arguably the presence of the particular quality 'Socrates' presupposes that of the universal quality 'man', while the opposite is not the case.

The relation of this Stoic theory to the one presupposed by the Cappadocian author appears to be quite complicated. By the time the *Epistle 38* was written, the original Stoic doctrine had been subjected to various influences by writers who wanted to use it (for grammatical purposes, for example) without sharing the Stoics' philosophical presuppositions. To follow this development in detail is difficult, as our sources are scarce, and perhaps not necessary for the present purpose. Some facts, however, seem to be evident.

Since from the late second century the Aristotelian *Organon* increasingly became the chief authority for logical questions (with the *Categories* understood as a treatise about logic!), we encounter a tendency to substitute its terminology for the Stoic one. Thus, many grammarians use 'common' and 'particular substance' (κοινὴ καὶ ἰδικὴ [or ἴδια] οὐσία) rather than 'quality'.[107] This, certainly, would bring about a considerable conceptual shift since Aristotle in the *Categories* is not concerned with aspects or parts of things, but with things. First substances would be individual things while second substances appear to be their classes. As for the precise understanding of the latter, the *Categories* are not as informative as one would wish. It seems, however, likely that the relation between first and second substances was thought of as that of parts to a whole (see pp. 85–6 below).

This, however, means that in those 'Aristotelian' grammars names were thought to indicate things (πράγματα) while the Stoic theory had them refer to parts of things. The view presupposed by the Cappadocian author seems to be some kind of synthesis of the two theories. On the one hand, it emerged that he held names to indi-

---

[106] Cf. e.g. Diogenes of Babylon, ap. Diogenes Laertius VII 58 (= SVF III, 213,27–31).
[107] Cf. already Dionysius Thrax, *ars gramm* 12 (33,6 Uhlig); Scholia Vaticana, *in art Dion* (232,19f. Hilgard).

cate things; in this regard his view follows the 'Aristotelian' theory. On the other hand, though, the Stoic doctrine, too, seems to have left its traces in the *Epistle 38* in so far as it recognises a relation of the names to universal and particular elements (via the respective account).

A very similar position we find in Boethius. In his *Commentary on De Interpretatione* he writes, commenting on Aristotle's famous definition of the universal (*de int* 7 [17ᵃ38–17ᵇ1]), that both the individual and the whole race can be called 'man' since the universal quality (*universalis qualitas*) humanity is both one in them all and whole in each single individual.[108]

Boethius certainly was not a Stoic. The reason why he was nevertheless able to use this originally Stoic idea seems to be that the Stoic notion of corporeal qualities could apparently be adapted to the Platonic and Peripatetic notion of (incorporeal) immanent forms with relative ease. Boethius would thus have conceived of those qualities not in the Stoic way as of bodies of some kind, but as of intelligible being which, for this reason, could be both entirely present in the individual and one in them all.[109]

It is remarkable that Boethius makes a clear difference between universal and particular, which he views as class and individual and as such the object of the names' indication, on the one hand, and universal and particular qualities on the other. The universal thing (*res universalis*: 138,18–9 Meiser) is man (*homo*), its extension being indicated by the presence of the universal quality *humanitas*. The particular thing or particular substance (*particularis substantia* = οὐσία μερική: 137,16 Meiser), Plato, is, again, distinguished from its particular quality for which Boethius invented the name *Platonitas* (137,3–7 Meiser). If we say, 'A man is just,' this predication 'takes one part out of man who is universal both in name and in nature (*partem . . . tollit ex homine qui est universale vel vocabulo vel natura*: 140,9–12 Meiser). If we just hear the word 'man' 'the mind turns to the many whom it knows to be contained (*contineri*) in humankind (*humanitate*).[110]

This approach seems to concur perfectly with the view apparently held by the Cappadocian author of the *Epistle 38*. The difference consists primarily in their terminology: while the *Epistle 38* has *phusis*

---

[108] Boethius, *in de Int* II,7 (137,18–138,3 Meiser).
[109] Boethius, *in de Int* II 7 (136,23–4 Meiser).
[110] *In de Int* II 7 (137,16–8 Meiser).

and *pragma*, *ousia* and *hupostasis*, Boethius uses particular substance and universal thing, universal and particular quality.

Now as for the latter pair, Boethius' terminology would not appear to be very Aristotelian; it could well be possible that other commentaries on the *De Interpretatione* employed terms more germane to the philosophy underlying their text. The Cappadocian author, on the other hand, had good reasons to employ his terminology of *ousia* and *hupostasis* as this was required by neo-Nicene orthodoxy. Neither should we be surprised that he used *phusis* and *pragma* for the Aristotelian first and second substances as, again, he was bound by theological concerns to employ *ousia*-terminology as unequivocally as possible. Thus I should suggest to discard the terminological difference between Boethius and the Cappadocian author as an impediment to the identification of their views.

It would appear, nevertheless, that the quest for the philosophical background of the *Epistle 38*'s theory should not end here. Obviously, Boethius cannot have been the Cappadocian author's source, but a blanket claim of his Porphyrian background would not, I think, settle the case satisfactorily either. It is possible, of course, perhaps even likely that Basil or Gregory read Porphyry's commentary on *De Interpretatione*; again, something can be said to support the idea that, like the bulk of Boethius' material, his explanation of Aristotle's definition of universals in chapter seven of the treatise was derived from Porphyry also. In any case, however, it is impossible to get beyond probabilities here.

It may be more promising, then, to trace back to Aristotle the interpretation Boethius offered to the problem of universals in *De Interpretatione* 7. Why is it that a philosopher in late antiquity, commenting on an Aristotelian text, comes up with such a theory? Is there anything within Aristotle's own philosophy that could be seen as giving rise to this kind of thinking?

The first answer to this question must be, I think, that the very text of *De Interpretatione* 7 should be seen as causing severe difficulties to students of Aristotle. For it is here that Aristotle expressly refers to universals as to 'things' (*pragmata*); Abaelard will later cite this passage to support his claim that Aristotle, too, must be called a 'realist'.[111]

Aristotle's express juxtaposition of universal and particular things is not easily explained on any count. What kind of thing could the

---

[111] Peter Abaelard, *Logica 'Ingredientibus'. Glossae super Porphyrium*, ed. Geyer (1919), 9.

universal be? As it seems clear from a number of texts that in his *Metaphysics* Aristotle did not consider the topic of universals a subject matter relevant to the search for *ousia* (cf. esp. *met* Z 13), students of the Stagirite would be forgiven for turning to the *Categories* in search of an answer to this question. For in the latter writing the problem of universals and particulars occupies a prominent place. It is here, and only here (*cat* 2 [1ᵃ20–1ᵇ9], that Aristotle offers his well-known division of all things into such as are not predicated of a subject and such as are predicated of a subject. The other division of things, introduced alongside, into such as are in a subject and such as are not, as well as its relation to the former division may be left aside here.

As far as substances (*ousiai*) are concerned, the above division becomes relevant as that between first and second substances (*cat* 5 [2ᵃ11–9]). First substances are such things as are neither in a subject nor predicated of a subject (the former being the property of all substances: *cat* 5 [3ᵃ7–8]), while second substances are not in a subject, but can be said of a subject. While it seems clear that this theory somehow corresponds to observations made at simple predications (individuals never occur as predicates there), it is also obvious that for Aristotle substances are a kind of thing which can be thus divided. This means that both first and second substances are things which, while being different *qua* universal or particular, share those properties that were said to be characteristic of substances in general.

If it were possible, then, to find out what kind of thing second substances were conceived of, this might be thought to provide for a clue to the riddle of *De Interpretatione* 7, too. There are indications now that what Aristotle had in mind in the *Categories* was that second substances are wholes composed of first substances as their parts. This would most distinctly appear from the following statement:

> The species in which the things primarily called substances are, are called second substances, as also are the genera of these species.[112]

It must be admitted that a conclusive interpretation of these lines is nearly impossible. However, a number of distinguished scholars have come to the conclusion that 'the species in which the first substances are' means that the species are wholes whose parts the individuals

---

[112] Aristotle, *cat* 5 (2ᵃ14–7); ET: Ackrill (1963), 5–6.

are.[113] This interpretation is supported by the more general observation that, originally, it was taken for granted in the Academy
that the relation of universal and particular was that of a whole and
its parts.[114]

This interpretation of Aristotle is, it appears, bluntly asserted by
Porphyry in his *Isagoge*, which, it may be recalled, was written as an
introduction to the study of Aristotelian logic:

> The individual is contained by the species and the species by the genus,
> for the genus is a whole, the individual a part, and the species both
> a whole and a part.[115]

Similarly, in his shorter *Commentary on the Categories* he explains:

> The individual thing (τὸ ἄτομον πρᾶγμα) partakes of the universal in so
> far as the individual is *in* the universal as in its species or genus. Thus
> Socrates is in the species 'man' and in the genus 'animal'.[116]

Prophyry seems to have expressed the same opinion in his *Commentary
on the Sophist* also, as emerges from Boethius' writing *On Division*. The
passage was cited above (p. 69 above). Its special interest for the
present inquiry lies in the fact that the notion of the universal as a
whole is combined with semantic theory: 'the whole man' (*totus homo*)
is the proper designation of the species as an aggregate of individuals.

All those Porphyrian writings have this in common that they draw
specifically on the Peripatetic tradition. In both the *Isagoge* and the
essay on the art of division this is explicitly asserted;[117] as for the
Commentary on the Categories, the same would there seem almost self-
evident. It might, therefore, appear not entirely unjustified to surmise that the notion of 'man' or 'the whole man' as the totality of
humankind has its origin in the Peripatetic exegesis of Aristotle.

This I would venture to substantiate by adducing two pieces of
evidence for a pre-Porphyrian, Peripatetic use of this notion. The
first of those is an argument contained in Alexander of Aphrodisias'
Commentary on Aristotle's Metaphysics. Commenting on *Metaphysics* Δ 26,

---

[113] Frede (1978), 23–4 with n. 2; Graeser (1983), 43–6; Krämer (1973), 155–9.
See also: Aristotle, *phys* A 1 (184ª23–6).
[114] Cf. Graeser (1983), loc. cit.
[115] Porphyry, *Isagoge* (7,27–8,4 Busse).
[116] Porphyry, *in Cat* (72,25–7 Busse).
[117] Porphyry, *Isagoge* (1,14–6 Busse); *fr* 169f., 779–82 Smith.

Alexander expounds Aristotle's claim that to some nouns both πᾶς and πάντα can be added as follows:

> But he also says that the term 'all' in the plural (πάντα) is applied to those things to which the term 'all' in the singular (τὸ πᾶς) is predicated as of one thing: 'all the number' when the aggregate (ἄθροισμα) of monads is taken as one, 'all the monads' when the monads from which all the number is (constituted) are again taken as separate, but in such a way that they make up all the number; so that the term 'all' in the plural is predicated of the parts as separate, but the term 'all' in the singular of the parts as united. So too, (we say) 'all men', or, in the sense that (they are) under one thing, 'all man' (πᾶς ἄνθρωπος).[118]

The claim that πᾶς ἄνθρωπος is said of men as 'under one thing' left the translator puzzled: he remarks in a footnote that this phrase should mean 'every man'. In principle, this is undoubtedly true. Still, why does Alexander choose this illustration? Aristotle himself had argued in the paragraph in question (met Δ 26 [1024ᵃ1–10]) that 'all' in the singular (πᾶν) is paired with continuous wholes like a sheet of water, in which case the order of the parts is irrelevant. 'Whole' (ὅλον), on the other hand, would designate an entity whose integrity is destroyed by rearrangement of the parts as, for example, a scale. That number is counted by Aristotle as an example of the former type reminds us that whole numbers were thought of by the ancients as aggregates of monads. Aristotle then adds that

> to things, to which *qua* one the term 'all' in the singular (πᾶν) is applied, the term 'all' in the plural (πάντα) is applied when they are treated as separate; 'all the number', 'all these monads'.[119]

Aristotle seems to have been confused here: in fact, 'all' in the plural (πάντα) is never added to mass terms, but to count nouns; it designates the entire number of the class' elements.[120] His embarrassment becomes apparent at once by his example of number: πάντες ἀριθμοί would naturally mean 'all numbers'; as this is not what he means he writes 'all the monads' instead. The point, apparently, is that certain entities can be looked at in two ways: as wholes of identical parts and as the totality of those parts. Thus all the monads make up one number which thus is 'whole' (πᾶν); at the same time the

---

[118] Alexander, *in Met* (426,19–26 Hayduck), ET: Dooley (1993), 113–4.
[119] *Met* Δ 26 (1024ᵃ8–10); ET: Ross (1928).
[120] Cf. LSJ, s.v. πᾶς.

monads can be viewed by themselves, when their totality is focussed upon as an aggregate.

One must see, I think, both this apparent intent of Aristotle's and his obvious failure to come up with a satisfactory example to understand Alexander's commentary on this passage. To all appearance he intended to make things clearer by introducing 'man' as a further (and better) example for the case Aristotle would have had in mind. One may wonder whether he did.

Be this, however, as it may, it would seem obvious that Alexander would have perceived an analogy between man and number in that both can be looked at as a whole and as an aggregate of parts. However, 'man' in this case could only be universal man, Aristotle's second substance. *Pas anthropos* would, then, mean 'the whole man' exactly in the sense we saw Boethius use it drawing on Porphyry.

It would be strange, however, to think that Alexander should have introduced this example without any precedent of such usage. Since πᾶς ἄνθρωπος does normally mean 'every man' Alexander's example makes sense, in my view, only if his readers could be expected to be familiar with this special usage of the phrase.

I should venture to argue that, indeed, it is possible to trace the notion of 'the whole man' as composed of individuals as its parts back behind Alexander; this will provide the second piece of evidence for pre-Porphyrian use of this concept. To this end we have to turn again to Boethius' treatise *On Division*. At the outset of that writing the Roman philosopher admits that for the argument he is heavily indebted to Porphyry. This is normally understood to indicate that the entire treatise is something like a paraphrase of one section from Porphyry's *Commentary on the Sophist*, probably the introduction.[121] Porphyry himself is explicitly cited in the proem as expressing his indebtedness to predecessors, mentioning in particular Andronicus of Rhodes.[122] With regard to this statement, Paul Moraux argued that, ultimately, it indicates only that Andronicus contributed in some way to the art of division; the precise character of Andronicus' argument, Moraux held, could not be elicited from the Boethian writing.[123] However this may be in general, I should venture to argue that the notion

---

[121] Moraux (1973) vol. I, 127; cf. also: A. Smith, *Porphyrius. Fragmenta*, Stuttgart/ Leipzig 1993, X–XI.
[122] Porphyry, *fr* 169f., 1–8 Smith.
[123] Moraux (1973) loc. cit.

of the species as a whole that is composed of parts must go back to a Peripatetic predecessor of Porphyry's, most likely to Andronicus.

The reason is this: In its second part the treatise compares the kinds of division in general (108ff. Smith). There the point is made that, while the genus is ontologically prior to the species, the whole is posterior to its parts (144–57 Smith). This is then illustrated by the example of a house which, having been dissembled, is not a house (i.e. a whole) any more although its parts may continue to exist. One thus wonders why the species is considered to be a whole and as such different from the genus: could the author have thought that the species is ontologically posterior to its individuals and at the same time ontologically posterior to its genus? The species, then, would be, in the author's view, the lowest ontological level. It would seem difficult to ascribe such a view to any philosophical author.

A reasonable explanation of this rather astonishing fact may be advanced, I would suggest, if we allow that the person responsible for the schema of divisions, in whose context the statement about the *totus homo* occurs, is different from the person who wrote the explanatory part of the writing. As for the latter this must have been Porphyry.[124] It would be perfectly possible, however, that the initial exposition of the kinds of division, if anything, goes back to his Peripatetic predecessor, in all likelihood Andronicus. I would thus conclude that it is the latter to whom we owe the schema of divisions presented in Boethius' text and thus the assortment of the species-individual relation to that of wholes and parts.

If, however, the originator of this schema was a Peripatetic,[125] there appears to be a convenient way of accounting for his approach. We only need to assume that he understood Aristotle as giving the species, but not the genus, an ontologically prominent role. He could then be seen as arguing that the whole, including the species, is some kind of thing while the genus, as an abstraction, is—in Aristotle's words (cf. *de an* 402^{b}7)—either nothing or virtually so.[126]

In summary, it would appear that within the Peripatetic tradition the notion of *man* or *the whole man* as the entirety of human individuals played some role from early on. This was most likely a way of accounting for Aristotle's phrasing in *Categories* and *De Interpretatione* 7.

---

[124] See Moraux (1973) vol. I, 127–8 who compares the structure of the *Isagoge*.
[125] About Andronicus cf. Moraux (1973) vol. I, 97–142.
[126] For such a view cf. Themistius, in d An (3,36–4,9 Heinze): see pp. 91–2 below.

In this tradition, it seems, both the Cappadocian author of the *Epistle 38* and Boethius belong where they see the universal term 'man' as indicating the totality of human individuals.

I noted above that Boethius ascribed the unity of the universal man to some 'universal quality' that was said to be present in all human individuals at once, while being whole in each single one of them. Corresponding to this, he introduced a universal quality, *Platonitas*, which should be unique to one individual. This, I suggested, was a parallel to the Cappadocian author's defintion of *ousia* and *hupostasis* in the *Epistle 38*.

From Boethius' terminology it was apparent that this theory had—to some extent—Stoic precedents. How could it be integrated into the interpretation of Aristotle? I should suggest that both the need and the opportunity for this arose from an attempt to harmonise Aristotle's teaching on *ousia* in the *Categories* with that of the central books of his *Metaphysics*.

That the ontology underlying those two writings is different is, I think, beyond reasonable doubt. *Categories* present individual things as first substances, which are ontologically prior to all other being, and their species and genera as second substances. The *Metaphysics*, on the other hand, appear to have given up entirely the idea of universal being and offer instead an analysis of the individual (which is thus no more in-divisible) into matter and form, of which the latter is now called first substance.

Modern scholarship would perhaps explain this discrepancy by a developmental theory;[127] Aristotle's ancient commentators, however, normally held an eclectic theory treating both terminologies as equivalent. Such an eclectic explanation could, it appears, result in the four entities characteristic both of Boethius' theory and of the *Epistle 38*: the individual, the first substance of the *Categories* would be a compound (σύνολον) of form and matter. The second substance from the same writing is the totality of these individuals. Form (εἶδος) would be a specific universal, but it cannot simply coincide with the extensive second substance of the *Categories* since it is only part of the individual. Matter could easily be understood on the lines of what Aristotle had written as the individuating principle.[128]

---

[127] Cf. for such a theory Frede (1978), 27–9.
[128] Cf. Lloyd (1970) for a modern interpretation of Aristotle along those lines.

That this fourfold division of substance did indeed occur to students of Aristotle appears from Porphyry's shorter *Commentary on the Categories*,[129] where it is pointed out that Aristotle called substance three kinds of being: matter, form and the compound of both. It is then asserted that the *ousia* of the *Categories* coincides with the last named. Finally, this latter group is subdivided into first and second substances. This last division is crucial; it shows that Porphyry did not harmonise Aristotle to the extent of proposing a simple identity of the second substance of the *Categories* with any of the items dealt with in *Metaphysics*. This ought to be pointed out as there were others who apparently did. Such identification was, of course, especially tempting in the case of the form, which is given the same name (εἶδος) as one second substance. It is suggested, I think, wherever the second substances are referred to as 'complementing the *ousia*' (συμπληρωτικαὶ τῆς οὐσίας)[130] for this they could only be as effectively parts of the individual compound, not as their totality. There is at least one passage where Porphyry seems to expound the latter theory too.[131] Since Porphyry's coherence, however, is not at issue here, there is no need to pursue this any further.

What remains to be explained, then, is on what basis the Stoic notions of universal and particular qualities could be inserted into that schema. I noted earlier that this integration could be accomplished by both Aristotelians and Platonists without much effort. The reason for this is that, apparently, the Stoic notion of corporeal universal qualities had corresponded to the Platonic and Aristotelian notion of (incorporeal) enmattered forms from the very beginning.[132]

An example for this integration is provided by one text from Themistius' *Paraphrase of Aristotle's De Anima*. Commenting on *De Anima* 402^{b}7, the celebrated statement that the universal animal is either nothing or posterior, Themistius draws a sharp distinction between genus and species. He relates the problem of 402^{b}7 to the question—also posed by Aristotle in that context—whether all souls form a species or rather a genus. He explains that, in order to decide on

---

[129] Porphyry, *in Cat* (88,8–29 Busse); cf. Simplicius, *in Cat* (74,18–22 Kalbfleisch); the text there has a lacuna, but the upshot must be the same; see ibid. (78,4ff. Kalbfleisch).

[130] So, e.g., Simplicius (*in Cat* 82,28–35 Kalbfleisch) who probably draws on Iamblichus here: cf. Dexippus, *in Cat* (45,27–31 Busse).

[131] Ap. Simplicius, *in Cat* (79,19–21 Kalbfleisch = *fr* 59f., 10–2 Smith).

[132] Frede (1987b), 348–9; *pace* Rist (1971, 49–51).

the latter question, one has to ask whether one and the same definition and one essence (τὸ τί ἦν εἶναι) fits every soul:

> For the consideration makes not a small difference: for the genus is a non-existent thought collected from the dim similarity of the individuals, and the genus is either nothing or by far posterior to the individuals, but the species (εἶδος) he wants to be a nature (φύσις) and a form (μορφή): for the *logos* of man requires only matter to *be* man.[133]

It seems clear, then, that Themistius interprets Aristotle as having spoken about the genus 'animal' *qua* universal as opposed to the species; in his view, Aristotle could not have said the same of the species 'man'. This differentiation of genus and species rests obviously on an identification of the latter with the form which, together with matter, makes up an individual.

From this it would appear that the *eidos* could be seen as a specific universal with matter as the individuating principle. The two would thus function as principles of universality and particularity in a way similar to that of the Stoic universal and particular qualities.

A similar phenomenon can be observed with regard to the individual quality. Here it seems clear that the view of a set of properties that is unique with an individual and thus marks out its individuality goes back to the Stoic idea of an individual quality.[134] The idea is substantially accepted by both Porphyry (*Isagoge* [7,21–3 Busse]) and the Cappadocian author (*ep* 38,6,4–6). However, its non-Stoic use must antedate these authors since Proclus rejects the theory as Peripatetic[135] with his wording strongly reminiscent of Porphyry's. It would thus appear that the latter had found this theory already in a Peripatetic source. In such a Peripatetic interpretation, then, the two notions of matter as the principle of accidents and of individuation would have merged into the notion of a set of inseparable accidents responsible for the thing's individuality which was the notion we had detected in the *Epistle 38*.

I would thus conclude that the philosophical background of the understanding of human nature in the *Epistle 38* cannot be elucidated by comparison with one particular author, let alone with one piece of writing. Viewing it against certain developments of late

---

[133] Themistius, *in d An* (3,36–4,9 Heinze).
[134] Dexippus, *in Cat* (30,23–6 Busse).
[135] Ap. Olympiodorus, *in Alcib I* (204,8–11 Creuzer).

ancient philosophy, however, in particular the growing dominance
of the Aristotelian *Organon* with regard to logical and related questions, it can be satisfactorily explained. Stoic theories played a role,
but mainly in so far as their remnants became part of the Neoplatonic-
Aristotelian mainstream and as such continued to exercise some philosophical influence.

It will be the task of the remainder of this chapter to show that and
to what extent the theory found in the *Epistle 38* underlies the trinitarian thinking of Gregory of Nyssa. To this end, his statements
bearing on this topic have to be considered. These are mainly to be
found in two contexts: first, in his extended polemics against Eunomius,
secondly, in his defence against the charge of tritheism.

2.4   *Gregory of Nyssa's anti-Eunomian polemics*

As far as we can judge from those of its remnants that have been
preserved, the *Second Apology* of Eunomius seized with great dexter-
ity upon the apparent weaknesses in the Cappadocian position. To
do this, however, Eunomius did not have to expand far beyond those
arguments which he had already presented in his *First Apology*. His
primary charge is, not surprisingly, that Basil's way of distinguishing
between unity and plurality in the Godhead makes God a composite
being. This is, I take it, the background of his claim that

> whatever is united by an account of being (λόγος τῆς οὐσίας) this will
> necesarily exist in bodies and be subject to corruption.[136]

This statement, I think, shows that the principal Cappadocian doctrine was known to Eunomius beyond what had been contained in
Basil's books against his *First Apology*. Naturally, in his *Second Apology*
Eunomius devotes greater care to the proof that the co-ordination
of divine Persons results in absurdity: as we have seen, he had initially taken this for granted, but after Basil had decided to opt for
this view, he had to dwell on this point at some length.

As for Gregory, he was normally content to set his own claims
against those made by Eunomius; fairness was no concern of his in
this context. To illustrate his point about the one *ousia* of God he

---

[136] Ap. Gregory, *Eun* III/5 61 (GNO II, 182,26–183,2).

cites the human analogy frequently. There is no need here to discuss each of those passages; some of them will suffice to show their basic agreement with the conceptual framework laid out in the *Epistle 38*.

A rather surprising point, which, to my knowledge, has hitherto escaped scholarly attention, will emerge incidentally: those passages reveal something like a hidden agenda in Gregory's polemic in that they are much more immediately directed at the traditional derivation theology than at Eunomius' own thinking. While expressly contesting Eunomius' denial of a substantial relationship between Father and Son, Gregory scores points against upholders of the former view wherever he argues for the co-ordinate relationship within the Deity, often rather disingenuously confusing their position with that of Eunomius.

In the following I will concentrate on three arguments from Nyssen's work: the first (*Contra Eunomium* I 172ff.) is to show how Gregory himself invoked Aristotle to bring home his point of substantial equality; the second (*Contra Eunomium* III/1,73ff.) is interesting in that it shows quite distinctly how Gregory opposed not only the Eunomian doctrine of unlikeness, but also the Apollinarian one of a derivative *ousia*. Finally, I shall look at *Contra Eunomium* III/5, which is important for the relationship between Gregory's and Basil's trinitarian theologies.

2.4.1   Contra Eunomium *I 172–86: 'Eunomius does not even know* the *Categories'*

This passage, like those immediately preceding it, is directed at the strongly hierarchical element in Eunomius' initial theological exposition.[137] Eunomius had written of a

> ... supreme and proper *ousia* and one which is by the former and after it, but prior to everything else' (ibid. 1–4).

For this Gregory takes him to task on a number of counts: first he argues that calling the Father alone an *ousia* proper would deny the other two Persons their hypostatical reality.[138] Next, after dismissing a possible materialistic 'misunderstanding', he develops his famous theory of God's infinity:[139] as there is no opposite to the good con-

---

[137] Cf. *Eun* I 151 (GNO I, 72,1).
[138] *Eun* I 162–5 (GNO I, 75,21–76,15).
[139] *Eun* I 167–70 (GNO I, 77,1–26); cf. for this passage: Mühlenberg (1966), 118–22, but now Uthemann (1993), 170–5.

ceivable in any of the Trinitarian Persons, it cannot be limited (for a limit is always set by an opposite) and is thus infinite. If it is, however, infinite, how could one argue about more or less within the Godhead?

Perhaps, Gregory seems to concede, with regard to time? Now it is clear that and why Eunomius found this particular idea absurd: it was, as we have seen, one of his key tenets that this kind of subordination would presuppose the pre-existence of an entity (in this case, time) prior to God. Gregory, then, certainly does not reply here to an argument which Eunomius had set forth or could have set forth.

Nyssen's chief claim is that, even if such a temporal priority of the Father were granted, this would have no bearing on the decisive question of substantial equality:

> But even if this were so—it may be stated hypothetically for the moment—what more *is* the one who came prior in time than the *ousia* that was generated later, with regard to the account of being (ὁ τοῦ εἶναι λόγος) itself I say, so that we call the one highest and most authentic, while the other one is not so?[140]

That Gregory here writes λόγος τοῦ εἶναι rather than λόγος τῆς οὐσίας does not mask the concept's identity. Rather, it confirms the above analysis regarding the meaning of *ousia* in this phrase: the account is about the being of man or of God, i.e. what it means for each of them to be what they are. This, it is claimed, would be the same in the Godhead even *if* (and, of course, he does not really concede this: cf. *Contra Eunomium* I 176 [GNO I, 79,2–8]) there were a temporal priority of the Father.

As an illustration for this claim he introduces humanity:

> What did David, who was proclaimed fourteen generations later, have less than Abraham with regard to the formula of being (τῆς οὐσίας λόγος)? Could humanity have been changed in the former so that he was less of a man because he was later in time? Who would be silly enough to say this? For the formula of being is one in both of them, in no way changed with the course of time. One would not say that one is more man because he came earlier in time, while the other partakes less of that nature (φύσις) because he came to life after the former so that either in those who preceded the nature had been used up or the time had exhausted the power (δύναμις) in the past. For it

---

[140] *Eun* I 172 (GNO I, 78,4–8).

is not time which defines the share of the nature for each individual, but nature remains on its own account (ἐφ' ἑαυτῆς), preserving itself by means of those who are born later. But time is moved in its own way, either embracing or flowing past the nature, which remains steadfast and unchanged in its own boundaries.[141]

By way of comparison with the doctrine of *Epistle 38* it appears that Gregory concentrates here on the item that was referred to as *ousia* there, i.e. a thing that is the same in all human beings and is responsible for their being this. Both writings concur in their apparent terminological dependence on *Categories*. In the present passage, however, the same item is called without apparent differentiation both *ousia* and *phusis*. What is more, δύναμις too seems to be used equivalently. The emphasis is on its universal character: although it is, apparently, passed on from generation to generation, it nevertheless is not influenced by this process.

The overall thrust of the argument is clearly directed at establishing the identity of substance or nature in all men. This is remarkable as Eunomius had not doubted this; he certainly would have argued that this analogy was just not applicable to the Deity. Much more, it seems, the present passage is aimed at a doctrine like the one held by Apollinarius attempting to denounce the possibility that the share of human nature could vary in the individuals. This impression is reinforced by a remark Gregory makes a little later in the same context. He there states that the name 'man' is truly applied only to the 'real' man:

> This one is not a likeness of man, but he himself is the archetype of the likeness.[142]

In the same context the image (εἰκών) is relegated to the state of a homonym, bearing only the name of that after which it is named. All these words (archetype, likeness, image) ring bells: with a few words Gregory disowns a long-standing theological tradition. But this tradition, one would think, is not what is at issue here. Gregory's opponent is rejecting it himself no less than the Cappadocian. Should Gregory not have been aware of this? He seems to charge Eunomius personally with ignorance about the issue of co-ordination within an *ousia*:

---

[141] *Eun* I 173–5 (GNO I, 78,11–27).
[142] *Eun* I 178 (GNO I, 79,17–8).

But since he likes being wise in such things, and spits on those who without logical skill try their hand at writing, let him tell us, whom he despises, by what wisdom he learnt the greater and lesser degree of *ousia*. What reasoning produces a difference of such a kind that one being exists more than another being?[143]

What is remarkable about this text is, first of all, that it provides perhaps the clearest indication in Gregory's writings that knowledge of the *Categories* was taken for granted by educated people of that time. Jaeger notes that 'Gregory attempts to show that Eunomius does not know Aristotle's *Categories*, i.e. the fundaments of logic' (ad loc.). This conclusion seems appropriate.

Less appropriate seems Gregory's own conclusion that rejecting the co-ordination of the Trinitarian Persons would be equivalent to denying the Son being a substance, as he could not be a substance without being on the same level as the Father. This, surely, is more than a little disingenuous: of course, if it was allowable to call God an *ousia*, this would mean calling him the most authentic *ousia*. This would be true for Gregory as well as for Eunomius, and Gregory would probably not accept for himself the charge that he deprives, say, man of any hypostatic reality.[144]

On the other hand, however, the Aristotelian statement that there is no more or less in a substance is expressly not meant to say that substances cannot relate as prior and posterior (*cat* 5 [3^{b}34–5]) although, admittedly, this point had come to be nearly forgotten as soon as *ousia* itself was treated as a genus term.[145]

The crucial difference between Gregory's and Eunomius' position is certainly that for the former 'being God' with all its implications is the *ousia* of the Father (I am using the orthodox terminology here) while for Eunomius it is 'being ingenerate'. Gregory's alternative seems to presume his own understanding of the *ousia*: under this presupposition, arguably, one could cite Aristotle for the claim that the Son either was or was not this *ousia*. But Eunomius' position was not affected as he would argue that the *ousia* of the Son was 'being generate' and could easily be this without being on the same plane as the Father.

---

[143] *Eun* I 180–1 (GNO I, 79,28–80,3), ET: Hall (1988), 61, with changes.

[144] Cf. Stead (1976), 116–7 who points out that Gregory's teaching elsewhere actually requires increasing degrees of perfection.

[145] Cf. Porphyry, *Isagoge* (4,21–2 Busse), Plotinus' argument in *Enn* VI 1,2 and pp. 37–8 above.

Thus, while Eunomius' alleged denial of the Son's subsistence should be altogether dismissed, it appears that again the natural target of Gregory's argument would be such a theory as allowed the substance to be the same in both Persons, but insisted on a subordination within this substance. This brings us back to the earlier question of whether Gregory could have assumed that Eunomius held such a theory.

This seems all but impossible: provided that Gregory had read Eunomius' writings he must have noticed the latter's distaste for such views. This leaves us with a number of possible explanations: one would be that Gregory simply was so used to this kind of argument that it slipped into his polemics almost unconsciously. One also might think that, for rhetorical reasons, he was content to convey the impression that all his theological opponents held the same position. Further, it would be possible to think that he did not really care about Eunomius' own theology at all, but treated it primarily as an object that had to be destroyed.

These explanations are not mutually exclusive; in fact, I believe that the last named has to be taken quite seriously. My overall impression from Nyssen's anti-Eunomian treatises is that, whatever these books are, they are certainly not an attempt to meet and disown Eunomius' theology on its own ground.

2.4.2   Contra Eunomium *III/1,73–6 and the rejection of the derivative model*

In this text the observation that in introducing the analogy of human nature in his anti-Eunomian polemic Gregory argues simultaneously, if not primarily, against a derivative understanding of the Godhead, can be made even more distinctly than in the previous passage.

Its polemical context is Gregory's seizing on Eunomius' use of the phrase 'begotten *ousia*'. By doing so, he argues, Eunomius effectively deviates from his normal claim that the Son's *ousia* is 'being begotten'. Citing John 16,21 ('A woman in labour is in pain because her time has come; but when the child is born she forgets the anguish in her joy that a man has been born into the world.') Gregory claims that the notion of 'being born' and the notion of 'being man' are clearly distinct. Thus, he concludes, the use of this phrase should henceforth forbid the anomoians to refer the distinction 'unbegotten-begotten' to the *ousia* of Father and Son.

Incidentally, this is not a very plausible argument. If rigidly applied, the principle put forth by Gregory here would ban from his own language expressions like 'divine *ousia*' which are very dear to him.[146] On the other hand, why do the Cappadocians themselves avoid expressions like 'paternal *ousia*' or 'begotten *ousia*' if such usage were in accordance with their trinitarian theology?

More interesting than its context, then, is an illustration Gregory advances for his claim. Citing human nature as an analogy, he attempts to demonstrate that 'being begotten' or 'unbegotten' is irrelevant for being man, i.e. for the human *ousia*. For, he writes, while Abel undoubtedly was begotten no one would object to the description of Adam as unbegotten:

> Now, the first man had within himself the entire definition of the human *ousia*, and the one who was begotten from him equally is circumscribed by the same formula of being. But if the begotten *ousia* were proved to be different from the one not begotten, the same formula of being would not apply to both of them. For those whose *ousia* is different will not have the formula of being in common. Since, then, the *ousia* of both, Adam and Abel, is characterised by the same properties, it is necessary to conclude that there is one *ousia* in both of them, while what shows itself in one *phusis* is one or the other (sc. in *hupostasis*). For the two, Adam and Abel, are one in the formula of *phusis*, but in the properties which are seen with each, they preserve their mutual difference unconfused. We cannot therefore properly say that Adam generated another *ousia* besides himself, but rather that of himself he generated another self, with whom was produced the whole *logos* of the *ousia* of the one who generated him.[147]

While this passage confirms a number of conclusions that have been reached earlier in this investigation, it is of particular interest in that it enlarges considerably our knowledge of Gregory's precise understanding of the unity of human nature.

To begin with, it appears that Gregory's argument in these lines develops quite cogently in a sequence of steps. He effectively presupposes three facts: (1) that Adam and Abel would be accepted as unbegotten and begotten respectively; (2) that in both the definition or formula of man is the same, and (3) that a common formula necessarily indicates community of substance. The last premise is particularly important: since Gregory leaves this unmentioned elsewhere some scholars have concluded that his notion of substantial unity is

---

[146] Cf. e.g. *graec* (GNO III/1, 26,2); *Abl* (GNO III/1, 55,2); *Eun* I 316 (GNO I, 121,1); *Eun* II 93 (GNO I, 254,12) and passim.

[147] *Eun* III/1 74–5 (GNO II, 30,7–24).

essentially conceptual.[148] The present passage shows that this is not the case, thus substantiating an argument presented earlier (see pp. 74, 90–2 above).

From these premises, then, Gregory constructs the following proof: from (2) and (3) it follows (4) that there is one *ousia* in both of them. From (4), finally, and (1) it appears that unbegotten and begotten can be in one substance.

Let us now look at some details. As for terminology, it is interesting that again *phusis* apparently bears the same meaning as *ousia*. Both designations correspond to the item which was termed *ousia* in the *Epistle 38*. The clearest indication for this concurrence is perhaps that λόγος τῆς φύσεως appears once for the formula of being. The extensive aspect of the common nature does not seem to play any role.[149]

One also may note that ἰδίωμα is employed here indiscriminately for the property of both *ousia* and individual. Generally, it seems to me that there is less evidence than textbooks suggest for a Cappadocian use of the term strictly limited to individual properties.

The main importance of this passage lies, in my view, in its explanation of the relationship between *ousia* and generation. To be sure, on the surface it might appear that the author's only interest was to show that the *ousia* is not changed by generation. However, by implication he also makes clear that generation is the way the *ousia* is transmitted. This had been found to be implied in previous texts. However, the present passage seems to be much more informative about this fact.

To determine the specific profile of the present theory, it may be worthwhile to compare it once more to the concept behind Apollinarius' use of human nature. The latter view, apparently, depended heavily on the assumption that the *ousia* is passed down from the primogenitor to his descendants. It is clear from elsewhere, as we shall see (pp. 131–2 below), that Apollinarius regarded this as a quasi-material process which made 'being man' essentially equivalent to 'being a descendant of Adam' and Adam himself the archetype of men. In comparison, Nyssen's theory seems to concur perfectly, but only up to a point. For, although in Gregory's view, too, the human *ousia* is

---

[148] Cf. Meredith (1988), 342–3.
[149] One might, perhaps, find this meaning in the phrase ἐν τῇ αὐτῇ φύσει δεικνύμενον (loc. cit.).

handed down by means of the procreative process, and 'being man' is thus *practically* equivalent to 'being a descendant of Adam' this fact is in reality only accidental. Essentially, the condition which needs to be fulfilled for something to be man is the presence of human nature or *ousia*, which is indicated by the applicability of a particular formula. *As things are*, this condition is fulfilled only in Adam and his descendants. But this is not necessitated by human nature itself which seems, quite generally, more independent of the individuals than in Apollinarius' understanding. The clearest indication of this independence is perhaps that human nature is the same in Adam and in his descendants: this, as I noted earlier (see pp. 36–8 above), Apollinarius would not say. Thus, while the Cappadocian *ousia* is still immanent in the individuals, it is not tied directly to any one of them. This observation will be of some relevance in other areas of Gregory's theology.

2.4.3 Contra Eunomium *III/5 and the relation between Basil's and Gregory's conception of substantial unity*

The fifth tome of the third book against Eunomius has been thought to provide for some important evidence in favour of a significant conceptual disagreement between Gregory and his older brother with regard to the meaning of *ousia*. Balás was the first to draw attention to a passage[150] where Gregory, while purporting to quote literally from his brother's book,[151] makes in fact what appears to be a decisive correction to Basil's wording. Where Basil had written of *ousia* as of the material substratum ('*ousia* I now call the material substratum'),[152] Gregory quotes him to the opposite effect:

> For of Peter and Paul and, generally, of men appellatives are different, but the *ousia* of them all is one. Therefore we are identical with each other in most (properties), and differ only in those properties that are seen around each individual. Wherefore also appellatives are not significant of *ousiai*, but of those properties which characterise the individual. Upon hearing Peter, then, we do not think of his *ousia* (*ousia* I now call *not* the material substratum), but an imagination of those properties, which are seen around him, is imprinted upon us.[153]

---

[150] *Eun* III/5 22 (GNO II, 168,2). Cf. Balás (1976).
[151] *Adv Eun* II 4 (PG 29, 577C).
[152] Loc. cit.
[153] *Eun* III/5 21–2 (GNO II, 167,22–168,4).

I have argued earlier in this chapter (see pp. 61–2 above) against the far-reaching consequences Balás and others have drawn from this observation, and there is no need to repeat this here. However, I do believe that Balás was mistaken also in his interpretation of the relevance of this change for the present argument. Balás had, albeit with some hesitation, expressed his belief that Gregory had consciously changed Basil's text; Eunomius would have seized on Basil's materialism which Gregory wished to avoid.

Now there is, naturally, no knowing whether and, if so, why Gregory himself changed the text; in my view, it seems perfectly possible that he considered the original reading a scribe's error. As for Eunomius' criticism, however, it seems clear from the preserved fragments that this was directed not against Basil's materialism, but against his rather disingenuous limitation of 'appellatives' to proper names.

Basil's argument is, indeed, rather astonishing in this respect, particularly if one takes into account the frequent references in his later writings to the distinction of two kinds of name: if proper names differ with men although the latter are one *ousia*, there is still the universal name 'man' which is indiscriminately employed for all of them.

This inconsistency, then, ought to be regarded as a further, rather major indication of the immature character of Basil's *Adversus Eunomium*, and it appears that it was equally this inconsistency which Eunomius seized upon. Gregory cites his 'praising words which signify the subject' (ὑποκείμενον)[154] and quotes a scornful remark[155] to the effect that no sane person would, talking of men, call one a man, the other a horse. The latter I take as saying that, of course, those who are of one *ousia* are all given the same, not a different, class name.

It is not difficult to see, then, that Eunomius' argument caused Gregory some pain. The latter does, indeed, concede its justification, but only to turn the tables on his opponent once more: admittedly, the same name indicates sameness of substance, but then Eunomius ought to concede that Father and Son are of one *ousia* as both are called God. It is noteworthy and marks a crucial difference of Gregory's position here from Basil's position in the *Adversus Eunomium*, that the anomoian dictum that like names indicate like substances and, *vice versa*, unlike names indicate unlike substances, which Basil had quoted

---

[154] *Eun* III/5 24 (GNO II, 168,11–2).
[155] *Eun* III/5 26 (GNO II, 169,10–3).

as infinitely blasphemous,[156] is effectively adopted and employed for the orthodox cause. A further point on which anomoianism seems to have influenced the eventual formulation of orthodox theology.

It is truly regrettable we know practically nothing of that part of the *Second Apology* which immediately follows, for it is in this part that Eunomius appears to have dealt with the Cappadocians' neo-Nicenism. Only in passing does Gregory quote his phrase that

> whatever is united by a formula of being (λόγος τῆς οὐσίας) this will necessarily exist in bodies and be subject to corruption,[157]

generously letting us know that he intends to bypass this 'like morbid stench'. Balás refers to this statement as evidence of Eunomius' capitalising on Basil's materialism.[158] However, Eunomius' remark clearly is not aimed specifically at a Stoic model of *ousia*, but, more generally, indicates his rejection, in Aristotelian language, of earthly species as an analogy for the Deity. The most logical connection with the preceding words would, to my mind, be provided by the assumption that Eunomius, after exploiting the shortcomings of Basil's argument for his own ends, now felt he had to make clear that a community of *ousia* as in the case of men could not be thought of in the case of the Godhead.

Things then being as they are, the best we can do is to look at Gregory's reply to Eunomius' claim that the *Categories* could only be applied to sensible reality. Not surprisingly, Gregory flatly denies such a claim. He argues from the consubstantiality of souls which, he claims, nobody would question:[159]

> For who does not know that there is an infinite multitude of human souls, but one *ousia* underlying (ὑποκεῖναι) all of them, and the consubstantial substratum (ὁμοούσιον ὑποκείμενον) in them is alien to bodily corruption?[160]

Thus, he concludes, although bodies may be both *homoousios* and corruptible, they are not the former because they are the latter, and it is therefore wrong to say that consubtantiality is to be found in bodies only.

---

[156] Loc. cit. (n. 151 above); cf. *spir sanct* 2 (18,17–19,10 Johnson).
[157] *Eun* III/5 61 (GNO II, 182,25–183,2).
[158] Balás (1976), 277.
[159] It is, perhaps, interesting that one of the few uses of *homoousios* by Porphyry refers to the consubstantiality of souls: *abst* I 19,1 (vol. I, 56 Bouffartigue).
[160] *Eun* III/5 62 (GNO II, 183,5–8).

The argumentative value of this statement can hardly be rated higher than that of the passages analysed before. If Gregory was acquainted with the debate among philosophers about the applicability of the *Categories* to the intelligible realm,[161] he gives no indication of his awareness.

What is interesting, in my view, about the quoted statement is that it very clearly underlines once more the character of *ousia* in this concept as an entity which is immanent in, but different from, the individuals. Gregory expresses this by saying that one *ousia* underlies all these souls and makes his point even more strongly by referring to a 'consubstantial substratum' within them. The latter phrase, I think, makes this as distinct as one could wish.

In summary, the following conclusions may be drawn:

(i) Gregory's *Contra Eunomium* provides for a number of valuable clues towards his understanding of the unity of human (and divine) nature, although the respective passages do not appear to reply conclusively to Eunomius' elaboration.

(ii) The presupposition underlying all these passages is an 'Aristotelian' understanding of the human *ousia*; the derivative model is clearly rejected. This reinforces observations made earlier in this chapter.

(iii) In comparison with the theory that was found to stand behind the *Epistle 38*, Gregory concentrates in *Contra Eunomium* on the item that was called *ousia* there, i.e. an entity immanent in the individuals and responsible both for their unity and for their specific identity. In *Contra Eunomium* this item is referred to above all as *ousia*, but on a number of occasions *phusis* and other terms (ὑποκείμενον, δύναμις) are employed equivalently. The extensive aspect, which *phusis* was found to indicate in the *Epistle 38*, did not appear to be prominent in the present books.

(iv) As for the character of this universal item, it was learned that (in human beings) it is thought to be passed on through sexual generation. Nevertheless, it was emphasised that this process does not by any means change the universal nature, which is expressly said to be the same in *all* human beings, including Adam.

---

[161] Cf. Simplicius, *in Cat* (76,13–78,5 Kalbfleisch).

2.5   Gregory's defence against the charge of tritheism

It is sometimes thought that the charge of tritheism was prompted merely by the assumption of separate *hupostaseis*. Such a view could draw on Socrates' account of the immediately post-Nicene controversy between Eusebius and Eustathius of Antioch.[162] The church historian claims that in the wake of the Council of Nicaea the supporters of the *homoousion* were charged with Sabellianism, while themselves accusing their opponents of polytheism.

However, Socrates may not be an ideal guide to a proper understanding of fourth-century doctrinal controversies. His assumption of debates between defenders and critics of the *homoousion* of which, as we have seen (see pp. 21–2 above), there is no evidence prior to the 350s, should suffice to rouse suspicions about the accuracy of his perception. Equally, the idea that the *homoousion* would have prompted charges of Sabellianism has not found much support in fourth-century sources.[163]

As for the charge of tritheism, then, I would suggest that we mistrust his authority too, the more so as there are a number of fourth-century witnesses who appear to provide a rather different picture. Their evidence seems to suggest that tritheism was the label conventionally given to theories based on the co-ordination of divine *hupostaseis* and as such rejected both by Eusebians and by monarchians like Marcellus.

The former would, for this reason, always insist on the derivative nature of the Son's divinity as indeed they do in the Macrostichos:

> But confessing three things (πράγματα) and three Persons (πρόσωπα) of Father and Son and Holy Spirit according to Scripture, we do not therefore make them three gods. For we know the self-willed and ingenerate and eternal (ἄναρχος) and invisible God to be the only one, (the) God and Father of the Only-begotten. He (sc. the Father) alone has his being out of himself, and he alone ungrudgingly gives a share of this to all others.[164]

A similar statement is to be found in the homoiousian epistle preserved in Epiphanius' *Panarion*. There the authors argue that saying 'three *hupostaseis*' does not imply a confession to three principles

---

[162] Socrates, *hist eccl* II 18 (74,7–24 Hansen).
[163] See p. 28 above with n. 26.
[164] Hahn (1897), §159,IV.

(ἀρχαί) or three gods.[165] Again, it seems clear that the suspicion of tritheism is equated with a belief in three principles (ἀρχαί) and, consequently, countered with the assertion of the principal nature of the Father.

That fundamentally the same view could be taken on the basis of Nicenism is borne out by a statement of Apollinarius[166] which seems to be no more than a corollary of his derivative understanding of the *homoousion*.

A different approach is encountered, of course, in Marcellus. The relevant passage from his letter to Pope Julius has been quoted earlier (see p. 58 above). Marcellus' line is that any assumption of the Son's hypostatic reality (he speaks of separating the Logos from the Father) results in either Arianism or ditheism (he ignores the Holy Ghost): the former, we may gather, is apprehended wherever there is subordination, the latter, consequently, where *hupostaseis* are co-ordinated.

From this the conclusion seems cogent that in the case of the Cappadocians the charge of tritheism ensues inevitably from their emphasis of both equality *and* hypostatic independence of the divine Persons.

It also seems natural to assume that more than one party was able to throw this accusation against them, as apparently did indeed happen. Since, however, most of their theological opponents would try to maintain a hypostatic distinction between the Persons by means of some sort of subordinationism, it is not surprising that charges of tritheism alternate with accusations of Sabellianism. We have one vivid description from Gregory's pen of such an interaction of these two charges:

> They accuse us of teaching three gods and spread the rumours of the many and do not cease to make up this slander. But truth is fighting on our behalf since we have demonstrated—in public to everybody and privately to those who approached us—that we condemn anybody who teaches three gods and do not even judge him to be a Christian. But when they hear this they have Sabellius at hand against us, and the disease initiated by the latter is brought out against our teaching. And again to this also we direct the accustomed weapon, truth, showing that we shudder equally from Judaism and from the latter heresy.[167]

---

[165] *Haer* 73,16; (vol. III, 288,20ff. Holl/Dummer).
[166] *KMP* 18 (173,13–22 Lietzmann).
[167] *Eust* (GNO III/1, 5,3–14).

What Gregory presents here as a disingenuous sophism on the part of the pneumatomachi[168] must, from their point of view, have appeared to be no more than a logical reply to the Cappadocian rejection of any subordination, saying that this would necessarily result in either tritheism or Sabellianism. It apparently corresponds to Marcellus' claim that any theory of a personal Logos was either Arian or ditheistic and, indeed, to Basil's obsession with Arianism and Sabellianism.

Given Basil's unequivocal opposition to subordination and Sabellianism, however, the charge of tritheism must have been the one most difficult to disown. What, then, would have been the most effective defence against it? In the context just quoted Gregory makes no mention of any particular argument he employed, but elsewhere, of course, he does. In fact, he devotes two entire treatises, *Ad Graecos* and *Ad Ablabium*, to proving that his trinitarian teaching is not tritheistic. His argument in both these writings, that strictly speaking there *is* only one man, has not found much sympathy amongst scholars. Indeed, quite often it has simply been derided.[169] In the following I shall argue for a more balanced view. Although I do not believe that Gregory's approach can ultimately salvage the Cappadocian theory from the smack of tritheism, I shall contend that it is the best one he could have chosen on the basis of the Cappadocian doctrine as it has emerged from our reconstruction.

To be sure, at times the Cappadocians (in particular Nazianzen)[170] seem to offer a different approach, arguing like the Eusebians and Apollinarius from the 'archaic' property of the Father. However, it seems to me that this argument had altogether lost its force once the 'Aristotelian' paradigm of specific co-ordination had been introduced to combat subordinationism: ingeneracy having been made a property with no bearing on the Father's divinity, it could not be used to uphold a derivative sameness any more than any other property. If the Cappadocian theory was to be defended against tritheism at all, this could only be approached by showing that within the

---

[168] That this is what his opponents must be has been recognised by Jaeger (1966), 6; cf. Stead (1990), 150–1.

[169] Cf. Holl (1904), 219 who calls it 'tasteless'; Stead (1990, 149) opines 'that it resembles an accomplished conjuring trick more nearly than a valid theological demonstration'. Cf., however, now: Frede (1997), 49–50.

[170] E.g. at *or* 20,7,1–5 (70 Mossay); cf. Holl (1904), 173–8. For Basil, see: Holl (1904), 142–8. I take it, however, that this does not put into question their principal commitment to the co-ordinate model (see p. 19, n. 4 above).

'Aristotelian' paradigm the concept of substantial unity could be maintained; and this, I think, is what Gregory attempts.

This is not to say, of course, that Gregory's argument is beyond blame. However, it deserves to be taken more seriously than it frequently has been. In the following I shall therefore start from an analysis of the two writings concerned in so far as they are relevant to the present quest. I will be asking whether they are consistent in their use of human nature both with themselves and with the views that have been found to underlie the Cappadocian position in general.

In a further step the question will be raised whether or to what degree their pledge against tritheistic implications of the Cappadocian trinitarian teaching holds theologically.

2.5.1   *The* Ad Graecos

For a number of reasons this brief treatise appears to occupy a singular place among Gregory's writings: to begin with, it gives us no indication of its addressees or, indeed, its purpose. Without a proem it begins directly with a syllogism stating under what condition a trinitarian confession would be tritheistic. The bulk of the writing is then devoted to the proof that the Cappadocian teaching does not fulfil this condition and, therefore, steers clear of that charge.

The next peculiarity is the restriction of the writing to what one may call philosophical arguments; the entire treatise does not make use of Scripture as of an authority.[171] It is therefore in a sense not surprising that in the manuscripts it has the title *Against the Greeks. From Common Notions.* Nevertheless, this title is probably secondary: in spite of its lack of biblical references the contents of the treatise points to the trinitarian controversy, not apologetics, as its context.

From these observations it might appear that there would be no chance of fitting *Ad Graecos* into a particular historical situation. There is, however, a further observation to be made which, while raising new questions, partially helps to answer those that are otherwise left unanswered by the treatise: Gregory's text shows in its first part the most extraordinary similarity with the extant fragment from Eustathius' *Against Photinus* (see pp. 58–60 above). Comparing those two texts, as I have done elsewhere,[172] reveals that the first part of *Ad Graecos*

---

[171] No scriptural references are given in Mueller's edition except for those related to the problem of the Bible's plural use of 'man' (ad GNO III/1, 26,6.23).

[172] See my paper 'Gregor von Nyssa und das Schisma von Antiochien' in: *ThPh* 72 (1998), 481–96.

is largely a paraphrase of the Eustathian argument in that fragment. From this it would appear (or so, at least, I have argued) that *Ad Graecos* was written as part of attempts towards a settlement of the Antiochene schism, perhaps as a contribution to the 379 synod at Antioch, which we know Gregory attended.[173] As that synod marks the high tide of conciliatory endeavour with regard to that schism in the late fourth century,[174] one could well imagine Gregory delivering *Ad Graecos* there.

In the present context, however, the precise elucidation of the historical background of *Ad Graecos* is perhaps not as important as the tackling of questions concerning its contents and theology.

In the second part of the writing (which does not appear to draw on Eustathius' text any more) Gregory raises the problem that Peter, Paul, and Barnabas are called three men.[175] That this usage becomes a problem is, of course, obvious only from the conceptual framework into which the question is imbedded. Gregory had started his treatise from the following alternative (the phrasing almost literally coincides with the Eustathian fragment):

> If the name 'God' were indicative of the Person, then we would, saying three Persons, necessarily also say three gods; but if the name 'God' is indicative of the *ousia*, then, confessing one *ousia* of the holy Trinity, we consequently teach one God since 'God' is the one name of the one *ousia* (19,1–5).

It seems clear that what this statement has in mind is the juxtaposition of universal and proper names; what it suggests, then, is that if 'God' can be shown to be a universal name, the charge of tritheism is void.

However, this apparently misses the real problem, which is in what sense the universal is used for the individual member of the class or, indeed, the applicability of the human analogy.[176] It is therefore not surprising that Gregory, having established 'God' as a universal

---

[173] This view had already been taken by Hübner (1971, 208–9). However, his conclusion that the Eustathian fragments were really extracts from Gregory's writing has become untenable with the publication of the full fragment by Lorenz (1980).

[174] Cf. Schwartz (1935) 197–9.

[175] *Graec* (GNO III/1, 23,13–4). In the following, page numbers in the text refer to GNO III/1.

[176] Gregory himself remarks rightly (GNO III/1, 22,24–23,3) that if 'God' were a proper name, the consequence would not be a multiplicity of gods, but one God, that is he whose name it would be.

name at the end of the first part of *Ad Graecos*, finds himself confronted with the argument of *de facto* plural use of those names. But perhaps this way of putting it is misleading: if it is clear that the first part of *Ad Graecos* reproduces Eustathius' arguments, one might as well suppose that it is Gregory himself who raises the question of the *de facto* plural use to indicate where he finds Eustathius' theory in need of improvement.

Be this as it may, Gregory answers the question first of all with the flat assertion that this plural use is catachrestic (23,21–5). He then goes on to argue in a rather oblique way that there are reasons which explain this wrong use with regard to man, but not God. The following three reasons can be discerned:

1. 'The definition of man is not always seen in the same individuals, i.e. persons' (24,1–2). Men are born and die, there are at times more of them or less, which accounts for counting them; all this does not occur in the Godhead, which in all eternity consists of three Persons only (24,3–26).
2. Not all human individuals have their existence immediately from the same person. Again, this is different in the Deity where the Father is the only cause of Son and Spirit (24,26–25,8).
3. There is no spatial, temporal or other separation between the divine Persons, which, however, exists between men (25,8–17).

It seems clear that for Gregory all these are reasons that explain, but do not justify, the improper use of 'man' in the plural: this is what he explicitly says (25,17–9) and it also comes out, I think, from the reasons he gives. For, for example, although men do not have their origin *immediately* (κατὰ τὸ προσεχές) from the same person, we know that ultimately they do, as they are all descendants of Adam.

Is it possible, then, to elicit the underlying concept of the one human *ousia* from these arguments? This seems to me to be the case; indeed, I do think that what Gregory has in mind here must be the item referred to as *phusis* in the *Epistle 38*, i.e. the totality of human individuals. This item, corresponding, as has been shown, to the second substance of *Categories*, was in the *Epistle 38* thought to be indicated by the universal name, which would provide for a first, important parallel with the present writing.

The most explicit statement supporting this interpretation is, in my view, contained in the following sentence:

Therefore, then, we call the one cause together with the two (beings) that are caused by him rightly and boldly one God, since also he co-exists with them (25,6-8).

With this Gregory draws the conclusion from the argument numbered as (2) above. The 'cause' is therefore not to be understood as referring to a derivative theory, but simply as stating that the genetic relation between the three Persons is crystal clear. The crucial word for the interpretation of the passage appears to be 'with' (μετά): the three together are said to constitute the one God.

Once this interpretation is allowed, it seems easy to find this view behind the other arguments as well. Indeed, there are many more or less relevant observations which support this reading.

In the first argument I find important the distinction made between 'man' and 'the definition of man'. The latter, I take it, represents here what is called elsewhere the λόγος τῆς οὐσίας, and this was said to indicate the immanent form, the item responsible for men being what they are in the *Epistle 38*. This 'definition' is said twice to be seen *in* the individuals (24,1-2.9-10), thus emphasising the difference between this immanent item and 'man' as the compound of the individuals.

Interesting also is that Gregory here regularly uses 'individual' (ἄτομον) for the person as opposed to *ousia*. This again points to the *Epistle 38* where I have argued that *pragma* would bear exactly that sense.[177] Now, *pragma* was there paired with *phusis*, which again would confirm that the extensive meaning of the latter term is also the meaning of the present *ousia*. Also remarkable in this context are phrases like 'all the persons of man' (24,26; cf. 25,18) or 'the Persons of the Godhead' (25,8) where the genitive seems to underline the supposed relation of a whole and its parts.

As for the second of the above arguments, it appears that the assumption of the human 'family's' size as a reason for not comprehending its unity is equally best understood if we think of *ousia* in an extensive way: the idea seems to be that, if we *could* perceive humankind as genetically related, its unity would be much easier to understand. The same, I think, applies for the third reason Gregrory adduces: that 'man' as a whole is one would be obvious if we could

---

[177] Cf. also Aristotle's *Categories*; this treatise is the origin of this use of ἄτομον: Frede (1978).

transcend the temporal and spatial differences between the human individuals.

One could, moreover, adduce arguments from elsewhere in the writing: thus, Gregory repeatedly equates not only person with 'individual', but also *ousia* with 'species' (εἶδος: this is, I think, the only meaning the word can have here).[178]

I should thus conclude that in *Ad Graecos*, like in the *Epistle 38*, the one man, who is indicated by the universal name, is the whole of humankind. There remains the problem of terminology: why is it that Gregory employs *ousia* here in a sense different not only from the *Epistle 38* (where we do not know how far he was responsible for the formulation), but also from *Contra Eunomium*? In the latter writing, it is true, Gregory would not consequently distinguish *ousia* and *phusis*, but this amounted there to an assimilation of the latter term to the *ousia* of *Epistle 38*. In the present writing we see the opposite happen. One possibility to account for Gregory's phrasing would be to assume that Gregory's language is influenced by the Eustathian fragment, which would have employed this terminology. This would, I think, be a rather satisfactory explanation; in the last part of *Ad Graecos*[179] one can observe how the language of a question could indeed influence Gregory's own phrasing. And Gregory's use of the term 'person' throughout the first and second parts of the writing (19,1–28,8) does in all likelihood mirror his Antiochene source.

The problem with *ousia* is that the translated Syriac of the Eustathian fragment seems to point to *phusis* rather than *ousia* in the Greek original.[180] The original *could* of course have been different, but in the absence of stronger reasons one should probably not doubt the accuracy of the translation. I should then leave this problem unaccounted for, concluding that *Ad Graecos* confirms the analysis of *Contra Eunomium* in that Gregory does not make a terminological distinction between *ousia* and *phusis* throughout.

---

[178] Cf. *graec* (GNO III/1, 31,1–5).

[179] Beginning at *graec* (GNO III/1, 28,9) with the introduction of a wordy counter-argument which uses οὐσία and ὑπόστασις. In his reply Gregory equally employs this pair while earlier in the treatise he had based his argument on οὐσία and πρόσωπον.

[180] Cf. Schwartz' Greek retranslation of those fragments which had been available to him in: id. (1925), 60–1.

2.5.2 *The* Ad Ablabium

The treatise *To Ablabius. That There are not Three Gods*, commonly known as *Ad Ablabium*, is not easily fitted into a particular historical context. The writing presents itself as an answer to an otherwise unknown (or, at least, virtually unknown)[181] cleric, who had raised the problem of tritheism as the seemingly logical consequence of the human analogy.

Many scholars have assigned the treatise to a later period of Gregory's activity, which indeed seems likely for a number of reasons:

1. The absence of obvious polemic; this points to a time well after 381 when the Cappadocian position, though criticised, was in fact established orthodoxy.[182]
2. Gregory's authoritative position; the setting makes it clear that Gregory considers himself entitled to settle a doctrinal difficulty like the present one for a lower rank. What is more, he seems to intimate that it would have been more appropriate had Ablabius himself answered those critics on Gregory's behalf (31,1–5). This is reminiscent of the way Plotinus had his pupils rebut critics of his own position.[183]
3. The absence of any reference to Basil as the supreme authority on any such question points into the same direction.
4. Finally, mention is made of Gregory's advanced age (37,5).

I should thus tentatively assign the treatise to the latter half of the 380s; anything more specific would be too speculative. This, however, ought to be sufficient for maintaining that it is, in all likelihood, several years later than *Ad Graecos*.

As for the character of the writing, a rather striking feature is its almost complete lack of the technical jargon so characteristic of all the writings with which we have dealt so far. This, I take it, indicates that the addressee was not thought to be highly erudite. It does not necessarily imply, I think, that Gregory did not bother about the refinements of theological discourse here. His answer may just as well represent an attempt to give a non-technical account of a philosophical view he held.

---

[181] Cf. Pasquali's note on *ep* 6, *tit* (GNO VIII/2, 34,9).
[182] Cf. the frequently cited Theodosian edict, issued after the Council in 381, making the communion with Gregory a requirement of orthodoxy; cf. May (1966), 120.
[183] Cf. Porphyry, *vit Plot* 18.

Moreover, we have no reason to doubt that the argument put forth in the writing coincides *in principle* with what Gregory argues elsewhere in a more elaborate way. Indeed, from what has been found so far it should be clear that such a view could be held by a philosophically educated author of that age and, further, that in more than one place Gregory explicitly or implicitly refers to it. Its striking similarity, in particular, to the central tenet of *Ad Graecos* serves to substantiate this presumption.

What has to be asked, then, is first of all whether the explanations given, and the illustrations adduced, by Gregory in *Ad Ablabium* give us a consistent picture of the precise nature of the 'one man'.

Their evaluation, I think, ought to take into account the consciously non-philosophical, popular way in which they attempt to explain what appears to be a rather subtle theory. This, of course, cannot mean that Gregory is exempt from the usual requirements of consistency here; nevertheless, it may be that bearing his assumed purpose in mind helps the better understanding of the writing.

The question raised by Ablabius is quoted by Gregory as follows (38,8–11):

> We call Peter and James and John three men although they are in one humanity: and there is nothing inappropriate if those, who are connected in their nature (κατὰ τὴν φύσιν) are counted as multiple by the name of the nature if they are many. . . .

The question is straightforward: from the common use of language it is argued that, granted the legitimacy of the human analogy, we could say 'three gods' as well as 'three men'.

Gregory's reply consists of two groups of arguments, and it is not quite clear how they are interrelated. On one hand he *defends* the human analogy by arguing that it is only by popular misuse that we speak of many 'men', on the other, he apparently reduces the applicability of that analogy by claiming that 'God' unlike 'man' does not signify a nature, but an activity. The structure is somewhat curious as the arguments of the former group seem to from an *inclusio* of the latter, which occupies the central part of the treatise.

Be this as it may, what concerns us here is the former group, that is those arguments by means of which Gregory seeks to establish the monadic character of the *phusis*. All these arguments are adduced to substantiate Gregory's claim that strictly speaking a word like 'man' should not be used in the plural.

The first of them, which I have in a way pre-empted, is that say-ing 'many men' would in effect mean 'many human natures' (40,7–8). What Gregory implies here is his tenet, well known from elsewhere, that 'man' indicates human nature and, secondly, that human nature is one with all human individuals.

Next (40,10–7) he points to actual usage: in addressing a person we do not employ the universal but the proper name in order that he is not confused with some other man. As such, this argument does not seem to bear out much philosophically. It is, however, rem-iniscent of the *Epistle 38* where in a similar way the 'indefinite' mean-ing of the universal term had been invoked. In that context I have argued that the author understands the universal as a quasi-collective noun, and the same thought may stand behind the present argument. However, we cannot get beyond speculation here, I think.

A further consideration is introduced then (40,17–21): there are many who partake (μετέχειν) of the nature, but *the man* in (ἐν) all of them is one, provided that the term 'man' indicates the common item, not the individual. This is one of the few rather technical pas-sages in the writing. For the combination of participation and being 'in' something compare Porphyry's shorter *Commentary on Aristotle's Categories*. In one passage Porphyry lists nine homonymous uses of 'in', among them the following:

> It is possible to be in something (. . .) as the genus is in the species, for the species participate (μετέχειν) in the genus: animal is predicated of man as of something that participates in it.[184]

Both, Porphyry and Gregory apparently see the presence of the more comprehensive class *in* the less comprehensive one safeguarded by the participation of the latter in the former. This should warn us against a rash identification of the present notion of participation with the well-known theory of Plato's middle-period dialogues:[185] the fact that sensible things 'participate in' ideas does, in the latter view, exclude the possibility of immanent forms thus creating the much-debated χωρισμός. At the same time, however, it seems to me that the relationship envisaged here cannot be that of a whole to its parts either, as in that case we would expect the formulation to be that the individual is *in* the species or the species *in* the genus. This,

---

[184] Porphyry, *in Cat* (77,27–30 Busse); ET: Strange (1992), 61.
[185] This is what Stead does: (1990), 158–9.

indeed, is cited by Porphyry as a further case of the meaning of 'in' immediately preceding the one quoted above:

> It is possible to be in something as the species is in the genus, as man is in animal, for the genus comprehends (περιέχειν) the species.[186]

In so far as the genus comprehends the species, they are all contained *in* it. The juxtaposition of the two concepts makes it, in my view, the only possible interpretation of Gregory's argument here that 'the man' which is one *in* all individuals is the immanent form, the *ousia* of the *Epistle 38* and the *Contra Eunomium*.

It would then appear that the immediately following characterisation of *phusis* as an indivisible monad does also refer to *this* item rather than to the concrete *phusis*:

> Yet the nature is one, united in itself, a monad completely indivisible, not increased by addition, nor diminished by subtraction, but in what it is, it is one and remains one even if it is seen in a multitude. It is indivisible, continuous and complete, and not divided alongside the particulars who participate (μετέχειν) in it (41,2–7).

This assumption, it seems, is confirmed by the wording of the statement which again mentions 'participation'.

But then Gregory goes on to illustrate this monadic character of the *phusis* with examples of collective nouns (λαός, δῆμος, στράτευμα, ἐκκλησία: 41,8–9). What, then, is this monadic *phusis*? Is it, to use the terminology of the *Epistle 38*, the *phusis*, i.e. the totality of individual men, or the *ousia*, i.e. the universal item responsible for their being man?

The latter interpretation, it seems to me, is supported by two more observations: first, the parallel of *Contra Eunomium* I 175[187] where nature is described as a monad in similar terms and, secondly, the example of gold which is introduced later in the writing (53,16–54,4). The upshot of that example also appears to be that human nature is the unitary element underlying all individual things.[188]

Finally, mention has to be made of a further argument which is not easily interpreted, on any count. Gregory at one point claims that human nature is not counted since 'only that which is seen in an individual circumscription (περιγραφή) is numbered by addition

---

[186] Porphyry, *in Cat* (77,27–8 Busse); ET: Strange (1992), 61.
[187] *Eun* I 175 (GNO I, 78,22–7); see p. 96 above.
[188] Cf. the concluding formulation: 'but the man *in* them (sc. the particulars) is one.

(κατὰ σύνθεσιν)' (53,9–10). He then goes on to relate that only items which are located in space and time could be counted at all (53,10–5).

It appears that this argument is easily dismissed;[189] Gregory's own example of souls at *Contra Eunomium* III/5,62 (GNO II, 183,5–8; see p. 103 above) and of angels at *De hominis opificio* 17 (PG 44, 189A) might be cited against it as well as his counting divine *hupostaseis*. I think that perhaps the most favourable interpretation for Gregory would be to understand it as affirming that human nature can be one in many due to its intelligible character: we do not count human nature because, although it is to be found in many individuals, it is *one* in all of them.[190] In this interpretation this argument would fall into the second of the above groups, supporting an understanding of *phusis* as an immanent, universal item.

So far, the arguments presented by Gregory all seem to point to either of the two concepts we have found to be present in other works as well, notably in the *Epistle 38*. The crucial question, then, is how the two concepts are thought to interrelate. There are, it appears, three possibilities to account for this: first, by ultimately discarding one in favour of the other; secondly, by charging Gregory with inconsistency; thirdly, by opting for a further concept which allows the integration of the two.

Quantitatively, the second group seems fairly dominant; only one argument, the example of collective nouns, could clearly be associated with the view of nature as the totality of individuals. Should we, then, altogether discard this latter view as accidental? Yet this would obviously collide not only with the theory of *Epistle 38* (where, again, we do not know for certain how Gregory was involved), but also with the view that was found to underlie *Ad Graecos*.

If, then, we cannot easily abandon either of the two views in favour of the other one, could we detect an overarching theory capable of integrating the two approaches into one? This, again, seems to me all but impossible. Surely, the two items as analysed above in the *Epistle 38* have much in common; they are not by any means independent of each other. Nevertheless, one cannot easily equate them, and if one could, we should certainly expect an author to show more refinement in that attempt than Gregory displays in *Ad Ablabium*.

---

[189] So Stead (1990), 153: 'This contention is clearly false.'
[190] Cf. Boethius, *in de Int* II 7 (137,18–26 Meiser) and pp. 83; 96 above.

Thus, for example, *Epistle 38*, *Contra Eunomium* and *Ad Graecos* all agree that it is the formula or definition that corresponds to the immanent *ousia*: in *Ad Ablabium* Gregory does not even bother to refer to it. What is more, the example of collective nouns and of a stuff (gold) are introduced as though they were to illustrate the same fact; but this would work (if at all) in a very subtle way, and there is virtually no indication that Gregory is concerned with subtleties here.

Thus I find it difficult to resist the conclusion that Gregory has to be charged with a number of rather disingenuous inconsistencies in *Ad Ablabium*. As to why it is that in this writing he falls so clearly behind his usual standard of perspicuity, we are left guessing: perhaps a gap of some years between this and earlier utterances on the subject could explain a certain alienation of Gregory from the topic; it is also possible is that the feeling of authority which so strongly permeates the writing had weakened Gregory's sense of self-criticism. Whatever the reason, and in all likelihood we will never know for sure, I should conclude that *Ad Ablabium* is not the most appropriate guide to a proper understanding of Gregory's teaching on human nature.

2.5.3   *The alleged tritheism of Gregory of Nyssa*

All this, however, has not yet answered what is perhaps the crucial question about those writings, that is, how far they are eventually able to disperse the suspicion that the Cappadocian doctrine is tritheistic in its consequences.

That Gregory's defence fails on logical grounds has been emphatically affirmed by Stead. He writes:

> If we ask what Gregory's logic actually establishes, the answer must be that it gets us no further than generic unity. Father, Son and Spirit can each be entitled 'God'; though the mere use of this title guarantees very little; the genus of gods includes some disreputable members (!).[191]

He then goes on to relate that a more favourable interpretation of Gregory's argument would draw on the disanalogies he concedes more strongly than on the analogies he claims: if men *were* the way they are meant to be, they might indeed provide for something like an analogy for the 'mutual enjoyment and self-giving of the divine Persons' (ibid.).

---

[191] Stead (1990), 161.

This is an interesting interpretation, as it suggests that what the Cappadocians intended was after all a *social* analogy. However, it seems to me that Gregory's argument does not really yield this interpretation. Nyssen clearly thought that human nature could provide for a limited analogy for the unity of the Godhead in a logical and ontological sense and the disclaimers he offers do not refer, I think, to the factual division of humankind in the first place, but rather to the principal ontological difference between created and uncreated being which limits the force of any analogy.

This, then, would, in Stead's view, leave Gregory exposed to the charge of tritheism. A similar conclusion was adopted by Hübner with regard to the *Epistle 38*.[192] And others, who, like Kelly,[193] Meredith[194] and Hanson,[195] have passed a more favourable judgment on the Cappadocian teaching, have done so by arguing that passages elsewhere in their writings would limit the force of the human analogy either by emphasising unity and simplicity of the divine substance or by general remarks about the impossibility of adequate conceptions of God. They all, however, agree on the 'inescapably tritheistic' implications of the 'unfortunate' human analogy[196] without much reflection upon the meaning of 'generic'.

Lebon and Ritter,[197] however, have questioned this presupposition, and while their 'Platonic' interpretation of the Cappadocian *ousia* has been shown to be problematic, in this they undoubtedly raised an important point. Can it, then, be said on the basis of the findings of this chapter that the interpretation of the 'generic' item by Gregory of Nyssa acquits him from the charge of tritheism?

Quite generally, it appears that the arguments contained in *Ad Graecos* and *Ad Ablabium* do not add substantially to the picture gained from the analysis of other writings, in particular of the *Epistle 38*. Gregory's anti-tritheistic writings have at best maintained the standard of that treatise, *Ad Ablabium* in fact fell considerably behind it. The evaluation to be given here cannot therefore differ fundamentally from the conclusions adopted with regard to the *Epistle 38*.

---

[192] Hübner (1972), 489.
[193] Kelly (1958), 267–9.
[194] Meredith (1972), 251–2.
[195] Hanson (1988), 696–99; 734–7.
[196] Kelly (1958), 267.
[197] Lebon (1953), 639–41; Ritter (1965), 285–91.

It seems to me, then, that on the basis of that theory the Cappadocian doctrine can indeed explain that there is only one man understood as the totality of human individuals. Its unity would be guaranteed by the underlying *ousia* which is one in all the individuals.

Yet, while the assumption of such an underlying substrate is needed to ward off the danger of tritheism, it is for a different reason obviously unacceptable in the case of the Trinity: its introduction into the Godhead would mean adding a further item to the three *hupostaseis*, thus effectively confirming a frequent suspicion of the anti-Nicenes.

A supporter of the Cappadocian theory might argue that this is not the case as this common *ousia* is not an independent item; there are only the three Persons which, in their community, form the common *phusis*; only *logically* can their *ousia* be separated while in reality it is immanent in them. But then there is the obvious reply, and we have seen that at least Eunomius apparently made it, that this presupposes an analysis of the individual into substance and accident, which should not be applied to God. Of course, these properties of the *hupostasis* are accidents only in a very limited sense, but even so, I think, this is the point where the Cappadocian theory ultimately collapses.

This, I believe, would apply even if the details of the present analysis were not accepted: the assumption of divine Persons being identical *qua* divinity and different *qua* individual property, however precisely conceived of, involves presuppositions which neither the Cappadocians nor their opponents would normally accept with regard to God.

It seems to me, then, that the Cappadocian theory basically suffers from some implicit presuppositions which are built into their human analogy but cannot easily be applied to the Godhead. Whether that leads eventually to some kind of tritheism or to a separation of *ousia* and *hupostasis* would depend very much on the emphasis put on the several elements of that theory.

In elucidating the use of human nature in Gregory of Nyssa's trinitarian teaching the present part of this study has had two main objectives: first, it was attempted to explain *historically* and *theologically* why the analogy was adopted the way it was.

I hope to have demonstrated that the primary purpose of this cannot have been to reconcile homoiousians with the Nicene Creed, as has often been thought, because the main emphasis of the analogy in both Basil's and Gregory's usage lies on the co-ordination of divine Persons or *hupostaseis*, to which the homoiousians were openly hostile. Nor, indeed, can it be said that the Cappadocian Nicenism follows directly from Athanasius' or Apollinarius' derivative interpretation of the Nicene formula.

Rather, I have argued that it was the anomoian theology of Euno-mius which prompted the adoption of co-ordination as implied in the Cappadocians' use of the human analogy. Apollinarius' use of the human analogy is drawn on only with a characteristic reinter-pretation of it which makes humanity an 'Aristotelian' rather than a 'Neoplatonic' genus. If there is any immediate precedent for the Cappadocian position in post-Nicene theology, it is to be found in the Eustathian fragment from *Against Photinus*, a fact which may shed new light on the vicissitudes of Basil's involvement in the Antiochene conflict.

The second main interest of this part, approached in the second chapter, was to analyse the Cappadocians' own understanding of the unity of human nature in this analogy, including its philosophical background. To this end, the *Epistle 38* was taken as the main witness, and I hope the remainder of the chapter has proven this decision adequate. There a remarkably subtle theory was detected, distinguish-ing a common *phusis* as the totality of individuals, and as such indi-cated by the universal name, from *ousia*, conceived of as the universal element in all individuals of one species and indicated by the defini-tional formula. Correspondingly, the epistle discerned *hupostasis* as the individualising element from *pragma*, the individual being. This theory was then traced back to a particular late ancient interpretation of Aristotle's logical writings.

Given that the *Epistle 38*'s authorship is debated it had to be shown that, as far as the present theories are concerned, it agrees with Gregory's views. This was the main purpose of the remainder of the second chapter. Such a concurrence could be demonstrated on the basis of some statements from Gregory's *Contra Eunomium* and his minor trinitarian writings although, in comparison, it appeared that the terminological framework of *Epistle 38* was not treated by Gregory as obligatory. With regard to the central topic of this study, Gregory's use of *phusis* terminology, it emerged that Gregory could employ such expressions in two ways:[198] on the one hand, *phusis* was used

---

[198] This corresponds largely to the results reached by Balás (1979), see p. 5 above.

for the immanent item, present in all human being and responsible for their being men. This meaning was predominant in the anti-Eunomian writings; it corresponds to the use of *ousia* in the *Epistle 38*. In fact, *phusis* in this meaning appears to be interchangeable with the latter term throughout. On the other hand, *phusis* could mean the extension of the class, the totality of human beings. This meaning was found, apart from the *Epistle 38*, in the *Ad Graecos* and, to some extent, also in the *Ad Ablabium*, although there some lack of consistency was noted. The *Ad Graecos*, in particular, confirmed the observation made in the *Epistle 38* that the universal term, man (ἄνθρωπος), stands for this entity. At the same time, however, it appeared from this writing that, contrary to the findings of Balás,[199] *ousia* could take on this meaning too.

In spite of everything which may be said in its favour, however, it seems to me that the Cappadocian solution to the trinitarian problem, as expressed by their distinctive use of the human analogy, provides perhaps for more new problems than it helps solve: notably, the distinction of *ousia* and *hupostasis* in the *Epistle 38* recalls fatefully the frequent anti-Nicene argument that *homoousios* would require the imposition of an *ousia* as a fourth element, perhaps even prior to the Persons. This, to be sure, was balanced by their complementary theory of *phusis* and *pragma*, but then this theory smacked of tritheism. While thus the Cappadocian solution is perhaps not as bad as is sometimes thought, it certainly is not free of serious tension and unevenness.

---

[199] Balás (1979), 122.

PART TWO

HUMAN NATURE IN THE DIVINE ECONOMY

CHAPTER THREE

HUMAN NATURE AND THE THEOLOGICAL
REQUIREMENTS OF SALVATION HISTORY

3.1 *Preliminary considerations*

The use Gregory makes of human nature in his trinitarian theology could be explained by his dependence on Basil and, more generally, by a number of theological interests shared by all three Cappadocian theologians. It is clear, however, that Gregory's use of human nature is not confined to this doctrinal field. In numerous passages Gregory cites the 'whole human nature' to bring home his particular theological argument. Following Balás,[1] I shall subsume these passages in the following categories:

1. Theology of creation: Gregory frequently states that God created human nature;
2. Universal sin: on some occasions Gregory seems to say that human nature fell in Adam and that therefore anybody possessing human nature is subject to the consequences of the Fall;
3. Soteriology: Gregory can argue that in the Incarnation the whole human nature has been effectively saved;
4. Eschatology: in Gregory's constant definition, 'resurrection is the *apokatastasis* of our nature in its initial state'.[2]

While the sheer bulk of the passages concerned makes it difficult to deny that Gregory often employs *phusis*-terminology, the precise meaning of this terminology in many of those texts and their conceptual and theological impact are a matter of substantial scholarly disagreement.

All these cases seem to have this in common, that they apply human nature to the divine economy (οἰκονομία), i.e. the account of God's history with his creatures, comprising the creation, Fall, salvation and restoration. It might therefore appear that with the help of a

---

[1] Balás (1979), 124–8.
[2] E.g. *an et res* (PG 46, 148A).

concept of universal human nature Gregory aims at a systematic treatment of this history: God created 'man' who afterwards fell but was saved from his fallen state through the assumption of human nature by Jesus Christ. This I shall term the 'systematic' interpretation of Gregory's use of human nature. It seems to be suggested by passages like the following from *Against Eunomius* III:

> We say that the only begotten Son through himself led all things into existence and rules all things in himself. One of the things generated by him is human nature which, having slid into evil and therefore become [subject to] death's corruptibility, is again drawn towards immortal life through him. Through the man in whom he dwelt (κατεσκήνωσεν: cf. John 1,14) he assumed the whole human item to himself, mixing his own life-giving power with the mortal and perishable (ἐπικήρος) nature and changing our mortality into living grace and power through the amalgamation with himself. And this we call the mystery of the Lord's Incarnation, that the unchangeable was in the changeable in order that, having changed for the better and turned away from the worse, he consumed from the nature evil, which was blended with the changeable condition (διάθεσις), having destroyed evil in himself. For our God is a consuming fire (Hebr 12,29) by whom the entire matter of evil is consumed.[3]

It would appear from such a text that what Gregory has in mind is something like a meta-process of salvation history taking place on the level of *phusis* and determining what happens historically to the individuals. While many scholars have embraced this very interpretation,[4] others have remained sceptical or even opposed to this idea.[5] They would argue that Gregory's statements on the subject are not of such a kind as to allow far reaching systematic conclusions; those statements should rather be taken as metaphorical *ad hoc* illustrations of Gregory's theological thinking.[6]

It would appear that a central question for a decision on this issue is the precise understanding of human nature in those texts. Is this of such a kind as to substantiate the systematic interpretation? Or, more generally, what kind of theory would be needed for a systematic application of human nature to the economy? Let us start from a consideration of the latter question.

---

[3] *Eun* III/3 51–2 (GNO II, 125,28–126,15).

[4] Balthasar (1995), 50–5; Leÿs (1951), 78–92; Skouteris (1969); Gregorios (1980), 185–93; Hauke (1993), 664–70.

[5] Holl (1904), 222–5; Hübner (1974); cf. op. cit., 3–25 the exhaustive though biased account of research on the topic up to the date of his thesis.

[6] Hübner (1974), 105–6 and passim.

Upholders of the systematic interpretation have often argued with Gregory's alleged Platonism. Thus, for example, Harnack writes about Gregory's soteriology as follows:

> Gregory was able to demonstrate the application of the Incarnation more definitely than Athanasius could (. . .). But he does so by the aid of a thoroughly Platonic idea which is only slightly suggested in Athanasius, and is not really covered by a biblical reference. Christ did not assume the human nature of an individual person, but human nature. Accordingly, all that was human was intertwined with the Deity; the whole of human nature became divine by intermixture with the divine.[7]

Harnack does not tell us what this Platonic understanding of human nature was. If we assume that by 'Platonic' he meant the doctrine of ideas in Plato's middle-period dialogues, the universal human nature would probably be something like the universal Man known from Philo's account of creation:

> . . . he that was after the (divine) image was an idea or type or seal, an object of thought (only), incorporeal, neither male nor female, by nature incorruptible.[8]

Scholars have, of course, argued that Gregory's views were similar to those of Philo,[9] but without pursuing this at the moment it ought to be stated that, whatever this theory may help to explain, it certainly cannot serve to set salvation history in a universal framework: this Platonic man of Philo's cannot fall, and whatever earthly human beings do, this would not affect him. Philo's account seems, indeed, not least designed to yield an interpretation of Genesis directly opposed to that required by later generations of Christian theologians: the contradiction of the image mentioned in Gen 1,26 and the somewhat less exalted human state at present is not explained by the dialectics of original and fallen state, but by those of archetype and participant.[10]

Quite generally, it appears that the Platonic paradigm of a universal form and its individual participants would not allow for the kind of dynamism the systematic interpretation of the economy would

---

[7] Harnack (1894) vol. III, 297. Gregory's Platonism is also cited by Skouteris (1969), 9.
[8] Philo, *op mun* 134; ET: Colson/Whitaker (1929) vol. I, 107.
[9] Cf. p. 168; n. 77.
[10] *Op mun*, loc. cit.

call for: what was needed, apparently, was a universal nature capable of change, not a changeless one as the Platonic idea is by definition. This difficulty would not be removed, I think, by allowing that in Christian thought the paradigmatic entities are changeable due to their created status.[11] For as such also they would be ontologically prior to the individuals: so again who should change them?

Nor would this problem be remedied by the application of Stoic instead of Platonic theories as some have suggested.[12] For the Stoic universal nature, although immanent rather than transcendent, is no less prior to the particulars than the Platonic one; this principle was indeed applied by them with such rigidity that it caused in turn some Platonists to rethink the priority of the universal at least in the case of man in order to account for individual freedom and self-determination.[13]

The same overall difficulty can be seen in attempts to argue for a systematic interpretation without specific reference to a philosophical system. Thus P. Gregorios commenting on Gregory's use of the term πλήρωμα writes:

> The *pleroma*, the fullness of humanity is thus a limited entity with a beginning and an end, and when that limit is reached history itself as we know it must come to a close. (. . .) It is this whole *pleroma* which was created at first. It is this *pleroma* that Christ has leavened, like leaven hid in three measures of flour. It is this whole *pleroma* and not merely individual man that is in the image of God.[14]

This passage demonstrates, I think, quite clearly the logical problem. If God created a *pleroma* in the beginning,[15] this ought to be prior to its individuals. Yet as such it cannot be subject to history. One might, of course, argue that it has something like a meta-history which would in a sense prefigure and determine the history of its earthly participants. However, such a suggestion would apparently entail disastrous theological consequences: for responsibility for the course of this meta-history would no more be borne by the individuals, but—since this *pleroma* is not a subject—ultimately by God himself.

---

[11] For this view, cf. Gregory of Nyssa, *op hom* 16 (PG 44, 184C–D).

[12] Balthasar (1995), 53–4, n. 39; Hübner (1974), 146–59.

[13] Plotinus, *Enn* III 1, passim esp. III 1,8. Cf. Nyssen's *fat* (GNO III/2, 37,12–38,1) for a sketch of the Stoic view.

[14] Gregorios (1980), 187.

[15] But see p. 156 below on the meaning of πλήρωμα in Gregory's account of the creation of man.

Given this *status questionis* one might wonder whether there is any concept of universal human nature that would be able to function in a systematic way to expound the economy? Perhaps those difficulties indicate that any search for such a theory is void and should no longer be pursued. In this case the question with regard to Gregory would be reduced to asking for his *intent*: it could, after all, be that he wished to make systematic use of human nature, but that attempt would inevitably have been bound to fail.

It appears, however, that there is one theory which may be able to fulfil the requirements of a systematic interpretation of the economy in the above sense; and it seems furthermore that prior to Gregory this theory had indeed been used by Christian theologians to precisely that end. This is the interpretation of humankind as a derivative genus with Adam as both the first individual and the *ousia*, the very interpretation we found Apollinarius offer to Basil in the trinitarian context. This theory, it seems, is extremely useful far beyond its value as a trinitarian analogy. Applied to the exegesis of the early chapters of Genesis, for example, it could satisfy both a literal reading of those stories and the theological interest in their universal interpretation: by creating Adam God would have created the paradigmatic Man whose Fall, consequently, affected the entirety of humankind. Further, one might imagine that an interpretation of Christ as the second Adam would allow an understanding of him as the primogenitor of a new humankind begotten not by material, but spiritual procreation.

These speculations, as I said, existed prior to Gregory. As far as we are able to make out, they took their starting point not in the first place from the exegesis of Genesis, but from that of Ro 5,12–21 and 1 Cor 15,45–9. An author like Origen, who elsewhere could offer an allegorical exegesis of the creation story,[16] felt obliged to reach out for a different explanation while commenting on Ro 5,12:

> But in order that it may become clearer what we are saying, let us adduce also what the same Apostle wrote to the Hebrews (Heb 7,9): 'For even Levi, who received tithes, has himself been tithed. For he was still in his ancestors loins' (that is, Abraham's) 'when Melchizedek met him'. If then Levi, who was born four generations after Abraham, was allowed to be in Abraham's loins, how much more were all human

---

[16] *C Celsum* IV 40 (vol. I, 313,17–24 Koetschau). Cf. Bammel (1989), passim.

beings, who are, and have been born into this world, in Adam's loins when he was in paradise. And all human beings were expelled with him or in him from paradise when he was evicted from there.[17]

Origen, admittedly, does not here develop a full-scale theory of derivative genera as we have seen Apollinarius do in his epistle to Basil. It would not even be possible to state with certainty that such a philosophical theory was known to him or that it stands in some clarity behind the present passage.

It appears, however, that the unequivocal words of the apostle provided for a strong exegetical need to move towards such a theory. Doctrinally, on the other hand, it is apparently the assumption of universal sinfulness which for Origen necessitated the first theological steps into this direction: as has been observed long ago it was the practice of infant baptism which in his view called for a theological justification along these lines.[18]

3.2   The teaching of Apollinarius

There is some evidence that in the fourth century such a theory was developed into a much more elaborate form and applied to the economy by Apollinarius of Laodicea. This evidence, which is scattered and not wholly conclusive on some points, I shall now present as it seems of rather high relevance for the subject under inquiry here:

1. From his letter to Basil it appears that Apollinarius knows of derivative genera and finds it natural to interpret humanity that way.
2. A number of texts confirm that he understood the creation of man as the creation of Adam, the paradigmatic Man.
3. It seems that Apollinarius taught some kind of traducianism.
4. There also are indications that he could have held a theory of universal sin based on that conception although some considerations might seem to count against this assumption.
5. Apollinarius' christology, in particular his interpretation of the virgin birth, draws on the assumption that the human *ousia* is handed down as part of the procreative process.

---

[17] Origen, *in Rom* V 1 (PG 14, 1009C–1010A).
[18] Bigg (1913), 246–7; cf. Origen, *in Rom* V 9 (PG 14, 1017B); *in Lev hom* VIII 3 (396,7–399,8 Baehrens) and Williams (1929), 219–31. Bammel (1989, 83) rejects Biggs' developmental theory.

6. In his soteriology Apollinarius uses derivative humanity as an analogy for the derivative character of the Church as new humankind.

I am not going to dwell on (1), since I take this as established by
the above analysis of the relevant section from Apollinarius' letter.[19]

Ad (2): this seems perhaps most of all like an inevitable logical
conclusion from that view which needs not much further confirmation.
Moreover, it would appear that to a writer, who is committed to
the historicity of the Genesis account (and Apollinarius is counted by
Socrates as a critic of Origen!),[20] the idea of Adam as the paradigmatic
Man would have been very attractive as it can account alongside,
as it were, for the biblical idea that each of us is a creature of God.
I take it, therefore, as *prima facie* likely that this is what Apollinarius
thought.

Two texts can confirm the legitimacy of this assumption. Let us
begin with a fragment from Apollinarius' commentary on the Psalms
preserved in the catena. There the writer argues (commenting on Ps
144,1 LXX) that

> in the present life of man, who is one *qua* succession (διαδοχή), these
> things may be possible that, with the preceding generation departing,
> their successors take their place. Therefore also we are all called by
> the name of Adam, as indeed we are him, and God says 'I made the
> earth and man upon it' (Is 44,12), conceiving of them all as of one.[21]

First of all this passage strongly underscores the interpretation of
humankind as a derivative genus with Adam as its origin. However,
it also leads directly to theology of creation as an obvious application
of that theory. What is more, it here seems as if the author employed
the biblical evidence for God's universal creation to support his own
derivative interpretation of humankind. The former view would thus
appear to be a given which could be presupposed rather than being
itself in need of support.

A second passage is even more explicit in that regard. This text
is a further fragment from the catena, on Ps 118,73 LXX ('your
hands made and formed me').[22] There Apollinarius strives to account

---

[19] See pp. 35–40 above.
[20] Socrates, *hist eccl* VI 13,3 (334,13–6 Hansen). Cf. Apollinarius, *in Ps* 118,50
(*fr* 224, 88,12–4 Mühlenberg) and Cattaneo (1981), 168–9.
[21] Apollinarius, *in Ps* 144,1 (*fr* 301, 113,8–12 Mühlenberg).
[22] Apollinarius, *in Ps* 118,73 (*fr* 227, 89,1–6 Mühlenberg).

for the seemingly inappropriate word 'to form' (πλάττειν) with regard
to God's creative activity. He points out that, wherever God seems
to 'form', he does in fact complete his work at once; this is why, in
Apollinarius' view, human beings can say that they are individually
created by God (Jer 1,5; Job 10,9) thereby referring to the creation
of Adam. This is particularly striking in the case, adduced by
Apollinarius, of Job, who refers to his being formed from clay. The
point must be that Job is entitled to this claim because the creation
of Adam *is* the creation of Man.

I should thus take it as established that Apollinarius held this view
of the creation of humanity.

Ad (3): the evidence for Apollinarius' traducianism is provided
partly by a passage from Nemesius of Emesa's *De Natura Hominis*[23]
which states this expressly. A fragment from Apollinarius' *De Unione*
confirms this conclusion:

> The ordinary man is animated and lives by the will of the flesh and
> by the will of man (ἀνήρ) the spermatic matter, charged with vivify-
> ing power, being emitted into the receptive matrix.[24]

Again, general considerations about the requirements of a theory of
derivative generic identity would also seem to support it.

The crucial problem, for a number of reasons, is the origin of
mind, the intelligible part of man. It seems now clear that Apollinarius
held a trichotomy of body, soul and mind throughout his career.[25]
As for the last of these, some have argued that it could not possibly
have been thought to be handed down *ex traduce*.[26] However, it
appears that the latter is precisely Apollinarius' view. To be sure,
he asserts that the 'intelligible' is 'from above', not 'from the world',
yet he maintains in the same context that as such the highest principle in man enters the individual as part of the procreative process.[27]

Ad (4): from what has been found so far it would appear rather
likely the notion of universal sin as a direct result of Adam's Fall
played some part that in the overall framework of this theory.
However, there is surprisingly little evidence pointing to this partic-

---

[23] Nemesius, *nat hom* (32,3–6 Morani) = Apollinarius, *fr* 170 (269,23–7 Lietzmann).
[24] *De unione* 13 (191,4–7 Lietzmann).
[25] De Riedmatten (1957), 222–34; accepted by Norris (1963, 87–8) and Mühlenberg
(1968, 109–10). *Pace* Lietzmann (1904), 5–6.
[26] Raven (1923), 171.
[27] Cf. for the whole problem: Apollinarius, *in Ez* 37,9 (90 Mai).

ular doctrine, and such evidence as exists is, in my view, not entirely conclusive.

The most clear-cut statement, as far as I have found, positing a connection of universal sin and Christ's incomplete humanity is to be found in the ps.-Athanasian *Contra Apollinarium*:

> For he became not, as it were, a complete human being. For where there is a complete human being, there also is sin.[28]

A similar argument is apparently implied in Nyssen's account of the controversies in which he became involved during his stay in Jerusalem.[29]

This argument has been thought to imply that Christ could not assume a human mind since the latter, responsible for sinning as the centre of decision making, was necessarily sinful; thus Christ assuming it would himself have sinned.[30]

In this interpretation the argument would be in stark contrast to Apollinarius' strong emphasis on human free will as the token of godlikeness which he appears determined not to undermine. In this attempt he can go as far as to state that Christ did not assume a human mind because in the resulting mixture of human and divine the human would have been effectively deprived of its capacity to decide freely: and this, he writes, is a humiliation God would not inflict on his image.[31]

Elsewhere[32] Apollinarius writes of universal sinfulness in definite terms, but strikingly avoids any mention of Adam's Fall in that connection.

Should one thus conclude that the aforesaid argument from the sinfulness of human nature is not genuinely Apollinarian? This might be tempting as an Apollinarian origin of the argument in both texts seems far from certain.[33] However, I do not think that this consequence is necessary, for the above interpretation of the doctrine envisaged in the ps.-Athanasian writing is by no means cogent. From

---

[28] (Ps.)-Athanasius, *c Apoll* I 1 (PG 26, 1096B).

[29] Gregory of Nyssa, *ep* 3,17 (GNO VIII/2, 24,19–24).

[30] Gwatkin (1900, 252–3) and Raven (1923, 231) accept this assumption as genuinely Apollinarian. Cf. also Bethune-Baker (1929), 250–2.

[31] Apollinarius, *in Rom* 7,7 (64,22–3 Staab); cf. de Riedmatten (1957), 210–2.

[32] Apollinarius, *KMP*, long recension (178,10–179,4 Lietzmann).

[33] For the opponents of *ep* 3, see pp. 218–20 below. The ps.-Athanasian treatise mentions Apollinarius only in the title which, if Athanasian origin is rejected, may well be secondary.

the argument preserved by ps.-Athanasius[34] it would rather appear that his opponents held a view according to which sinfulness was due to a lower, 'carnal soul'. This latter was said to have been passed down from Adam and to be responsible for sinning. The ps.-Athanasian author does, of course, insinuate that this is tantamount to making the intelligible *phusis* of man prone to sinning (1144C), but it seems clear that he there is misrepresenting his opponents' case.

Now, a theory explaining human sinfulness by reference to a lower soul is known from elsewhere, and Origen in his *De Principiis*[35] finds something to be said in its favour. What is more, if we allow a basic identity of the view related by Origen with the one presupposed in *Contra Apollinarium* II 5, as has been suggested by Raven,[36] it would appear that the latter is both consonant with a doctrine of free will and in agreement with Apollinarius' traducianist teaching.

A further doctrine that appears to be relevant in this connection is Apollinarius' exegesis of Gen 2,7: he identifies the *pneuma* breathed into Adam with the Holy Ghost which would explain, in his view, Adam's prophetic gift immediately after his creation.[37] This Spirit, it appears, was lost with the Fall.

However, judging from a further fragment, Apollinarius does not consider human participation in the Holy Spirit to be the possession of another, as it were, hypostatic reality. Rather, receiving the Holy Spirit means to have mind in a different disposition (ἐνέργεια):

> Thus the apostles having the life-giving Spirit from the insufflation of the Lord, acquire the principal Spirit, who is sent from heaven, not Spirit upon spirit, one upon the other, but another disposition of the same spirit as the apostle says (1 Cor 12,4–14).[38]

So human beings would have lost this disposition of their mind with the Fall, and were consequently no longer able to resist the evil impulse of their lower souls:

> Evil then extends until it embraces the intellect (λογισμός) subjecting it to serve the passions, which is what Paul calls 'doing the will <of the flesh>' (Eph 2,3).[39]

---

[34] *C Apoll* II 5 (PG 26, 1144B–1145B).

[35] *Princ* III 4,2 (264,17–267,22) cf. Raven (1923), 196–8.

[36] Raven (1923), 198.

[37] *In Ioh* 20,22 (*fr* 153, 62,1–7 Reuss). Nyssen apparently rejects this view; with him the passage refers to the human mind: *antirrh* (GNO III/1, 146,23–7). Cf. Cattaneo (1981, 169–75).

[38] *In Num* 27,18 (147 Devreesse); cf.: de Riedmatten (1957), 209.

[39] *In Lev* 13,4–6 (134 Devreesse); cf. Cattaneo (1981), 178; <> add. Cattaneo, ibid.

If a conclusion, which I should wish to be regarded as tentative and provisional, rather than ultimate, may be drawn from all those separate strands it might perhaps be as this: within the human constitution the soul as the principle between mind and body is the origin of evil. Human spirit, on the other hand, is in itself not strong enough to suppress the evil instincts that arise from that soul and to govern the flesh according to its insight. In order to achieve the latter, human mind is therefore always in need of assistance from God, which was given to Adam in the form of an insufflation of the Holy Spirit which he received at the moment of his creation.

This gift being lost after the Fall, there is thus, in spite of the mind's retained freedom of choice, nothing preventing it from coming ever more under the influence of man's lower instincts except for a renewed interference on the part of the Godhead in order to let human beings again participate in the Holy Spirit as a supporter of their own, weak, human spirit.

This exposition, to be sure, does not answer all questions relevant for Apollinarius' understanding of the Fall, but nor is this the purpose of the present study.[40] It does, however, allow us a glimpse of the relevance of his concept of a derivative human nature for the universality of the fallen state. This would appear to consist in the fact that both the 'weakened' spirit and the sinful soul are passed down from Adam and thus inherited by each individual human being.[41]

Ad (5): Apollinarius' christology has always been seen as the most conspicuous feature of his theology. After all, his doctrine of an 'incomplete' humanity in Christ accounted for his repeated condemnation, and the bulk of his literary remains are dedicated to an elucidation of his position on this subject. Thus it is not surprising that various and different hypotheses have been ventured upon to explain this feature: while some[42] cited Arian christology as the ultimate background of Apollinarius' thinking, others opted for the developing Antiochene two-nature christology which would have prompted the Apollinarian response.[43] Others again wanted to see particular philosophical, notably anthropological, theories behind his christological views.[44]

---

[40] Cf. in general: Cattaneo (1981), 168–86; Hauke (1993), 478–80.
[41] Cf. further: Apollinarius, *in Ps* 50,7 (*fr* 90, 34,14–35,6 Mühlenberg).
[42] Dorner (1862), 359–60; Grillmeier (1975), 341–2.
[43] Raven (1923), 177.
[44] Norris (1963), 81–122.

For the present purpose de Riedmatten's interpretation is of particular interest. This interpretation, contained in two articles,[45] stresses the relevance of Apollinarius' understanding of a derivative human *ousia* for his christology.

De Riedmatten starts from observations concerning the virgin birth in Apollinarius' thought. That Christ had been born to a virgin was, of course, accepted by the entire church. It appears, however, that the Laodicene had a special theological interest in this fact. In one of his writings against Diodore of Tarsus he effectively charges the latter with making the virgin birth void:

> And he is not ashamed to say that there is the same *phusis*, but a different (mode of) generation: but the birth from the virgin is rendered void and superfluous if that which is begotten does not conform to the (mode of) generation, but is (regarded as) identical with that which is begotten of man and woman.[46]

In the light of the aforesaid theory the point can only be that the supernatural generation of Christ marks his decisive difference from man and that is, from human *nature*: not being a descendant of Adam, Christ does not partake of the human *ousia* in the strictest sense. The same point is made in a similar way elsewhere;[47] particularly interesting in the present context is a passage in the ps.-Athanasian *Quod unus sit Christus* which, although perhaps not Apollinarian, is certainly early-Apollinarist:[48]

> For it is impossible for a woman to become pregnant without a man since God deposited the *ousia* of those to be begotten in the fathers. So also Scripture says that Levi was in the loins of his father Abraham (Hebr 7,9).[49]

The parallel in the use of Scripture to Origen (cf. pp. 129–30 above) is remarkable. The present text apparently identifies the 'spermatic matter charged with vivifying power' of the above passage from *De Unione* (p. 132) with *ousia*. The latter is handed down through the generations by means of the procreative process.

In the text following this quotation the author asserts that in the case of Christ the virgin conceived from the divine *ousia*. Therefore,

---

[45] De Riedmatten (1948, 1957).
[46] *Fr* 142 (241,19–26 Lietzmann).
[47] Cf. De Riedmatten (1948), 240–5.
[48] Cf. Richard (1945), 10; 15–6.
[49] *Quod unus sit Christus* 11 (301,13–6 Lietzmann).

he did not receive the human *ousia*, but only the σχῆμα, which is the flesh.[50]

With regard to Apollinarius' christology the consequences seem to be obvious: the fact that Christ was not a descendant of Adam but born from a virgin is vital both for the negative point about his 'incomplete' humanity and for the positive point of his being the one *phusis* incarnate.

This is not to say, of course, that there are no problems connected to this theory. These become apparent as soon as one enquires somewhat more closely into the relevance of the contribution made by father and mother respectively to generation: if it is accepted that the *ousia* comes from the father and is supposed to be universal with all human beings, one might expect that the female ingredient is somehow responsible for individuality. Such an approach might perhaps be combined with some kind of form—matter dualism as has been discussed above (pp. 90–2); it would, however, be very difficult to combine it with the soul—body dualism as that would entail a view of the human individual as a compound of universal soul and individualising body.

It appears, however, that precisely the latter would be required by Apollinarius' christological application of the derivative *ousia*. Moreover, Christ as born from a virgin would really lack the human *ousia* entirely as the overall theory does not seem to opt for a joint contribution of father and mother towards the human nature of the child.

Ad (6): looking, then, finally at Apollinarius' soteriology, it is first of all his sacramental theology, his interpretation of the Eucharist, that is of relevance for the present enquiry. For the elucidation of this point I am again drawing on de Riedmatten and Cattaneo.[51]

From what has been shown so far it seems clear that in Apollinarius' view the restitution of men's original participation in the Holy Spirit must form a central part of their salvation, and that, furthermore, the gift of the Spirit is a fundamental datum in the history of Christianity. It is now interesting to see that, in his exegesis of the Lord's Prayer, Apollinarius explains the notoriously difficult ἐπιούσιος ἄρτος (Mt 6,11) to be the Spirit,

---

[50] Ibid. (301,16–8 Lietzmann).
[51] De Riedmatten (1948), 248–50; id. (1957), 220–1; Cattaneo (1981), 141–65; cf. also Bates (1961).

that is, life-giving food in the world to come, and 'the bread which I will give' to you 'is my flesh for the life of the world' (John 6,21).[52]

Apollinarius thus equates the gift of the Holy Spirit, for which Christians are to pray daily, with the reception of sacred bread at the Eucharist. The logic of the argument is, of course, partly drawn from John 6, but the spiritual interpretation of the Lord's Supper as based on the combination of Mt 6,11 and John 6,51 is, it appears, Apollinarius' own. It would thus appear that for him the Christian participation in the Holy Spirit is closely connected with their participation in the 'flesh of Christ' at the Eucharist.

What brings us back to the issue of derivative humanity is the specific notion of Christ's flesh which is apparently implied in Apollinarius' theory: this, it seems, is understood to be the 'divinised' flesh of the resurrected Christ, the notorious 'heavenly flesh'. As de Riedmatten has convincingly argued, Apollinarius' sacramentalism is consistently bound up with his christology.[53] Note how the above fragment continues:

> the food, then, and the drink have revealed a participation which would not exist without the body: for, if the divine power had not been linked to a body and united with blood, we would not have participation, through it, with God.[54]

Without the Incarnation, that is, in the precise interpretation Apollinarius gives to it, salvation would not be possible. Participation in the Spirit, which is the ultimate purpose of the Eucharist, would be impossible were it not for the deification of Christ's own flesh in the Incarnation. For it seems clear that, if one does not wish to let Apollinarius contradict himself in one and the same passage, the 'spiritual' interpretation of the Eucharist must underlie the present assertion as well: the bread is both, flesh of Christ and Holy Spirit.[55]

It would thus appear at least possible that the heavenly Adam, Christ, is the originating principle of new humankind in much the same way that the first Adam was the *arche* of old humankind, his spiritual *ousia* being passed on to his 'descendants' by means of their birth from spirit (cf. John 3,8). Thus, Apollinarius could, as in the

---

[52] Apollinarius, *in Mat* 26,26–8 (*fr* 134, 47 Reuss).
[53] De Riedmatten (1948), 248–50.
[54] Apollinarius, *in Mat* 26,26–8 (*fr* 134, 47 Reuss).
[55] Cattaneo (1981), 146.

case of Adam and humanity so also in the case of Christ and his Church, argue for the comprehension of the descendants in the originating principle:

> we are contained (περιέχειν) in the body of Christ as in the tabernacle (. . .).[56]

The latter notion would, of course, be suggested to any Christian author by the Pauline description of the Church as the 'body of Christ' (Col 1,24; 1 Cor 12,27; Eph 4,15–6).

This understanding of Christianity as a new, spiritual humankind with Christ's humanity as its originating principle, which has been supposed to stand behind certain Apollinarian texts, is to be found in a much more explicit form in a writing whose authorship is uncertain, the ps.-Athanasian *De incarnatione et contra Arianos*, which Tetz has attributed, rashly, to Marcellus of Ancyra.[57] Cattaneo has pointed out that its treatment of the Eucharist is practically identical to that of Apollinarius,[58] and I think that the soteriological and ecclesiological consequences it draws are very likely to correspond to those of Apollinarius also.

I shall treat it as anonymous here; I am sure that it is not Apollinarius', and to investigate its precise relationship to his theology would require an independent investigation. After all, it is not the present task to elucidate the details of Apollinarius' theology, but to trace a particular interpretation of derivative nature which he appears to have substantially furthered. At the same time, *De incarnatione et contra Arianos* is of special interest here since Gregory has been said to depend on it in his exegesis of 1 Cor 15,28.[59]

It may provide for an interesting starting point to note that the ps-Athanasian author apparently understands humankind as a derivative genus along Apollinarius' lines as he expressly equates 'from the *ousia* of men' with 'from the seed of Adam'.[60] Furthermore, it has already been mentioned that his interpretation of the Eucharist agrees with Apollinarius':

---

[56] Apollinarius, *in Num* 7,1 (138 Devreesse).
[57] Tetz (1964), but cf. Simonetti (1973), 324.
[58] Cattaneo (1981), 156–8.
[59] Hübner (1974), 53; 288; cf. pp. 207–12 below.
[60] *D inc et c Ar* 8 (PG 26, 996C). Cf. also ibid. (996A): 'οἱ υἱοὶ τοῦ ἀνθρώπου, τουτέστι τοῦ Ἀδὰμ . . .'

And again, while the Lord says about himself, 'I am the living bread which has come down from heaven,' (John 6,51a) he elsewhere calls the Holy Spirit the heavenly bread saying, 'give us this day our *epiousion* bread'. For he taught us in that prayer to pray in the present world for the *epiousion*, that is, for the future bread, whose first fruits we have in the present life having received the flesh of the Lord as he himself says: 'the bread which I will give is my flesh for the life of the world' (John 6,51). For the flesh of the Lord is life-giving Spirit as it has been conceived from life-giving Spirit: 'for that which is born from Spirit, is Spirit'.[61]

Beyond this the author makes clear that for him *pneuma* is more than a divine gift for each individual Christian. He asserts that the spirit mentioned in Lk 23,46 ('Father, into thy hands I commit my spirit') refers to all human beings who have been made alive in Christ; they are handed over to the Father:

> for they are his (sc. Christ's) members, and the many members are one body, which is the Church.[62]

Here the spirit is identified with the entirety of Christians and they in turn, as the Church, with the body of Christ. The identification of the body of Christ with the spirit is thus recurrent, but the Church is added as a further element in that equation. This latter identification, the biblical notion of the Church as the body of Christ, seems indeed to be axiomatic for the author of the treatise. Thus he can explain Acts 22,36 as said of Christ's humanity, 'which is the whole Church'.[63] The repeated reference to Gal 3,28 ('You are all one in Jesus Christ') in that connection further underlines that he thinks of a unified entity: they are all one.

The originating principle of this entity, however, is Christ's humanity. Not only does the author use the Pauline notion (1 Cor 15,23) of Christ as the first fruits (ἀπαρχή), he also explains Prov 8,22 ('The Lord created me the beginning of his ways') as said of the Church which was created in Christ.[64] What is more, he combines v. 22 with v. 25 ('Before all the hills he begat me') to argue that the Church is first created, then begotten by God.[65] And in the same context he expounds John 1,12–3 by asserting that 'all those who

---

[61] *D inc et c Ar* 16 (PG 26, 1012B).
[62] *D inc et c Ar* 5 (PG 26, 992B–C).
[63] *D inc et c Ar* 21 (PG 26, 1005C). That Hübner (1974, 53) finds here an equation of the body of Christ with the whole of humankind is beyond my comprehension.
[64] *D inc et c Ar* 6 (PG 26, 992C–993A).
[65] *D inc et c Ar* 12 (PG 26, 1004C–1005A).

are born from the Holy Spirit are begotten from God'.[66] Finally, in this connection, attention has to be drawn to a passage linking Incarnation and salvation as follows:

> And therefore the Logos and Son of the Father was united to flesh and became flesh (cf. John 1,14), [a perfect man][67] in order that human beings, having been united with the Spirit, are begotten in the Spirit.[68]

From all this it would appear legitimate to draw the following conclusions: in Christ a new, pneumatic humanity was created (Prov 8,22); this humanity is related to Christ as to its (ἀπ)αρχή, that is, as humankind is to Adam; the propagation of the seeds is described, in analogous (but biblical: John 3,3–8) terminology, as spiritual begetting; as humankind can be called 'Adam', in Apollinarius' view, so the new humankind can be called 'the body of Christ' and 'one Spirit'.

There thus emerges a practically perfect analogy between the derivative understanding of humanity, as it was encountered in Apollinarius, and the present ecclesiology of the one body of Christ, which is to illustrate the transmission of salvation from Christ to the Christians. Given this concurrence both with the elements of Apollinarius' own soteriology that can be extracted from his extant writings, and with his use of derivative genera which has been found to underlie practically the entirety of his theology, there can, in my view, be but little doubt that the details of ps.-Athanasius' theory go, in one way or another, back to Apollinarius as well, although at present any more far-reaching statement would belong to the realm of speculation.

Be this as it may, with regard to the theological use of universal human nature one crucial observation seems to be that its present soteriological application is an analogous one: the relationship between Christ and the Church is seen *in analogy to* the relationship between Adam and human beings. The universality of humanity is not as such used to prove the reality, let alone the universality, of salvation: indeed, there is no salvation of universal human nature in this soteriological concept. Both Apollinarius and ps.-Athanasius employ the traditional 'physical' deification terminology;[69] yet this is, as far as I see, never used to a universalist end, but to press home the need

---

[66] *D inc et c Ar* 13 (PG 1005C).
[67] [ἄνθρωπος τέλειος] om. Tetz (1964), 244.
[68] *D inc et c Ar* 8 (PG 26, 996C–997A).
[69] For Apollinarius cf. *KMP* 31 (179,6–9 Lietzmann), for ps.-Athanasius, *d inc et c Ar* 8 (PG 26, 996A).

for a 'real' Incarnation: God had to become *flesh* in order that our carnal nature could be saved from corruption (see pp. 188–9 below). It would not therefore, I think, be accurate to ascribe to Apollinarius the view that universal nature first fell and then, as such, was saved: salvation as the renewal of humankind takes place only within the Church; only those who are begotten in the Spirit are members of new humankind.

In summary, then, it appears that Apollinarius, probably drawing on Origen, developed the theory of humankind's seminal inclusion in Adam, and of its unity as a derivative genus, into its most elaborate form. Although there is no evidence that, like Origen, he took Ro 5,12–21 as his starting point, it seems most likely that he did.

At the same time, he seems to have realised the considerable systematic potential for an application to the economy inherent in this theory. There are grounds for believing that he employed it for a variety of theological topics.

What are the consequences of these results for the elucidation of Gregory's thought? From the preceding analysis of his trinitarian theology it emerged that, while the Apollinarian interpretation of humanity as a derivative *ousia* would have been known to him, it was admitted not as such, but, in the interest of avoiding subordination within the Trinity, in an 'Aristotelian' reinterpretation.

As regards its application to *economic* topics, then, three main possible explanations seem to offer themselves: Gregory could have employed humanity as a derivative genus there, thus drawing on Apollinarius while not being perfectly consistent with himself; or, secondly, he could not have employed human nature systematically at all. A third possibility might have been an attempted reconstruction of Apollinarius' systematic use of human nature based on his tenet of co-ordination.

We should not expect the result to be unequivocal; Gregory was not systematic in the way a scholastic would be. Nevertheless, I think that an interesting pattern can be discerned in his treatment of the subject, for, while there are passages that seem to point towards a derivative interpretation and others in which no clear indication of whatever precise understanding of universal nature is given, texts dealing with creation and restoration reveal, in my reading, that Gregory does indeed envisage a systematic application of human nature to the economy which is in broad agreement with the 'Aristotelian' model that has been found to underlie his trinitarian theology. It will therefore be the hypothesis to be proved by the remainder of this study that Gregory's application of human nature to the economy points towards an attempt, in the interest, as will be seen, of a very specific theology, to achieve on the basis of the co-ordinate interpretation developed in the context of trinitarian theology what Apollinarius had done before based on the derivative model.

To this end I shall discuss the conceptual relevance of universal human nature in each of the subjects listed initially. That this cannot be done without any overlap needs perhaps not much explanation. At the same time I think that each of them poses a number of distinct and special questions justifying their separate treatment.

The three main questions to be answered in any of the following sections are: first, is there evidence that Gregory used human nature in a universal sense for his theological argument? Secondly, how precisely is human nature understood? In case the first question has been answered in the affirmative this question obviously amounts to asking what kind of universal it is.

This second question has, apparently, to do with Gregory's philosophical consistency: does he adhere to one particular model of universal nature or is he content to use philosophical concepts in a rather eclectic way? This will be decided in the first place by comparison with his established use of human nature in trinitarian theology.

In this, however, one should not be too rigid, I think: what appear to be conceptual differences can at times be merely the consequences of different requirements or interests regarding various topics. In trinitarian theology, the main emphasis had been on those aspects of universal nature that were relevant for the analogy drawn in that context. Other issues, in particular questions raised by the peculiar character of man as a mixture of sensible and intelligible were disregarded. Such questions are, on the other hand, likely to play a part in endeavours to come to terms with those theological subjects to which we are now turning. We may expect, therefore, to find, in any event, much more than a simple confirmation of those features of human nature that have so far been established.

In case the answer to the first question has been given in the negative, this second one will apply respectively.

The third question to be asked is how far the application of human nature actually supports, and is relevant for, the theological point

Gregory wishes to make. If the second question in a way asks for Gregory's *philosophical* consistency, the present one will rather enquire into the *theological* significance of his writings and, in particular, of the concept of human nature in them.

It goes without saying that these three questions do not correspond to any actual headings or subheadings of the relevant sections; they will be addressed in the course of each chapter according to the requirements of the argument.

While conducting my research, I found that most of the relevant material was centred around the first and the third of the above categories, i.e. the theologies of creation and salvation. As, on the other hand, the second and fourth seemed to be not only of rather subordinate importance in Gregory's thinking, but also somehow related to the other two, I decided to present the material in two main sections, of which the first will be dealing with creation, Fall and the universality of sin in Gregory's thought, the second with his understanding of salvation, eschatology and the person of Jesus Christ.

CHAPTER FOUR

GREGORY'S TEACHING ON CREATION
AND FALL OF HUMANITY

4.1 *The creation of human nature*

There is a single uncreate eternal *phusis*, the same for ever, which tran-
scends all our ideas of distance, conceived of as without increase or
decrease, and beyond the scope of any definition; (. . .) time and space
with all their consequences, and anything previous to these that thought
can grasp in the intelligible supramundane world, are all productions
of this substance.

  Well, then, we affirm that human nature is one of these productions; and a word of the inspired teachings helps us in this, which
declares that when God had brought all things else upon the scene of
life, man was exhibited upon the earth, a mixture from divine sources,
the godlike intellectual substance being in him united with the several
portions of earthly elements towards his formation, and that he was
fashioned by his maker to be the incarnate likeness of the divine transcendent power (reference follows to Gen 1,27).[1]

In the first part of his writing *On Infants' Early Deaths* Gregory gives
this as an account of what he thinks would be a common starting
point to all, who will discuss the problem under review there.

  A few points giving rise to further questions should capture our
attention right from the beginning: first, Gregory apparently takes it
for granted that 'human nature' is the object of God's creation in
the first place and not, for example, Adam. Why and in what sense
is it that Gregory here and elsewhere refers to the creation of human
nature? Incidentally, the passage tacitly presupposes that 'man' and
'human nature' are equivalent expressions.

  Secondly, there is no indication here that the creation of human
nature differs, in principle, from that of the world in general. Man
is simply one of God's creatures. Consequently, one will have to ask
how Gregory's understanding of the creation of man is imbedded
into his overall concept of creation.

  Thirdly, human nature's special property is that it is a mixture of

---

[1] *Infant* (GNO III/2, 77,4–20), ET: Moore/Wilson (1893), 375 with amendments.

two kinds of being, that is, sensible and intelligible substance. This, then, raises questions about possible peculiarities related to this particular feature of human nature.

While we thus learn from these lines that human nature is one of God's creatures and that it is a combination of sensible and intelligible being, the text does not expressly tell us whether or in what sense it is a universal item. Elsewhere Gregory seems to be more explicit in that regard. In a celebrated passage from his writing *On the Creation of Man* Gregory cites Gen 1,27a to the effect that 'man' (ἄνθρωπος) there does not refer to an individual, but indicates the entire human nature which would thus be the object of God's creation as reported by that verse.[2]

Admittedly, the precise meaning of those lines is a matter of substantial disagreement among scholars. Leaving aside for the moment all the particular ramifications caused by this text (for these see pp. 163–74 below), it seems *prima facie* difficult to deny that Gregory understands the biblical statement as saying that God created human nature in a universal sense.

Two further considerations serve to support this conclusion. To begin with, the assumption that 'man' indicates human nature agrees not only with the above statement from *De Infantibus*, but indeed with one important result reached in the first part of the present study. In the context of trinitarian theology, however, it was found that human nature as indicated by the universal term was conceived of as universal. Assuming some degree of consistency in Gregory's thinking, it is at least likely that he would have read Gen 1,27 in such a way.

This reasoning is supported by a more general theological consideration. It appears that Gregory would have had good theological reasons to interpret Gen 1,27 as dealing with universal human nature; whatever interpretation one gives to the creation story, this must be able to account for the theological presumption that all mankind is in the same way the object of God's creation.

I should therefore adopt as a working hypothesis that Gregory in his theological interpretation of the creation of man employed the concept of a universal human nature to precisely that end. To prove this hypothesis and to ascertain the exact nature of this concept will be the main task of this chapter.[3]

---

[2] *Op hom* 16 (PG 44, 185B).

[3] There have in recent decades been a large number of studies relevant for the

It appears that Gregory read Genesis primarily as a philosophical treatise on cosmogony.[4] This approach was not peculiar to him; many of the Fathers took it for granted following the example set by Philo, the great Alexandrine Jewish philosopher of the first century. Consequently, Genesis was thought to provide the ultimate answers to the main cosmological problem of the time, that is, how God, being single, simple, uniform, homogeneous, and unchanging, could have brought forth a world which, in its very essence, appears to be the exact opposite of him: multiple, multiform, heterogeneous, and changeable. This difficulty may be put into the proposition that the world ought to be conceived of as radically different from God, yet created by and dependent on him.[5]

For certain reasons this problem was substantially common to both Christians and Platonists in late antiquity.[6] It is therefore perhaps not surprising that philosophical influence is often found to be quite strong where the topic of creation was touched upon in Christian literature, although theologians would regularly claim that the biblical text testifies to the superiority of Moses over the Greek philosophers.

Gregory's attempt to untie this knot is to be found primarily in his *Apology on the Hexaëmeron*. There is every reason to believe that the solution developed in that writing holds good in principle for the creation of man as well, although the latter is not dealt with there. Thus I should start from an elucidation of the overall principles governing Gregory's approach to cosmology as they are set forth in that treatise.[7] The subsequent analysis of the creation of man will, I hope, justify that procedure.

---

present inquiry. I found especially useful: Balthasar (1995); Schoemann (1943); Armstrong (1948), (1954); Otis (1958); Ladner (1958); Hübner (1974); Balás (1979); Oesterle (1985).

[4] References to κοσμογένεια e.g. at *virg* 12,1 (GNO VII/1, 298,2), *hex* (PG 44, 61A), *cant* VIII (GNO VI, 245,18).

[5] For Gregory cf. his statement of the problem in *an et res* (PG 46, 121B–124A), esp. 121C–D: Ἐπεὶ οὖν ἡ μὲν τῶν ὄντων τὸ αἴτιον, οὐχ ὁμογενῆ δὲ τῇ ὑπερκειμένῃ φύσει τὰ δι᾽ ἐκείνης παραχθέντα εἰς γένεσιν· ἴση δὲ καθ᾽ ἑκάτερον ἐν τοῖς ὑπονοουμένοις ἡ ἀτοπία, τό τε ἐκ τῆς φύσεως τοῦ Θεοῦ τὴν κτίσιν οἴεσθαι, καὶ τό ἐξ ἑτέρας τινὸς οὐσίας ὑποστῆναι τὰ πάντα.

[6] Cf.: Alt (1993), 10–81.

[7] Gregory's cosmology has not, I think, received sufficient attention so far. Among the studies dedicated to this subject I should point out Corsini (1957), Wolfson (1970), Sorabji (1983, 290–4) and van Winden (1988), (1991).

4.1.1 *The creation of the world*

In order to appreciate Gregory's approach to creation in the *Apology on the Hexaëmeron* it is perhaps worthwhile to compare it to that put forth by Philo. That Gregory knew him is, I think, quite likely.[8] Philo's basic assumption, with which Gregory agrees, is that in his account of creation Moses reveals himself as the greatest philosopher, whose cosmogony is by far superior to that of Greek philosophers.[9]

Nevertheless, Philo's reading of the Genesis account is closely related to the way Plato's *Timaeus* was being understood at that time:[10] Philo is content to find in Genesis the typical triad of Demiurge, forms and matter, albeit monistically modified so that God, the Demiurge, is in fact the originator of the two other principles. According to Philo, forms are thoughts of God, which he compares to the plan in the mind of an architect;[11] the creation in six days would refer to this ideal creation which, however, took place instantaneously, outside time and space, the six days being only a symbol for the perfect order of this intelligible system.[12] The origin of matter is handled with some fickleness by Philo, and scholars disagree about whether or not he should be considered an advocate of the later Christian doctrine of *creatio ex nihilo*.[13] Leaving aside this particular point, however, it is quite obvious that Philo was willing to concede alongside other Platonists the principal function of matter in the process of creation.[14]

In comparison to this sketch the peculiarities of Gregory's approach become strikingly obvious, for with him there is, at first sight, no resemblance at all to the Timaean paradigm of creation.[15] There are

---

[8] Cf. Daniélou (1967), passim; for *op hom* esp. 335–43.

[9] For Philo: *op mun* 1–2; for Gregory: *hex* (PG 44, 61A) where Moses is referred to as an inspired philosopher (who, however, is matched by Basil according to Gregory: ibid.); *op hom* 16, 177D–180A (superiority of the biblical account over against philosophy).

[10] Cf. Runia (1986), 412: 'We can say (...) that Philo reads the account of creation and many other parts of the Pentateuch through Platonically tinted spectacles'. Cf. the same work, 476–519, for Philo's relation to the interpretative tradition.

[11] *Op mun* 20.

[12] *Op mun* 13–5.

[13] Cf. the contrasting conclusions by Wolfson (1947), vol. I, 300–9 (pro) and May (1978), 9–18, esp. 9, n. 32 followed by Runia (1986), 287–91, 453–5 (contra).

[14] *Op mun* 21–2; cf. for second century Platonism: Atticus (*fr* 26 des Places) and Alcinous (*didasc* 8 [162,29–163,10 Herrmann]). Cf. also Runia (1986), 452: '... in his (sc. Philo's) (Platonically influenced) interpretation of the cosmogony its presence is indispensable.

[15] *Pace* Cherniss (1930), 1–92, here: 25–8 esp. 26, n. 5.

no everlasting paradigms serving as models for the creation of the sensible world,[16] nor is there matter. Gregory must have felt the existence of the latter to be a heavy liability for a monistic theory of creation, for he devotes more than one section to the proof that matter as such is non-existent. According to him, 'matter' is but a name given to the total of qualities which, however, as they are in themselves purely intelligible, need not presuppose an origin other than the intelligible God.[17] Without entering into an exhaustive discussion of this rather complicated issue it should, however, be pointed out that what Gregory terms 'matter' in those passages is not what most philosophers used to call ὕλη, but simply a different word for 'bodies'.[18] If Gregory did indeed reject the existence of matter in that philosophical sense, he did so implicitly. He certainly eliminated matter as an independent principle of creation, following in this decision Neoplatonists like Porphyry.[19]

In Gregory's view there are two aspects which, taken together, explain how the present (and future) world can be thought to be God's work. On the one hand, he writes, everything has been created in the very first moment of the world's existence. This is how Gregory understands the statement in Gen 1,1 that 'in the beginning God created heaven and earth'. According to him this means that

> the *arche* of the world's condition is thus mentioned in order to indicate that God brought forth at once, in an instant (ἐν ἀκαρεῖ), the principles, the causes, and the powers of being, and that the substance (οὐσία) of every being concurred in the first act of his will.[20]

What are these elements that are said to be brought into existence in the first moment of creation? It might appear that they are to be

---

[16] At least not at first sight. Later (p. 153 below) it will become clear that the world of ideas has not simply vanished; yet its connection with creation has become more subtle. The place of ideas with Gregory is, I take it, the λόγος of God as it was with Philo and Origen before. Yet due to the further development of trinitarian theology this could not be thought to be the first creation in whatever sense any more, but was consubstantial and in all respects like God (cf. *Eun* III/7 8–9 [GNO II, 217,17–218,5] where Gregory accuses Eunomius of depending theologically on Philo). Its paradigmatic function for created being therefore had to be once again mediated.

[17] *An et res* (PG 46, 124C–D); *hex* (PG 44, 69B–C); *op hom* 24 (PG 44, 212D–213C); cf. Basil, *hom in hex* (PG 29, 21A–D); Plotinus, *Enn* II 4,11,1–13; Origen, *princ* IV 4,7 (357,29ff. Koetschau); see also Armstrong (1962); Sorabji (1983, loc. cit.).

[18] Cf. Sorabji (1983), 293 n. 23.

[19] For Porphyry see: *in Tim fr* 51 Sodano; *fr* 236F Smith.

[20] *Hex* (PG 44, 72B).

equated with 'matter' in the above sense, i.e. as the total of elements which are to make up the constitution of the world.[21] However, this interpretation should, I think, be discarded. What Gregory means by his statement that only the combination of accidents constitutes matter, must be that matter is not part of the first creation, but only a result of its further development. Elsewhere Gregory explains the description of the earth as 'empty and void' in Gen 1,2 ('invisible and without form' according to LXX) with the lack of any corporeal property at this stage of creation[22] (80A). I think this should not be understood as saying that the first creation is that of paradigmatic intelligible being, as it had been with Philo, but of a kind of intelligible being which is tied to the corporeal world. This is further supported by the fact that Gregory sees the creation 'in the beginning' as essentially an event outside time and space.[23] Given that the latter were thought to be basic constituents of sensible being, this suggests that things which have completely existed in this *arche* would have to be regarded as incorporeal beings, albeit of a particular kind.

So, since it must first be in their nature to develop into corporeal being, and, secondly, their initial perfection is only a 'potential'[24] one as that of a germ, an imagery popular with many philosophers[25] and

---

[21] Gregory names the following: 'light, heavy, firm, thin, soft, resistent, wet, dry, cold, warm, colour, shape, limit, interval' (PG 44, 69D). Had he formulated that they concurred (συνδραμόντα) to form matter (ibid.), he writes now that 'the οὐσία of each being concurred (συνέδραμεν) in the first act of his (sc. God's) will' (PG 44, 72B). Many exegets had, according to Origen (*princ* IV 4,6 [357,6–10 Koetschau]) interpreted Gen 1,1 as dealing with the creation of matter.

[22] *Hex* (PG 44, 80A). In the following, page numbers in the text refer to PG 44.

[23] This is how he understands the word ἀρχή: Διὰ δὲ τῆς ἀρχῆς δηλοῦται τὸ ἀκαρές τε καὶ ἀδιάστατον. Ἡ γὰρ ἀρχὴ παντὸς διαστηματικοῦ νοήματος ἀλλοτρίως ἔχει (PG 44, 72A).

[24] The notion of 'potentiality' in this context is not Aristotelian. Certainly, the germinative powers are not complete without their ensuing actualisation in sensible being, which is thus ontologically necessary. However, in Aristotle it is matter which is δυνάμει ὄν, and this is not how Gregory conceives of these λόγοι. The nearest approximation to Gregory's understanding seems to me to be found in the Neoplatonist doctrine according to which a higher ontological plane is the power (δύναμις) of the following level of greater multiplicity. For this reason it can be said to be the many 'potentially'. That Gregory's notion of 'potentiality' does not equal the Aristotelian doctrine can also be seen from unphilosophical applications. Thus, Gregory says that Moses's account of the creation is related to that of Basil as 'potentiality' to 'actuality': *hex* (PG 44, 61B); cf. van Winden (1991).

[25] As is well known, it originally belonged to the stock of Stoic imagery. Later, it could be used without problems by Neoplatonists as well. See, e.g., Plotinus, *Enn* III 2,2,18ff.; Porphyry, *sent* 37 (44,13–45,1 Lamberz). In one passage in his *in Tim* (*fr* 51 Sodano [38,30–39,14]) Porphyry adduces the development of the human

resounding in Gregory's account,[26] i.e. they find their full realisation only inside the sensible realm. I should thus conclude that what is created fully in the beginning are the principles of corporeal being which, however, are not bodies themselves, but the lowest level of intelligible being.

It should be noted at this point that this theory is similar to the Neoplatonic theory of *phusis* which is ascribed to Plato himself in Proclus' *Commentary on Timaeus*.[27] According to this theory *phusis* is the lowest kind of intelligible being, between soul and bodies, 'the limit (πέρας) of the intelligible plane' (11,11 Diehl). It is strictly immanent in the bodies, but ontologically prior to them as it contains 'the principles (λόγοι) of all things' (10,20 Diehl). It appears that, in spite of Proclus' protestations (10,13–5 Diehl), this theory has much in common with both the Stoic theory of universal *phusis* and the Peripatetic ἔνυλον εἶδος. In particular, the notion of *phusis* as containing all the principles (λόγοι) is of indubitably Stoic origin.[28] While the Stoics would not have accepted Proclus' interpretation of it as the lowest level of intelligible being, such an adaptation of Stoic views, as has been argued earlier (p. 83 above), was common practice, and the removal of those materialistic connotations from their theories could be achieved rather easily.

For the present investigation this observation is relevant because of some rather striking parallels with the theories underlying Gregory's argument in the trinitarian context. There, it was found, the item responsible for the unity of humanity was a kind of immanent form. While in the *Epistle* 38 it was referred to as *ousia*, elsewhere this term was employed alongside *phusis*. I have argued there (pp. 79ff. above) that its philosophical background is constituted by a fusion of Platonic, Aristotelian and Stoic notions of immanent forms or universal qualities. What we find in *Apology on the Hexaëmeron*, then, could be an attempt to fit the same theory into a cosmological framework. Thus

germ containing incorporeal λόγοι into a man to illustrate the generation of the world out of immaterial principles.

[26] In *hex* he writes of germinative powers (PG 44, 77D); for his use of the germ with regard to man see *op hom* 29 (PG 44, 236A–B).

[27] *In Tim* (10,13–26 Diehl): ὁ δὲ Πλάτων ὕλην μὲν ἢ τὸ ἔνυλον εἶδος ἢ τὰς δυνάμεις τὰς φυσικὰς οὐκ ἀξιοῖ πρώτως ἐπονομάζεσθαι φύσιν, ψυχὴν δὲ αὐτὴν αὐτόθεν ὀκνεῖ προσαγορεύειν, ἐν μέσῳ δὲ ἀμφοῖν τὴν οὐσίαν αὐτῆς θέμενος ... ὑπερέχουσαν δὲ τῶν μετ' αὐτὴν τῷ λόγους ἔχειν τῶν πάντων ... ἡ μὲν γὰρ φύσις σωμάτων ἐστί, δύνουσα κατ' αὐτῶν καὶ οὖσα ἀχώριστος ἀπ' αὐτῶν.

[28] Cf. SVF II, 328,13–25.

the present writing provides for a first indication that *Gregory might have attempted to carry through the idea of a monadic, universal phusis, which he had employed in the context of trinitarian theology, in a systematic way in other theological fields as well.* This, to be sure, is for the moment no more than a possibility that has to be checked against further details of Gregory's use of human nature, but it certainly would have the advantage of explaining his theory partly from his wish to be consistent with himself.

The present interpretation of the simultaneous creation 'in the beginning' helps us, I think, understand the second complement of Gregory's theory:

> But as alongside power wisdom too played a part towards the perfection of each constituent of the world, a necessary and ordered sequence was established at the same time.[29]

The creation of the world is thus constituted by the dialectics of a *phusis* which is completely produced 'in the beginning' and by the blueprint of its development into all the things which in their totality will make up the world as a whole. These, however, are not two different things, but two sides of the same kind of reality of which both its perfection and its necessary development are properties. *Phusis* is thus given here a dynamic element: it has the perfection of intelligible beings which are independent of time and space, while at the same time it develops, as it were, into time and space by producing a certain number of sensible individuals, a process which, of course, takes place in time and space.

It is important, though, that Gregory says more than simply (as a Platonist might) that *phusis* has an in-between status which makes it partly subject to the laws of sensible being. The idea of a necessary sequence, which philosophically owes more to Stoicism than to Platonism,[30] is introduced here, I think, as a requirement of Christian 'historicism': the creation is an event that took place once and for all, setting out the framework for the history of the world from its first to its last moment.

That blueprint, which as such is a property of the archaic principles, is here related to 'wisdom' (σοφία), which, I take it, is the

---

[29] *Hex* (PG 44, 72B–C).
[30] Cf. Daniélou (1953), 245–8.

wisdom of God. It thus appears, although Gregory does not really dwell on this point, that the paradigmatic forms of earlier Platonism have not altogether vanished in Gregory's theory; they have a certain parallel in God's wisdom which, as Gregory repeatedly asserts, 'knows all things before they come into existence'.[31] That is, in God things are already complete while in creation their completion is as yet to come.[32] Due to this foreknowledge of God the first creation is equipped with what Gregory calls an 'immanent *logos*'.[33] This *logos* is understood to cause a necessary order of events, bringing forth created beings one after another. This sequence, Gregory asserts, is described by the repeated commands of God which indicate the presence of *logos* in the entirety of creation.[34] What, then, is this *logos*? I take it that it cannot be a further, separate entity existing, as it were, alongside the universal *phusis*. Rather, I think, *logos* should be understood as an aspect, a property of the universal item, which is the object of the first, simultaneous creation, precisely what was called its dynamic element.

From Gregory's account, although it is unfortunately not a systematic treatment of the Genesis text, it becomes quite obvious why he found this paradigm so fitting for the exegesis of the biblical text: it made it possible to think of creation as starting from indeterminate being and moving towards ever greater determination: the 'world' as such is followed by the elements, with fire (76C–77A), naturally, preceding water (81A–85B) and earth (88C–89A; Gregory has to find reasons why the biblical text apparently misses air: 85D–88C) and only after these is the evolution of more determined beings dealt with.[35]

In this sense, Gregory can write that 'in the beginning' the whole world 'was there and was not there' (80A) or that 'potentially' it was

---

[31] Hist Sus 42, cf. *hex* (PG 44, 72B); *op hom* 16 (PG 44, 185A), 22 (PG 44, 204D), 29, (PG 44, 233D).

[32] See n. 16 above. Cf. also *inscr* I 6,42 (GNO V, 40,20–1): Ἀλλὰ μὴν ἴδιόν ἐστι τῆς θεότητος ἡ ἐποπτικὴ τῶν ὄντων δύναμίς τε καὶ ἐνέργεια.

[33] E.g., *hex* (PG 44, 73B, 88D) and passim.

[34] *Hex* (PG 44, 73A); cf. 113B: τὸ μὴ πρόσταγμα εἶναι διὰ ῥημάτων γινόμενον τὴν θείαν φωνήν, ἀλλὰ τὴν τεχνικήν τε καὶ σοφὴν δύναμιν ἑκάστου τῶν γινομένων (. . .) τοῦτο λόγον θεοῦ καὶ εἶναι καὶ λέγεσθαι.

[35] Here Gregory obviously leaves the common ground with Platonists. For them, following Aristotle, a development like this would mean to give chaos priority to order (cf. Porphyry, *in Tim, fr* 51 Sodano). That Christian cosmology found it more convenient to ally itself with stoicism at this point, has often been pointed out. Cf. the pathfinding books by Gronau (1914) and Jaeger (1914).

there, but not yet 'actually' (80B): it was there in the sense that with
the creation of universal nature all the presuppositions and initial
conditions were fulfilled for it to develop, it was not there in the
sense that none of its future parts had come into existence yet. It is
important to grasp this understanding properly because it provides
for the general paradigm according to which Gregory holds universal being to be prior to particular being.

In summary then, God created, according to Gregory, 'in the
beginning' a *pleroma*[36] of *logoi*, of intelligible being which, however,
can actualise itself only under the conditions of space and time in
order to reach the perfection which is only germinally provided in
it. This temporal and spatial development of those forming principles constitutes sensible being in the first place.

A further question to be addressed here is whether these intelligible *logoi* have ever existed independently of sensible being? Along
the lines of this argument the answer can only be that at no point
in time they have. The *arche* in which, it was said, corporeality did
not yet exist, was, as it were, the starting point of history, and as
such itself outside temporality; on the other hand, however, the nature
or substance[37] of the world exists and has always existed only as
immanent in bodies.

One may compare here the Neoplatonic theory of relation (σχέσις)
which was developed to account for the in-between status of ontological planes like soul:[38] such beings as are neither identical with
the supreme form of intelligible being nor with the lowest form of
material being, soul in particular, can be said to belong to either
realm as it were 'relationally'. Thus, looking at the *logoi* of the first
creation from the perspective of God, we can say that they are complete apart from time and space. Still, they also have the other relation which is to sensible being. In the latter, then, they depend on
time and space to develop into perfection.

4.1.2 *The creation of man*

At this point we may recall the observations made initially at the
passage from Gregory's *De Infantibus*. The creation of human nature,

---

[36] For πλήρωμα in this context cf. *hex* (PG 44, 113C).
[37] For the terms φύσις and οὐσία in this context see: *an et res* (PG 46, 124B).
[38] Cf. Plotinus, *Enn* IV 4,33; Porphyry, *sent* 3 (2,1–4 Lamberz), 29 (17,11–20,6
Lamberz).

we saw, was treated there as one part of the creation of the world. Thus we have no *prima facie* reason to doubt that the general paradigm of creation (which, we have seen, applies to both sensible and intelligible creation) is valid for this particular creation as well. Human nature would thus be an item whose creation implies the creation of humankind in its totality. It would embrace in itself all the forming principles constituting man. Finally, it would be quantitatively determined: the number of individuals into which it develops is part of its nature.

Textual evidence is found above all in Gregory's reference to the creation of human nature at *De Hominis Opificio* 16. This is a much discussed text which raises serious problems. However, I believe that they result from its context, that is from Gregory's attempt to explain the origin of evil with the help of that theory, more than from its immediate contents. As for the latter, I shall try to demonstrate that what Gregory offers here as an exegesis of Gen 1,27a is largely consistent with both his understanding of human nature in the trinitarian context and with his overall theory of creation as developed in *Apology on the Hexaëmeron*. Afterwards I will consider the function Gregory wishes to assign to this theory in his explanation of the origin of man's fallen state.

The crucial passage, which has to be given here in full, runs as follows:

> When the word says that God made man, the whole of humanity is indicated by the indefiniteness of the expression. For it is not named now Adam alongside the creature, as the history says in the following: but the name for the created man is not the particular (ὁ τὶς), but the universal (ὁ καθόλου). Now we are led by the universal name of the nature to understand it so that by the divine foreknowledge and power all humankind was encompassed in the first creation. For it is necessary that God does not conceive of anything made by him as indefinite (ἀόριστον): but that all being has a certain limit and measure taken by the creative wisdom. As now the particular man (ὁ τὶς ἄνθρωπος) is limited by the quantity of his body, and the measure of his existence (ὑπόστασις) is his size which contains the surface of his body: so I think is the totality of mankind (ὅλον τὸ τῆς ἀνθρωπότητος πλήρωμα) in a way encompassed by a single body through the foreseeing power of the God of the whole.
>
> And this teaches the word that says that 'God created man' and 'in the image of God he created him.' For the image is not in part of the nature, nor is grace only in some of those that are seen in the same way, but this power pervades the whole of the race equally, this

being indicated by the presence of mind in them all. All have the capability to think and plan and all the other things by which the divine nature is reflected in him that is made in its image. (. . .) Therefore, they all have been named one man since for the power of God there is neither past nor future, but even that which we expect is comprehended, equally with what is at present existing, by the all-sustaining energy. Our whole nature, then, extending from the first to the last is, so to say, one image of him who is.[39]

The exegetical starting point of Gregory's argument is, obviously, the observation that the verse mentions the creation of 'man', not of Adam. For this phrasing he gives an explanation which, whatever else one may think about it, is consistent with what he has been found to hold elsewhere: 'man' indicates the whole human item (ὅλον τὸ ἀνθρώπινον). While this phrase might be thought to be not quite unequivocal, the following makes clear that Gregory here again follows the view that the human race (πᾶσα ἡ ἀνθρωπότης), the *pleroma* of humanity, is the item indicated by the universal name. This is in accordance with his trinitarian writings, but provides for a difficulty in the present context: after all, Gregory does *not* want to say that God created the entire human race at once. This comes out, I think, quite clearly from his references here to God's foreknowledge: only from the perspective of God, transcending time and space, can humanity be said to be complete from the very beginning. This divine foreknowledge, on the other hand, cannot simply be a kind of divination; and it is not by chance that God's knowledge is paired here with his power: if God 'knows' the future number of men this really means that he determines it and, more precisely, that 'in the first creation' the future number of men, their *pleroma*, is already somehow included since, as Gregory writes, any creature must have its measure—a very Greek thought.[40] The whole first paragraph of the passage, then, would appear to be devoted to proving exegetically that Gen 1,27aα refers to a universal, first creation which, as was the case with the world in general, germinally embraces the entire future human race.

But what does this mean for the first creation? It is, I think, important to see that this first paragraph has as yet given no information about the precise character of that event; in particular, the item cre-

---

[39] *Op hom* 16 (PG 44, 185B–D).
[40] Cf. e.g.: Rist (1967), 24: "Being (for Plato) must be understood as finite Being. . . . this is the general classical view."

ated then has not yet been specified. It seems, on the other hand, that something must have been the object of that 'first creation'.

This, to be sure, has effectively been denied by Hübner. He advanced the influential argument that the 'man' of Gregory's argument is the Aristotelian 'universal concept' (*Allgemeinbegriff*).[41] However, this theory, fascinating though it may appear at first sight, is in its consequences so unlikely as to render it, in my view, almost absurd. For, given Gregory's exegetical starting point, what would be the meaning of Gen 1,27 if 'man' were to signify a mere notion? One might answer that God did in fact create Adam, and that the latter's universal human properties were abstracted into that notion in order to express the fact that Adam would become the progenitor of a whole race, a result, however, which would be only indirectly connected to the divine creative act. But this possibility collapses, not only because it seems perfectly anachronistic in its philosophical assumptions, but also because it cannot account for the obvious fact that Gregory himself insists that 'man' was created fully *before* Adam was there:[42] he would probably not have thought that God 'created' a mere notion. I should therefore suggest discarding this explanation.

We ought to allow, then, that God created something at the first creation, and that this something is 'man' in the sense that it necessarily develops into the human race. Yet this leaves us with the question of what *is* created at that first creation. I should suggest that the second paragraph of the present passage is meant to elucidate precisely this point. This paragraph starts from a renewed quotation of the biblical text. Note, however, that Gregory is now quoting the entirety of v. 27a, not only its first quarter verse; in fact, it seems as though he wants to put extra emphasis on the second quarter: 'the word says both (καὶ . . . καὶ) God made man *and* he made him in the image of God'. The crucial question then is: how does Gregory understand 'in the image' (κατ' εἰκόνα) here?

Leys, Urs von Balthasar and others have written about the importance of image-theology in Gregory, and it is now generally agreed to be of central importance for the entirety of his thought. However, in the present passage, I think, Gregory is not primarily concerned with his usual ideas of man as the image of God; rather, I believe, it is the specific force of κατ' εἰκόνα he is trying to account for. It

---

[41] Hübner (1974), 67–94.
[42] *Op hom* 22 (PG 44, 204D).

has often been noted that in Greek this is not the most natural way of saying that God created man in his image. An explanation frequently adopted since Origen was that, as Christ was said to be the image of God (Col 1,15), man was not himself the image, but 'made according to the image', i.e. an image of the image.[43] Yet this is not Gregory's interpretation; we have seen (see p. 96 above) that 'image' for him is no longer a term applicable to Christ's divine nature, and elsewhere he can apply Col 1,15 to Christ's humanity.[44]

Still, he too has to account for the wording of Gen 1,27aβ, and I think that in the present paragraph he offers his alternative explanation of that phrase by understanding κατ' εἰκόνα as the mode of the first, universal creation: to create man κατ' εἰκόνα would thus mean 'to create man in so far as he is the image' which, in the light of the meaning of 'man', makes the image equivalent to the germinally perfect form or *nature* of man as the object of the first creation.

This interpretation is confirmed by the very next sentence, which purports to give the reason for Gregory's interpretation of the biblical verse: 'for the image is not only in part of the nature (. . .), but this power pervades (διήκειν) the whole race equally'. The term employed for 'pervade' was a technical term of the Stoics;[45] while, of course, the power (δύναμις) thought of here is not to be identified with the material item of Stoic doctrine, this parallel strongly suggests that what Gregory has in mind is an immanent principle, equally present in all members of the species. And, I would suggest, on account of this immanent principle the entirety of humankind can later be referred to as 'one man': the principle of their unity would again be the immanent presence of the universal item in each and any of them. Yet this immanent power is clearly paralleled with the image which suggests that the latter itself is the universal item created by God in the beginning.

This same assertion is substantially repeated at the very end of the passage quoted: 'the whole nature pervading (διήκειν!) all men from the first to the last is one *image* of him who is'. The *phusis* (conceived here as the immanent form) is the image; Gregory's language is quite unequivocal. To create man κατ' εἰκόνα then, means nothing less than to create the immanent, universal nature of man.

---

[43] Origen, *c Celsum* VI 63 (vol. II, 133,6–12 Koetschau); cf. also, e.g., Didymus, *in Gen* 1,26 (58,3–15 Nautin).

[44] *Perf* (GNO VIII/1, 194,4–195,5).

[45] Cf., e.g., SVF I, 41,22–4; II, 155,24–30.

The upshot of Gregory's exegesis of Gen 1,27a would thus be that by creating the 'image' God created 'potentially' the entire human race (its *pleroma*), this being expressed by v. 27aα, while v. 27aβ would refer to the very creation of the universal item (φύσις) itself.

This interpretation appears to have a number of advantages. To begin with, it allows a very neat reconciliation of Gregory's argument here with his cosmological theories of *Apology on the Hexaëmeron* and, indeed, with his logical views on universals and particulars in his trinitarian writings: Common to all these texts is the assumption of an immanent universal form, termed nature (*phusis*) or substance (*ousia*), which is responsible for the substantial identity of generically related items. This, it was found, is clearly distinguished, albeit not terminologically, from the concrete universal which (in all these contexts) is indicated by the universal name. The two notions, of course, are mutually dependent; indeed, their connection has become clearer from the cosmological texts which assert that the immanent nature necessarily develops into a quantitatively determined totality of individuals. This fact may partly explain Gregory's ambiguous use of *phusis* terminology for both the extensive aspect and the immanent item which is recurrent in the present context too.

This broad agreement is furthermore confirmed by a brief comparison with the related argument of *De Hominis Opificio* 22. There Gregory expressly asserts that the 'image' 'which is seen in the whole human nature' was complete *before* Adam, the first earthly individual, was there (204D). Again, the term *phusis* assumes first the extensive meaning (the image is seen in the whole nature), while a little later it is equated with the universal image (204D). Otherwise, Gregory is somewhat less exact in that passage; he does not make as clear a distinction between the complete creation of the image and the 'germinal' completion of the entire human race as in the earlier passage. Notably, the whole *pleroma* of men is apparently equated here with the image rather than with the totality of men, which would be only potentially complete in the first creation.[46]

The second advantage of the present interpretation seems to be that it allows us at least a glimpse of Gregory's intention in employing this exegesis as an argument to explain the origin of evil. What he wants to maintain is that the two stages of the creation of man can account for the fact that man as the image of God nevertheless is,

---

[46] In the same meaning the term is employed at *hex* (PG 44, 113C).

in his present form, altogether different from his divine creator. I do not think that his argument is ultimately successful, but if he found in Gen 1,27 a hint that the object of the first, germinal creation was the image, then this helps us understand at least his intent. As there are, however, still many problems attached to this question it may be appropriate to offer a separate examination of them at the end of the present section (pp. 163ff. below).

So far I should conclude that the initially advanced hypothesis of a universal understanding of human nature in Gregory's theology of creation could be confirmed. Moreover, based on the analysis of the relevant sections in *Apology on the Hexaëmeron* and *De Hominis Opificio*, it has been possible to ascertain the precise character of this nature and its broad agreement with the theories employed in Gregory's trinitarian teaching.

For a further refinement of our understanding of that concept it may be worthwhile to start by comparing it with the Apollinarian model sketched above. Such a comparison has to note first of all the most astounding points of agreement between the two theories: in both of them, to begin with, the idea of humankind as germinally complete in the first creation is central. This notion is used to reconcile the quasi-historical account of Genesis with the theological requirement of a universal creation. While Apollinarius' theory sees Adam himself as the *arche* and Gregory stops short of that identification, both concur in the assumption that God creates the principles of being, which then necessarily develop into the particulars. It is true that in the case of Apollinarius we do not have positive evidence corroborating the assumption that he conceived of this as a necessary process or that his views about the *pleroma* were as strong as Gregory's. However, keeping in mind the incidental nature of our sources for the former's teaching, this lack of evidence makes it not unlikely that he held those views. While conclusions can only be drawn with care, it seems to me most natural that his theory would have required him to make assumptions very similar to those Gregory makes.

A further point of contact is the way the transmission of the nature is conceived of: both agree in making this a strictly immanent process, linking it to sexual generation and even allowing traducianism. This point has been dwelt upon on the occasion of *Eun* III/1, 73–6 (pp. 99f. above) and little needs to be added to what was said there. As for Gregory's traducianism, there is one pivotal passage in *De Hominis Opificio* that ought to suffice for a decision on this matter:[47]

> As nobody will deny that that which has been inserted (i.e. the germ), forms itself into the different joints and bowels without the addition of an outside power, but by the natural change of what lies in it, so the same has to be conceived analogously of the soul; that, while it is not recognised by any activities in what is seen, nonetheless it is therein. For the form (τὸ εἶδος) of the man who is to be composed is potentially in it too, though unseen, since, due to the necessary sequence, it could not appear plainly yet. So also the soul is in (the sperm), yet invisible, becoming visible, however, due to that activity which is its own and according to its nature, advancing alongside with the growth of the body. For, as the conceiving power (i.e. the germ) is not taken from a dead but from an animate and living body, we say it is sensible not to call dead and without soul that which proceeds from a living being towards the foundation of life. For whatever in the flesh is without soul is altogether dead; and death is the privation of soul. And no one should say here that privation precedes possession, making that which is without soul—and this is dead—precede soul.[48]

If the aforesaid concurrence would have rendered Gregory's acquaintance with Apollinarius' theory likely, the present one makes it, in my view, almost inevitable. What is more, these parallels seem to me to point to an attempt by Gregory to model his own concept of human nature on the Apollinarian one. For it would not be obvious that Gregory's theory of human nature requires this kind of immanent transmission. Rather, given the conceptual difficulties for psychology resulting from traducianism, one should think that Gregory would try to eschew this notion as far as possible. That he nonetheless embraces it would seem to indicate a strong indebtedness to the Apollinarian theory.

In the light of all this, however, the differences between the two conceptions deserve even greater attention. For, in spite of all those parallels, it is clear that the two theories are by no means identical. Their chief divergence appears to consist in the fact that with

---

[47] About Gregory's traducianism cf. also *op hom* 30 (PG 44, 253B); *an et res* (PG 46, 125C–128A). Recently, Hauke (1993, 662–4) has, not very convincingly, argued against this view. Balthasar (1995, 51) argues for a *via media*: 'We see that obviously *neither "creationism" nor "traducianism"* can be applied to this conception, for transmitted nature (body and soul) is not in the dimension of time, inasmuch as it is *the* human nature. But it is precisely human nature that is directly and immediately created by God' (italics in the original).
[48] *Op hom* 29 (PG 44, 236B–D).

Apollinarius the principle (ἀρχή) of humanity is identical with the first human individual, whereas with Gregory it is not. Thus, Apollinarius would see Adam as both, the *arche* and the first individual person, while for Gregory the *arche* is as distinct from Adam as from all other men.

How can this deviation be accounted for? It has to be recalled here that the most apparent reason for Christian theologians' adoption of the derivative interpretation of humankind's unity was precisely the advantage gained from the identification of 'man' and Adam. By removing this identity, then, Gregory appears to reduce this theory by the very element which had conditioned its original adoption.

Could Gregory simply have misunderstood it? This seems all but impossible; we have seen how Gregory spent much exegetical and philosophical skill on the construction of *his* theory of seminal identity. Assuming that the same person missed the comparatively simple point of an identification of Adam with the human *ousia* only to undergo in exchange the task of developing single-handedly[49] the complicated theories of *Apology on the Hexaëmeron* and *De Hominis Opificio* would, in my view, cause considerably more difficulties than attributing to Gregory the intention of changing that point.

Again, the reasons for that change can hardly be found in theological or exegetical requirements of the creation account. On the contrary, the idea that Adam is man would for a number of reasons appear much less far fetched than Gregory's interpretation.[50] Thus we are left with an occasion to be found from without creation theology which would have caused Gregory to adopt the present views.

This could have arisen in an area pertaining to the economy or within trinitarian theology or within both. Now we have already seen that within the latter field such an occasion did indeed arise in the Cappadocians' interest in co-ordinating the divine Persons. This interest, developed as part of the Eunomian controversy, would thus appear to provide one explanation for Nyssen's change of Apollinarius' theory of a derivative human nature. Whether Gregory's treatment of the divine economy provides another reason will have to be seen.

---

[49] According to van Winden (1988, 1262) Gregory's theory is fairly original.

[50] The fact that 'Adam' in Hebrew means 'man' was known, at least, to Origen (*c Celsum* IV 40 [vol. I, 313,17–24 Koetschau]). Gregory, to be sure, wishes to identify the name with the 'earthly creature' of the second creation: *op hom* 22 (PG 44, 204C).

4.1.3 *Further Considerations*: De Hominis Opificio *16 and the problem of double creation*

The main problem posed by the setting of the above passage in Gregory's *De Hominis Opificio* 16 is, in brief, that Gregory there employs this theory to explain the difference between the original, godlike, and the present, mortal and sinful, states of man by introducing the notion of a double creation of man. What has to be explained, then, is how he might have thought the idea of a universal creation of humanity *qua* image could function within such an overall argument. To this end I propose to start from a short sketch of the problem posed for creation theology by the existence of evil, and to proceed with an elucidation of Gregory's attempt of dealing with it in *De Hominis Opificio* 16.

1. The reality of salvation history confronted the Christian understanding of creation with a difficulty: how can the world as God's good creation be as faulty as it is? Why has it not simply been perfect from the beginning, but had to embark on that long and enduring journey towards its eventual, eschatological salvation? This, obviously, was due to the presence of evil in it. How, then, did evil enter the world? Granted that neither God[51] nor a being coeternal with him could be its originator, its source had to be found within creation itself. All fathers prior to Augustine blamed the free will of God's rational creatures in the first place; equipped with free will, which 'godlikeness' was often understood to include, they could, and did, sin. However, a monistic theism believing in an almighty God could not easily stop at this answer; more far-reaching explanations were being called for. In general, two patterns can be discerned: one would either be content to emphasise the contrast between the perfect and the fallen states of the creation; this tension would then provide for the dynamics of salvation history, with the eschaton being conceived as a return to the original state, the *apokatastasis*. This approach allowed God to be cleared of the charge of an imperfect creation; the shortcomings of the present world were thus entirely blamed on created beings and their free will. Yet it was open to criticism as it could not really explain how the Fall of a perfect

---

[51] Cf. for this Gregory's protestation against the suggestion of an unnamed exegete that the 'darkness over the deep' of Gen 1,1 would refer to fallen angels (*hex*; PG 44, 81D): Μήποτε οὕτω παρανομήσαιμι, ὡς ποίημα Θεοῦ τὴν κακίαν νοῆσαι.

creation would have been possible. Moreover, some would protest that it tends to suppress the anti-Gnostic Christian tenet of the present world's goodness.[52] This explanation is usually connected with Origen's[53] name.

The alternative attempt to solve that knot is normally attributed to Irenaeus.[54] It is based on an understanding of goodness as opposed to perfection: the present world is good as God's creation, but not (yet) perfect. This lack of perfection, however, is due to the overall inferiority of created to uncreated being.[55] Consequently, the tension driving salvation history is that between creator and creature,[56] the focus of this theology being on Incarnation and the ensuing process of a divinisation of mankind[57] rather than on the restoration of an original state. In their teaching on creation, accordingly, those theologians do not make much of the tension between the original and the fallen states: the Fall is the possible, if not necessary,[58] result of man's immaturity.

Both these approaches could be argued for on the basis of biblical evidence: the 'Origenist' type would find its justification in the duality of creation stories in Gen 1 and 2, which it would normally understand to refer to a duality of creations of man according to the duality of his constitution (body and soul). The second of these

---

[52] Cf. for this judgment: Augustine, *De civitate dei* XI 23.

[53] Cf. mainly *princ* II 9,1–6 (163,24–170,17 Koetschau) for this understanding. Cf., however, also *princ* III 6,1 (280,2–17 Koetschau) where Origen's opinion seems to be that man will be more perfect in the eschaton than he was in his original state.

[54] Again it has to be questioned how exact such an ascription can be. The text normally referred to is *haer* IV 38,1,6–15 (vol. IV/2, 944–6 Rousseau/Doutreleau). But there Irenaeus attempts to resolve one particular problem and the solution presented in that context need not be representative for the whole of his theology. On the other hand similar views can be found in other authors, including Origen (see previous note). One has to make allowance, I think, for the fact that the fathers in general are not as systematic as we sometimes think they are.

[55] Irenaeus, loc. cit.

[56] Cf. e.g. the juxtaposition of γενητός ἀγένητος in *haer* IV 38,1 *passim*.

[57] At *haer* III 19,1,18–21 (vol. III/2, 374 Rousseau/Doutreleau) he writes: Διὰ τοῦτο γὰρ ὁ Λόγος ἄνθρωπος καὶ Υἱὸς ἀνθρώπου ὁ Υἱὸς τοῦ Θεοῦ, ἵνα ὁ ἄνθρωπος (. . .) γένηται υἱὸς τοῦ Θεοῦ.

[58] I leave aside here a further possibility to solve the whole problem which would be that the Fall is indeed a necessary event in the development of mankind. According to Oesterle (1985, 107–14) this is, however, how Gregory ought to be understood. He combines the statements about man as the climax of evolution and as mediator between sensible and intelligible reality so that Gregory's teaching implies the necessity of the Fall. In his view, Gregory aims at an almost Hegelian concept in which God for his own eventual realisation is in need of the non-identical. The legitimacy of such an interpretation may be doubted.

was carried out with regard to the Fall. The 'Irenaean' type on the other hand would point to the different wording in Gen 1,26f.: whereas it is God's plan to create man in his 'image and likeness' (εἰκών and ὁμοίωσις), the actual creation of man depicted in v. 27 is only in the image (κατ' εἰκόνα). The likeness would thus be something additional which men will acquire only in the course of salvation history.

Overall, Gregory seems much indebted to the Origenist approach.[59] In fact, he nowhere uses the argument of Adam's infancy and, what is more, makes no use of the contrast between 'image' and 'likeness', thus being in a sense more Origenist than the Alexandrine himself.[60]

At the same time, his writings show that he was concerned to steer clear of certain alleged implications of the Origenist approach, such as the pessimistic view of man's corporeal state or the pre-existence of souls. Thus it is evident that in the account of man's creation given in the first chapters of *De Hominis Opificio*, man in his present constitution, mixed from sensible and intelligible substance, is the intention of God's work; summarising his explanation of why God created man last, Gregory writes at the end of chapter two:

> And therefore (God) laid down two principles in his (sc. man's) creation, mixing the earthly with the divine in order that he (man) may have relish of each, being akin and related to both, enjoying the divine through the divine nature, earthly good things through his kindred sense-perception. (PG 44, 133B)

In a similar way the elaboration on man as the climax of evolution, including all the properties of the more primitive creation,[61] makes sense only under the assumption that the mixture of sensible and intelligible in man was intended by God from the very beginning in the interest of both man and creatures.[62] More obvious still is the explicit attack on the doctrine of pre-existent souls which Gregory found in Origen's *De Principiis*; in the twenty-eighth chapter of *De Hominis Opificio* Nyssen sharply distances himself from that doctrine, clearly identifying it as Origen's (229B–233C).[63]

---

[59] E.g. *op hom* 17 (PG 44, 188C) and *an et res* (PG 46, 148A) where resurrection is defined as the *apokatastasis* of the original state.

[60] Balthasar (1995), 117–8; different: Leÿs (1951), 116–9. Cf. n. 53 above.

[61] *Op hom* 8 (PG 44, 144D–148B).

[62] Cf. also the explicit statement that mind needs bodily organs at *op hom* 8 (PG 44, 148B) and the elaboration of this view *op hom* 8–10 (PG 44, 148B–153C).

[63] The contrast between Gregory's and Origen's approach has been pointed out by Otis (1958, 108–9) and, especially, Oesterle (1985, 103): 'Gregors "De Hominis

2. The sixteenth chapter occupies a central place in *De Hominis Opificio*. With it we enter what can be regarded as a second part of the writing.[64] This part explores the more problematic side of man's creation, starting from the observation that man in his present state does not appear at all to be 'like God'.[65] In its course Gregory touches on a number of related questions: what was the Fall;[66] what about the resurrection;[67] why was the resurrection state not created at once,[68] and so forth.

Situated thus at a central juncture of the treatise, this chapter is the place where one would expect Gregory to present his solution to the dilemma sketched above. And indeed there can be little doubt that Gregory here aims at unveiling his settlement of the question why man as the perfect climax of a perfect creation can often be so unlike his divine artificer. This solution, it may be said, anticipating the result of the present analysis, is very much in line with the 'Origenist' approach, emphasising a duality of creations due to the Fall as foreseen by God. While Gregory's proposal appears to deviate in some points from Origen's view, there ultimately remains a grave tension between this theory and the role of man as a mediator between the sensible and the intelligible envisaged in the earlier parts of the writing. In fact, it appears, as will be argued at the end of the present section, that the rudimentary nature of Gregory's Origenism itself is responsible for a number of severe inconsistencies. An elaborate discussion of this problem being beyond the scope of this study, it may be said that a number of previous studies have equally led to the conclusion that Gregory fails to come forward with a theologically satisfying answer to the problems he proposes to solve.[69]

Opificio" ist durchgängig zu verstehen als immanente Auseinandersetzung mit der origenischen Anthropologie und Kosmologie.'

[64] With Laplace (1944), who regards the composition of the *op hom* as a drama (13), chapter sixteen constitutes the second act: '(La crise tragique) éclate avec violence dans le chapitre XVI, qui est le second acte: l'homme, dans sa condition présente, dit Grégoire, ne peut être ce qu'il est par nature: image de Dieu.' (15).

[65] *Op hom* 16 (PG 44, 180B).

[66] *Op hom* 20 (PG 44, 197C–201A).

[67] *Op hom* 25–7 (PG 44, 213C–229A).

[68] *Op hom* 22 (PG 44, 204B–209A).

[69] E.g. B. Otis (1958), 109f., 113. Cf. however Balthasar (1995, 71–87) who appears to be more optimistic about it.

Let us now look somewhat more closely at the argument.[70] Gregory sets out as his aim a further elucidation of Gen 1,26.[71] In these words, he writes, an esteem for man is to be found which is by far higher than that revealed by the Greek characterisation of man as a microcosm (177D–180A). However, he continues, is there not an apparent contradiction: man is at present not at all 'like' God, neither immortal nor impassible, neither eternal nor immutable; it rather seems that in very many respects man is opposed to the divine (180A). This is then stated as an apparent paradox: on the one hand we have to believe that the Scriptures do not lie, on the other hand man is indeed not like God. How can this be resolved?

To this end Gregory proposes a closer look at Gen 1,27, the verse depicting the creation of man in the image of God (181A). It teaches, according to Gregory, a duality of creations: it is one thing that is made 'in the image', another one that is created as male and female.[72] The latter, however, is no more the image of God, as Gregory points out with reference to Gal 3,28. In the following, Gregory refers this duality to the duality of intelligible and sensible substance in human nature. Of these the intellectual part has priority (or pre-exists: προτερεύειν, which is used in the Greek (181C), can, but need not have a temporal meaning here)[73] as would be evident from the biblical account.

Gregory's first and decisive answer to the question he had asked himself is thus that the image of God is to be found in part of man only. This is in line with our previous findings and, indeed, with the entirety of Gregory's teaching. In this view Gregory follows an exegetical tradition going back at least to Philo.[74] In the present context (and only here)[75] Gregory explains this duality in man with a double

---

[70] Among the studies devoted to this chapter the most thorough one to date is Corsini's (1971); cf. also: Hübner (1974), 67–94; U.Bianchi (1978), 83–115.

[71] *Op hom* 16 (PG 44, 177D). Earlier in the treatise (*op hom* 3 [PG 44, 133C–136A], 11 [PG 44, 153C–156B]) this verse had already received some attention.

[72] *Pace* Hübner (1974, 92) I do not think that it is Gregory's chief intention to argue that the image is asexual. Gregory rather wishes to employ this fact (based on Gal 3,28) as a basis for his exegesis of Gen 1,27, viz., that the latter verse reports a twofold creation. It is interesting to contrast this interpretation to that of Philo, who understands v 27b as 'neither male nor female' in order to press home the juxtaposition of 1,27 and 2,7 aimed at in his *op mun* 134; cf. Tobin (1983), 109.

[73] Cf. LSJ, s.v.

[74] *Op mun* 135.

[75] *Cant* XV (GNO VI, 457,19–459,4) which has at times been thought to contain a similar theory refers to soteriology (cf. p. 179 below).

creation (διπλῆ κατασκευή).[76] Again it is obvious that this idea is taken over from Philo and Origen.[77] However, what precisely is its meaning in Gregory's text?

To begin with, it seems obvious that the double creation of man cannot simply be the creation of compound being. The point of Gregory's argument cannot be that, as other beings may come into existence by, for example, mixing earth, water, and air, so man is created by mixing sensible and intelligible being: this would not be a double creation, but a single act of mixing these ingredients. The case here must be different.

Gregory's claim is that Gen 1,27a ('God created man in his own image, in the image of God he created him') depicts the complete creation of the image. Yet this statement tells us nothing about a creation of the soul or of any other *part* of man, but, taken at face value at least, reports the creation of man and nothing else; it also seems that this is what Gregory takes it to mean, as we have seen earlier.[78] In the present context too, Gregory pronounces quite clearly that '*man* has been divided into' male and female (181B). The term rendered here by 'divide' is διαιρέω, which was often used by philosophers (and by Gregory himself)[79] for the division of kinds. Although we cannot be sure that Gregory employs it as a technical term here, its connotation must be the splitting up of something which is already there. There are indications that for Gregory, quite generally, the *diairesis* of universal names follows the development of created nature in the process of creation.[80] Thus it would not appear far fetched

---

[76] Corsini denies that. He writes (1971, 115): 'Il (sc. Gregory) ne dit nullement qu'il y a eu deux créations pour les deux aspects (i.e. of intellectual and sensible in man): il dit tout simplement qu'il y a deux expressions de l'Écriture pour indiquer que l'acte créateur de Dieu s'est porté sur deux aspects différents de l'homme.' Against this interpretation Bianchi protests (1978, 103–111) whereas Balás (1979, 120–1) seems to agree with Corsini. The interpretation depends, I think, mainly on the way the 'duality' is conceived of. To my mind, Corsini is right in rejecting the view that in those lines a two-stages-theory of creation is to be discerned. On the other hand, Gregory explicitly writes of a 'twofold' or 'double' creation and there can be no doubt that he connects this duality with man's anticipated Fall.

[77] For Philo see, e.g., *op mun* 134–5, and in general the excellent treatment of the matter by Tobin (1983). For Origen cf. Haers (1992), 164–70. For Gregory's relation to these theories see: Bianchi (1978).

[78] See p. 156 above.

[79] E.g., *op hom* 8, (PG 44, 145A–B); *Eun* I 270 (GNO I, 105,19), III/6 66 (GNO II, 209,19); *cant* VI (GNO VI, 137,7). Cf. Balás (1966), 34–49; Mosshammer (1988).

[80] *Hex* (PG 44, 72C); cf. Balás (1966), 36–7. This theory has its antecedents in Philo: Früchtel (1968), 41–52.

to conclude that Gregory's account here is concerned also with a special kind of division, that of 'man' into 'male' and 'female', which entails that human beings receive, in addition to the general properties of manhood, in which they all partake, gender-specific properties by which men and women are differentiated.

The advantage of this approach to Gregory's argument seems to me that it presents him as attempting to fit the soteriological concept of a double creation, which he had found in Origen, into his own cosmological paradigm. For the two stages of the creation of man, which are called here a 'double creation', are not that different from what would have happened—in Gregory's theory—at the creation of other living beings too: one could thus, for example, discern between the creation of 'cow' and the ensuing division into male and female which can in theory be separated from the former as both, male and female are equally cows. Now in the case of cows this process is not reported as a twofold act in the Bible, but Gregory could argue that there would have been no point in doing so because the second step had to follow the first one: the only way to create the cow was to do precisely this.

With man, then, this would be different; here we hear about a first step which does not yet mention male and female because the second step, although it is more or less the same as in the case of the cow, is carried out for a different reason.

The chief difference is, of course, that the universal nature of the cow has not been made in the image of God, that is as a rational and thus *ipso facto* intelligible being. Such beings would obviously have their special mode of generation; they would not need sexual differentiation to reach their *pleroma*. This mode of existence, Gregory writes later in the treatise,[81] had been intended for man as well, but was not implemented. If it had been, the division of sexes would not have been necessary.

It is at this point, I think, where Gregory's understanding of Gen 1,27a slots in: according to his exegesis, as has been found, the complete creation of humankind is described in that half verse, both its germinal perfection as the image and its future development into the *pleroma* of humankind. Thus there would have been no need to add the division of sexes referred to in Gen 1,27b, were it not for a special reason.

---

[81] *Op hom* 17 (PG 44, 188D–189B).

The ensuing part of the sixteenth chapter is then meant to sup-
ply this very reason (181D–184A): as God is the entirety of all good,
it was his intention to give his image a share in all good things
(184A–B).[82] One of them, however, was freedom of will which for
this reason could not be withheld from man either (184B).[83] It was
thus in the power of man to do as he willed. Gregory then goes on
to show that there would also have been a difference between man
and God, which is the general one between creator and creature,
viz. that man unlike God is changeable (184C–D).[84] It would therefore have been possible for man to use his free will to do wrong
and fall from his destined position. As it was possible for God to
anticipate that precisely this was to happen, he devised the garment
of corporeality for man, in particular the division of sexes,[85] in order
that human beings would be able to survive and multiply under the
conditions in which they would find themselves after the Fall.

This argument is, I think, quite straightforward. The duality of
creations Gregory had found in Gen 1,27 is explained by God's
recognition of his creature's ambiguous and changeable character:
the 'second creation', the addition of sexual differentiation, becomes
necessary to supplement the purely intelligible creation man would
have been as the 'image'.

Again the similarities to Origen's approach are at hand.[86] More
important than this, however, is that the proposed interpretation of
the double creation has been confirmed. The anticipation of man's
Fall is, of course, the reason why God decided to add the animal
mode of creation, the division into male and female, to the creation
of the image. The 'double creation' of man was thus a means adopted
by God in order to prevent the worst consequences of the (anticipated) Fall.

---

[82] Cf. also Origen, *princ* II 9,6 (169,22–25 Koetschau) for the claim that God's
goodness was the only reason for him to create.

[83] Again the parallel to *princ* II 9 is remarkable.

[84] Many passages from Origen can be quoted to the same effect (e.g. *princ* III
1); besides, the property of free will belongs, of course, to the common stock of all
the Greek fathers (cf., e.g., Irenaeus, *haer* IV 37; Methodius, *autex*, passim).

[85] The text explicitly mentions the difference of the sexes only (PG 44, 185A).
However, in the light of what was said earlier (cf. esp. PG 44, 181B–C) it appears
that this stands *pars pro toto* here for corporeality as such; cf.: Oesterle (1985), 107.

[86] The relation between the two concepts seems to consist primarily in the dialectics of God's *foreknowledge* (πρόγνωσις) and man's or—in Origen's case—the rational creatures' free will. In a number of passages Origen indeed argues for this

In summary, then, the analysis of Gregory's argument in *De Hominis Opificio* 16 has, I hope, shown that the interpretation of his exegesis of Gen 1,27a offered above is not only not in contradiction to, but indeed in agreement with, the overall argument presented in that chapter. Gregory's line of reasoning requires that the first half verse is understood as referring to the complete creation of man *qua* image on the basis of his theory of simultaneous creation presented in *Apology on the Hexaëmeron*. On the basis of this exegesis he attempts to argue that the division of sexes mentioned in v. 27b is a separate act carried out by God on account of his foreknowledge of the Fall.

By way of evaluation it may be said that the main weakness of the theory as it stands appears not to be its identification of human nature with the image. This view, although theologically problematical (see below), is not in itself absurd and, moreover, as will be shown, dominates one strand of Gregory's thinking far beyond the present passage.

Rather, I think, it is the identification of the second stage of creation with the creation of man's sensible component in general (181B–C) which causes insuperable difficulties. It first of all poses serious theological problems; Gregory here effectively undermines his own previous argument that had emphasised the goodness of man's dual constitution: if the godlike nature of man is identified with man's intelligible component, it is difficult to believe that the mixture of the latter with sensible substance was designed by God as a necessary complement for the perfection of his image.

This identification also makes, I think, nonsense of Gregory's overall cosmological theory. In this view human nature is the sum total of *logoi* making up man. To these, more specific properties, which constitute individual human beings, would be added. Such a theory clearly does not allow for an understanding of man's nature without any corporeal properties.

Even within chapter sixteen there is, I believe, a tension to be observed resulting from that identification: Gregory starts from the consideration, related above, that human nature consists of two *parts*, that is, sensible and intelligible substance. Yet when he enters into the discussion of God's twofold creative act based on his exegesis of

---

concept with exactly the biblical quotation Gregory uses here and elsewhere, Hist Sus 42 e.g.: *in Gen* 3,3–4 = *Philocalia* XXIII (189,27–191,28 Robinson); *Comm I in Rom* 2 = *Philocalia* XXV (227,15–228,28 Robinson).

Gen 1,27 he introduces the notion that the creation of the image as such is the creation of *man*, thus tacitly moving from the creation of human nature as composed of two substances to an understanding of two consecutive creations.

This, however, could be remedied, it seems, by making a distinction between the corporeality human beings would have as part of their compound *nature* and those bodies, fitted with sexual organs, which they were given in a second act and which they have now.[87] If we allow, hypothetically, this slight correction to the present theory, it would appear not altogether unacceptable. What is more, in this form it would, as I shall show, be quite relevant for one important strand of Gregory's thinking.

There is, however, a further question to be asked about the present text which would equally apply if the correction suggested above was accepted: why does Gregory, addressing the problem of humanity's fallen character, refer to a double creation rather than to the Fall? This question derives its relevance from the force of a number of theological gravamina apparently connected with that fact: thus one might easily construct a case arguing that in Gregory's concept God himself is ultimately made responsible for the existence of evil. After all, the changes made to human beings would seem to increase the danger of sinning at least as much as they might prevent its worst consequences.[88] Also, there is no consideration whatever given to the relation between God's gifts to human beings for the needs within the present world and the malediction incurred by man against himself on account of his Fall, i.e. death. The latter, at least, appears to have been different in Origen.[89]

Ultimately, while being aware of the necessarily speculative character of any supposed explanation, I would suggest that these serious theological shortcomings in the present passage are best ascribed to what one may call Gregory's rudimentary Origenism. Where Origen develops the theme of a double creation in a way similar to Gregory's (*princ* II 1) he has no difficulties in ascribing the creation of a sensible world to God's providential foreknowledge of the Fall, for with him this latter creation does not *per se* change the condi-

---

[87] Such a view apparently underlies other passages in Gregory's works: Holl (1904), 202.

[88] Cf., e.g., *inscr* II 12,176 (GNO V, 131,21–3): ὅτι τὸ πρῶτον αἴτιον τῆς τῶν κακῶν εἰσόδου τὸ ἀποκτηνωθῆναι τὸν ἄνθρωπον τοῖς ζῳωδεστέροις παθήμασιν.

[89] Bammel (1989), 72.

tion of God's rational creatures. Rather, their Fall is entirely due to the movements of their own free will. At the same time it seems clear that, if we allow the respective conceptual framework, in their falling the existence of materiality can save them from becoming completely extinct. Thus it appears comparatively easy to construct a theory of a providential second creation along those lines. Gregory, on the other hand, rejecting the notion of initially existing rational creatures who fell into corporeality, attempts some seemingly minor corrections to Origen's framework which, I think, result in the *aporiae* sketched above: his human nature, being neither itself a subject nor a multiplicity of subjects, cannot properly be said to 'fall'. Consequently, the creation of sensible substance becomes an addition of sensible substance to that *phusis*. At the same time, the providential act in Origen of providing human beings with a means of surviving within the physical world comes in Gregory's account very near to a punishment for a sin that has as yet not been committed, a punishment, moreover, that is likely to engender further trespasses.[90]

Along these lines another inconsistency, which has been pointed out by Cherniss,[91] can perhaps also be explained. Gregory repeatedly names as the reason for the division of sexes God's wish that humanity should reach its predestined number. Yet, if the development into a *pleroma* is something that happens successively, but by necessity, how could it have been hindered by any act on the part of the creature? Cherniss adduces this observation to argue that the *pleroma* can only be the complete number, bare of any Platonic sense; according to him the 'queer bastardy' of that theory is Gregory's own. The latter may well be true, nevertheless, I think that in this case too the tensions result mainly from Gregory's attempt to offer a modified Origenism sustainable under the requirements of late fourth-century orthodoxy. Part of those tensions, it is true, may be inherent in any philosophy positing a providential God: in Origen's thought also God would strictly speaking not have been 'free' to let his creatures fall into non-existence. Nevertheless, Gregory's special interest in humankind's reaching its full number is certainly a consequence of his rejection of an initial creation of an 'actual' *pleroma*.

The problem posed for Gregory by his partial rejection of Origenism is exacerbated by his wish to limit his alliance with Apollinarius'

---

[90] This is Gregory's own argument against pre-existent souls: *op hom* 28 (PG 44, 232B–C).
[91] Cherniss (1930), 33.

derivative theory. The latter, of course, could maintain both the potential completeness of humankind in the first creation and its Fall 'in Adam'. Thus Gregory's argument in *De Hominis Opificio* 16 (and even more so in chapter twenty-two) makes it once more clear that Nyssen is far from following Apollinarius unconditionally, but sticks to his tenet of distinguishing Adam and human nature even at a high cost.

4.2   *A Fall of human nature?*

From what has been found so far it would appear that within the framework of Nyssen's theory of universal human nature there is no room for a Fall of the 'nature': *phusis* as a monadic entity pervading all humankind was not the kind of thing to which an action responsible for the Fall, an original sin, could be ascribed. Human individuals, on the other hand, would not have been able to change that nature on account of its ontological priority (it was complete before Adam was there!). Furthermore, for obvious reasons, God could hardly be considered a possible candidate for such an act, although we have already seen Gregory getting dangerously close to this last position.

While there was also an extensive, universal meaning of human nature, indicating the totality of human beings (their *pleroma*), this sense was, in principle, inextricably intertwined with the former view of nature in that the *pleroma* would be the necessary product of that monadic *phusis*. With no change to the latter, then, there could not strictly speaking not be a change to the former either. One could certainly imagine a somewhat looser use of the extensive meaning indicating the factual universality of sin without commitment to the ontological necessity that would seem to be implied by physical terminology. Such a use by Gregory may be detected in passages like the following:

> As he (sc. Christ) in himself assimilated his own man to the power of the Godhead, being a part of the universal *phusis*, but not subject to those passions of the nature which lead to sin ('He committed no sin, he was not convicted of falsehood': 1 Pet 2,22): so also he leads those who are like him into communion with the Godhead if they do nothing unworthy of that union with the divine.[92]

---

[92] *Perf* (GNO VIII/1, 204,20–205,4).

The nature, of which the Christ's humanity is said to be a part, must be the totality of human beings. If, then, there is a tendency to sin in that 'nature', but not in Christ's humanity, this would appear to indicate that sinning is not, after all, 'natural' for human beings, but simply something they all, 'the whole nature', have done and are doing.

Would it, then, be adequate to assume that in Gregory's view a Fall of the nature in the strict sense never occurred? This might in some ways appear to be an attractive solution. Quite a number of texts could be adduced, I think, to substantiate such a claim. First of all this would seem to be presupposed wherever Gregory equates human nature with the image. That this is his view in *De Hominis Opificio* 16 has been demonstrated; but there are other passages which appear to make the same point.[93] Such a theory is, as I have argued above, not in itself absurd. It was primarily the apparent identification of human nature with the intelligible component of man at *De Hominis Opificio* 16 that was open to criticism.

There are more observations that would seem to underscore this interpretation: thus, Gregory's entire theology of asceticism appears to draw on the notion of the image in man as of something obscured but not destroyed by his habit of sinning. This is especially distinct in Gregory's elaboration in *On Virginity* 12 where he uses the image of iron darkened from rust.[94]

Yet it is, nevertheless, clear that such a characterisation of Gregory's theology as has just been given would be so one-sided as to render it practically inaccurate. For not only are there equally numerous passages dwelling at length on the notion that man as he is now is altogether different from his initial state and far from his original destination, there are moreover, and more decisively for the present inquiry, a number of texts where Gregory seems to make an explicit connection between that difference and a supposed fallen state of human nature.

Does Gregory, then, or does he not, know of original sin as a single act of disobedience which has caused human nature to be damaged in a way that has affected every human being since? It is this question that is to be mainly addressed in the present section.

---

[93] E.g. *beat* V (GNO VII/2, 129,3–8); *cant* VI (GNO VI, 198,8–10); *virg* 12 (GNO VIII/1, 300,5–8): that human nature is in the divine image is grace (ibid. 8–12; cf. *op hom* 16 [PG 44, 185C]).

[94] *Virg* 12,2 (GNO VIII/1, 299,20–1).

Previous scholarship has varied in its judgment on this question. While some have found clear evidence for a fallen nature in Gregory's work,[95] others have remained unconvinced, usually citing as counter-evidence Gregory's emphasis on free will and his express opinion that human beings can achieve sinlessness.[96] Those latter arguments, to be sure, raise a variety of questions pertaining to possible theories of universal sin different from Augustine's. Having briefly indicated above (pp. 132–5) the lines along which I think those questions might be approached, I will not go into them any further here, but will confine myself to a discussion of relevant texts for the sketched dilemma.

4.2.1 The Neoplatonic pattern

In his probably earliest extant writing, On Virginity, Gregory devotes an extended section[97] to an explanation of the origin of evil. The starting point is similar to that of De Hominis Opificio 16: the item created in God's image could not have been passionate and mortal, for that would have made it dissimilar to its archetype. Thus, passion must be thought to have entered man later, after the first creation (μετὰ τὴν πρώτην κατασκευήν: 298,9).

The solution given to that dilemma in the present context, however, is altogether different from that presented in De Hominis Opificio 16. The first creation is contrasted here not with a second one, but man himself, the earthly Adam, is cited as the creator of evil (κτίστης καὶ δημιουργὸς τοῦ κακοῦ: 298,20). Two reasons are given to explain why he is capable of being this: first, as in De Hominis Opificio 16, man's free will is adduced; secondly, evil is said to be only a privation.[98] It has not been created by God, but has its existence (ὑπόστασις) only in being chosen by man (299,12–16).

From this first origin, then, evil spread throughout the entire human race:

---

[95] Tennant (1903), 319–24, Daniélou (1953), 232–3 and now Hauke (1993), 642–70, who gives a useful survey of previous scholarship (575–8). I should like to express my indebtedness to the amazingly comprehensive collection of relevant passages from Gregory's works in the last named study.

[96] Williams (1929), 269–82.

[97] Virg 12,2 (GNO VIII/1, 297,24–300,13). In the following, page numbers in the text refer to GNO VIII/1.

[98] Cf. for this idea in Gregory: Mosshammer (1990).

But the habit (ἀκολουθία) of sinning entered as we have described, and with fatal quickness, into the life of man; and from that small beginning spread into this infinitude of evil (299,16–19; ET: Moore/Wilson [1893], 357).

On the basis of this passage Daniélou has argued for a strict theory of universal sin in Gregory. He contends that the term ἀκολουθία, employed here by Gregory, signifies a strictly necessary sequence of events.[99] Thus in Nyssen's view the spreading of sinfulness from the first individual to the entire nature would have been a quasi-physical process.

This may or may not be the case.[100] For the present inquiry, in any event, it seems crucial to ask on which principle this necessary sequence would have been based. Is it the principle of the coherence of universal nature? Gregory does not say so, but he certainly does not expressly contradict this notion either. From what he writes, however, it would appear most likely that Gregory here thinks of *akolouthia* rather as of a principle inherent in evil itself; once evil enters the world it has the tendency to spread further until it reaches its climax.[101]

If, then, *On Virginity* 12 does not necessitate the assumption of universal human nature as fallen and thus responsible for human sinfulness, there are, on the other hand, a number of observations to be made in that chapter which seem to count against such an assumption. To begin with, human nature is employed throughout in connection with God's creation, not with sin.[102] While this would not exclude the possibility that Gregory conceives of it at present as fallen, it certainly does not support it. Moreover, the underlying logic of the passage as part of an ascetic treatise is that the lost beauty of the image ought to be recovered by human endeavour.[103] Yet an interpretation of the Genesis story as implying the inevitable subjection of later humankind to universal sin would be averse to that intent. Finally, Gregory's dependence for his argument at the present

---

[99] Daniélou (1953), 232–3; accepted by Hauke (1993), 646.
[100] This interpretation has an interesting parallel in the liberal interpretation of Gregory's allegedly 'physical' doctrine of salvation; cf. p. 188 below with n. 1 on this problem.
[101] So also, if I understand it, Daniélou (1953), 233.
[102] *Virg* 12 (GNO VIII/1, 298,4, 299,8.10.22;300,6.11.20).
[103] This is made explicit at *virg* 12,2 (GNO VII/1, 300,5–15).

place on Plotinus' *Ennead* I 6[104] may be cited as indicating an influence most unlikely to lead to an adoption of such a theological view.

It thus appears rather unlikely that *On Virginity* 12 presents universal human sinfulness as a consequence of Adam's Fall on the basis of the coherence of universal human nature. Rather, it seems that here and in related texts the underlying logic is that 'nature', as the item created in the image of God has not been substantially altered, but damaged and its beauty obscured by the existence of evil. Gregory obviously follows Neoplatonic thinking here, but perhaps more important is that in those passages his teaching seems most consonant with the special understanding of human nature which was found in his account of creation.

4.2.2   *The Origenist pattern*

A large number of texts certainly do contrast the present with the original state, employing human nature to differentiate between the two. Not all of them, however, make it equally explicit that human nature *qua* universal is the principle of the universality of man's fallen state.

I shall look first at a group of passages which, in my view, do not necessitate the latter assumption. They are characterised by a stark juxtaposition of initial and fallen state, emphasising their *physical* differences. In those texts, I would argue, the Origenist theory of an initial creation of spirits which then fell into corporeality lingers on, although Gregory usually takes care to avoid the underlying anthropological assumption of pre-existent souls. It may therefore be appropriate to approach this aspect of Gregory's teaching by expounding a text, a passage from Gregory's *Homilies on the Song of Songs*, where that Origenist background is, in my reading, more obvious than elsewhere, although this particular text does not primarily deal with the problem of fallen nature.

Towards the end of the commentary, one of his latest by the common reckoning,[105] Gregory explains that the various classes of women mentioned by the bridegroom at Cant 6,8–9 ('There may be sixty princesses, eighty concubines, and young women past counting, but there is only one alone, my dove, my perfect one . . .') refer to

---

[104] Cf. Aubineau (1959), 198–9.
[105] Cf. Daniélou (1966), 168 (after 390); May (1971), 63–4; Dünzl (1994ª), 38–9.

different degrees of perfection amongst human beings. This exegesis calls, in Gregory's view, for a deeper philosophical exposition:

> It is not according to the same sequence and order that the universe is created and then recreated. When, in the beginning, the created nature came into existence through the divine power in each of the existents, the *arche* was co-perfected with the limit (πέρας) without interval (διάστημα); i.e. each of the beings brought from non-being into being received together with its *arche* also its perfection. One of these created beings is human nature; it also did not have to traverse a distance from its inception to its perfection; but, from the beginning of its first existence it was formed in perfection. For it says, Man came to be according to the image of God and his likeness, by which is indicated the utmost good and perfection; for who can find something surpassing that which is in the likeness of God? So then, in the beginning of creation itself the *arche* coincided without interval with the limit (πέρας), and the nature begins its existence from perfection. Afterwards, however, having become subject to death through the relation with evil in departing from remaining in the good, it is no longer, as in the first creation, instantaneously that it receives perfection, but by a kind of road along which it advances towards the greater in accordance with a sequence and order, little by little shedding its propensity for the opposite (of the Good). In the first fashion there was no hindrance or obstacle to prevent the course from the birth to the perfection of the nature, evil not being present, but in the second creation (ἀναστοιχείωσις) by necessity diastematic extension accompanies the reversion to the first good. Because our understanding having been bound together with material propensity due to evil, it is only little by little that it manages to shed itself of the bark or membrane that envelopes it, by a discipline of virtue.[106]

To begin with, it seems evident that the two creations referred to here are not a parallel to the concept of *De Hominis Opificio* 16, but refer to salvation as a second creation.[107] What is special, then, about the present reference to the 'first creation' is the claim that in this creation all beings were created at once, without *diastema*. This is, apparently, in plain contradiction to Gregory's cosmological theory in *Apology on the Hexaëmeron* and *De Hominis Opificio*.[108] A reconciliation with those texts is, in my view, excluded by the contrast which is drawn here between the immediate nature of the first creation, and the sequential nature of the second. That first, instantaneous

---

[106] *Cant* XV (GNO VI, 457,19–459,4), ET: Verghese (1976), 255–6.
[107] Cf. *Eun* III/2 52 (GNO II, 69,22–6).
[108] Cf.: Verghese (1976), 255–6.

creation was possible, according to these lines, because there was as yet no evil, whereas the fallen state of humanity now necessitates a long and painful process towards the restoration of that first creation.

From these lines, then, it would appear that the *pleroma* was actually complete at the first creation but then destroyed on account of the Fall and is now in the process of being restored. There certainly is something within Gregory's writings to support the view that the Fall has damaged cosmic harmony,[109] and thus one could imagine that the difficulty of perceiving the unity of the *pleroma* is also partly due to that event.[110] Nevertheless, it seems to me that ultimately the only explanation of the view expressed in the present passage is the reconstruction of an Origenist background for this particular argument.[111]

While a literary dependence is not easily proven—the extant versions of Origen's commentary break off well before the relevant section[112]—it nevertheless seems, on general considerations, at least likely that Gregory in his commentary was strongly indebted to his great Alexandrian forerunner.[113] From the internal logic of the passage, on the other hand, it would equally appear that the *pleroma* that is created at once in the first creation is a pre-existent community of rational beings of the kind which the theory of *Apology on the Hexaëmeron* and *De Hominis Opificio* 16 had apparently been meant to exclude.

In this framework, however, the universality of the Fall would simply be an inference from the universality of men's corporeal constitution without any further need to prove a descent of Adam's guilt into the entire 'nature'.

The relevance of this observation is, I think, twofold: on the one hand it shows quite clearly that in Gregory's thinking the Origenist equation of the fallen state with corporeality still looms large.[114] There are other passages that appear to make the same point without going as far as the present one in admitting an actually complete creation

---

[109] Cf. *op hom* 12 (PG 44, 161C–D) and Balthasar (1995), 77–8.

[110] Cf. *an et res* (PG 46, 157B): ἐπειδὴ τῇ τῆς κακίας εἰσόδῳ εἰς πλῆθος ἡ φύσις κατεμερίσθη . . .

[111] With Bammel (1989, 83) I think there is no reason to discard completely Origen's well-known allegoric exegesis of the Genesis story.

[112] The explanation of the women as souls is confirmed by an extant Greek fragment (PG 17, 277B–D).

[113] He mentions Origen's commentary in the preface (GNO VI, 13,3–8).

[114] The fact that the most obvious case occurs in his *cant* should forbid the application of developmental theories here; *pace* e.g. Daniélou (1966), 160–1; Kees (1995), 234–6.

in the beginning. Thus, Gregory writes in his book *On the Inscriptions of the Psalms*:

> There was a time when the dance of the rational nature was one, and looked to the one leader of the chorus, and, in its movement in relation to his command, interpreted the choral song in relation to the harmony exhibited thence. But later, when sin occurred, it put an end to that divine concord of the chorus, when it poured the slipperiness of deceit at the feet of the first humans who used to sing in chorus with the angelic powers and caused the Fall, wherefore man was separated from the angels.[115]

It is perhaps not too much to say that, in spite of his reference to the first human beings, Gregory's argument in this passage presupposes a quasi-Origenist conception of pre-existent rational beings. Evidently, the Genesis story is understood allegorically when, a little later in the same context, Gregory writes that 'the one who has fallen might again be restored' (ibid. 11.23–4) thus equating Adam with 'man' in general.[116] At the same time, however, it is clear that Gregory (deliberately, I assume) stops short of committing himself expressly to this interpretation.

The same applies, I would argue, wherever Gregory hints at a non-spatial interpretation of paradise or at any other allegorical interpretation of the Genesis story.[117]

On the other hand, the fact that Gregory thought he could make use of those ideas in spite of his repeated express renunciation of pre-existent spirits would indicate, in my view, that he was not always equally concerned with theories of universal nature. The text from the *Homilies on the Song of Songs* is undoubtedly an exception in that regard. Otherwise, I would argue, references to the 'Origenist paradigm' point to a rather individualistic perspective on the fallen state in the passages in question: it is the individual human being who is reminded by the inferior 'nature' of his present state of his original, spiritual destination. This idea conforms too deeply to Gregory's own existential experience to be purged by whatever doctrinal assimilation.[118]

For the present inquiry this would have the consequence that in many instances Gregory's references to our fallen or sinful 'nature'

---

[115] *Inscr* II 6,60 (GNO V, 86,14–22), ET: Heine (1995), 138–9.
[116] Cf. Origen, *c Celsum* IV 40 (vol. I, 313,14–314,2 Koetschau).
[117] Cf. Hauke (1993), 585–7. Cf. also Gregory's exegesis of Lk 15,4ff. at *Eccl* II (GNO V, 304,23–305,13) which will be discussed on p. 194 below.
[118] Holl (1904), 202–8. Cf., e.g., *an et res* (PG 46, 137B–140B).

could easily be understood in such an individualistic sense without a necessary commitment to universal humanity in whatever inter-pretation.

It is interesting to note how close in Gregory's view the Origenist and the Neoplatonic pattern seem to be; they often appear to coin-cide in his mind. Thus their characterisation as 'patterns' rather than independent 'theories' seems adequate. A good example for this coin-cidence is provided by *On Virginity* 12. In the very chapter that has been shown above to yield the 'Neoplatonic' pattern, Gregory uses notions which clearly indicate the Origenist pattern; notably he alludes to the celebrated 'tunics of skin' (Gen 3,21).

4.2.3   *The Apollinarian pattern*

There are, however, some texts which seem to require a universal interpretation of human nature as the principle of the universal effect of Adam's Fall. Perhaps the clearest indication of such a view in Nyssen's thought is to be found in one of his homilies *On the Lord's Prayer*. Commenting on the fifth petition, Gregory considers whether someone might rightly feel dispensed from asking for God's forgiveness:

> Let not him who is inclined to such an opinion speak impertinently like that Pharisee who did not even know his own nature. For had he known that he was a human being, he would have learned from Holy Scripture that his nature was by no means free from defilement (ῥύπος), for it says that there cannot be found among men one who lives one day without stain (Job 14,4–5) ... The passage enjoins us not to look at the things which have been accomplished but to call to mind the common debt of human nature in which even he would have a share, participating as a part in the common nature, and to beseech the Judge to grant forgiveness of sins.
>
> For since Adam is living in us, we all, the individual human beings (οἱ καθ' ἕκαστον ἄνθρωποι), see each and all these tunics of skin (Gen 3,21) round our nature, and also the transitory fig leaves of this mate-rial life which we have badly sewn together for ourselves after being stripped of our resplendent garments (...) For even though one be a Moses or a Samuel, or any other man of outstanding virtue, in so far as he is man, he does not consider these words less fitting for him-self, seeing that he shares Adam's nature and participates in his exile. For since, as the Apostle says, 'in Adam we all die,' (1 Cor 15,22) the words that are suited to Adam's penance are rightly applied to all who have died with him.[119]

---

[119] *Or dom* V (GNO VII/2, 64,14–65,5; 66,8–15), ET: Graef (1954, 76–7), with amendments.

It seems clear that Gregory here claims that 'participating' (μετέχειν) in human nature is tantamount to sharing in Adam's Fall. In what sense could that be conceived of? The text does not give an unequivocal answer, but several hints all point into the same direction. The crucial phrase is, I think, 'Adam is living in us': here, I would argue, we are confronted for the first time in Nyssen with the view, well known from Apollinarius and others, that partaking of human nature equals 'being a descendant of Adam'. While the text does not explicitly develop that theory it would be an unlikely coincidence that Adam is mentioned here in so obvious a connection with 'being a human being'. This interpretation is further supported by the phrase 'Adam's nature' (ἡ φύσις τοῦ 'Αδάμ), which seems to presuppose the terminological equivalence of 'Adam' and 'man'. Also interesting is the reference given here to 1 Cor 15,22 as this Pauline passage has been shown to be one of the roots of the derivative interpretation of human nature (p. 129 above).

Taken in isolation, the line about Adam's living in us could perhaps also be interpreted as pointing to the Origenist pattern. Allowing an allegorical interpretation of the Genesis story, one might argue that each of us is Adam in so far as we all repeat his transgression. For this interpretation one could draw on the mention of the 'tunics of skin' (Gen 3,21) in connection with our fallen state: our present material state in itself would thus be evidence enough for an earlier Fall for which, however, we ourselves are strictly responsible.

It seems to me, however, that such an interpretation of the present passage should not be upheld. The present text refers quite explicitly to universal nature in whose debt each human individual shares as its part. I should thus conclude that Gregory here employs universal human nature to press home a universal debt which humankind is said to owe to God on account of Adam's original sin. It appears most likely that the underlying conception of the unity of human nature is the derivative theory identifying Adam with man.

For a theological evaluation of this argument it is, I think, decisive to see that Gregory does not primarily wish to rule out the possibility of individual sinlessness.[120] Still less does he strive to construct a theory that would be in opposition to his understanding of human free will. He cites the universal affection of human nature from the sin of Adam in order to explain why every human being can be called to pray the fifth petition of the Lord's Prayer. We have to

---

[120] Although he gets close to that position by his reference to Job 14,4–5.

call to mind here that ὄφλημα, the word Gregory employs following the Matthean text of that petition, would in the Greek not naturally be understood as 'sin' but means 'debt'. What Gregory wishes
to show by adducing the common heritage of human nature, therefore, is not that each human individual inevitably sins during his
earthly life nor that sinfulness has become a property of the nature,
but only that on account of Adam's Fall human nature owes, as it
were, a collective debt to its creator.[121] This comes out quite clearly,
I think, from the fact that a little later in the same oration Gregory
all but dismisses his earlier argument about sinful nature as irrelevant for the interpretation of the biblical passage on the grounds
that *in fact* each human being ought to be able to think of some
fault in his own life.[122] He does apparently make a much sharper
distinction between the debt of the nature and the individual sins of
human beings than the West would become wont to do in the
Augustinian tradition.

It would also appear evident that Gregory in the present passage
sees the 'tunics of skin' and physical death as consequences of Adam's
sin. This, I think, indicates a further problem which may well explain
why Gregory here and elsewhere feels the need to speak of fallen
humanity in 'physical' language. For both, those 'tunics'—whatever
precisely they may have meant with him[123]—and death—if the latter is not included in the former[124]—would appear to be features of
human nature now, but were obviously not intended by God for his
image. That is, in some sense fallen humanity is a reality. Gregory,
it is true, often seems to deny this implicitly: in the present passage,
for example, he formulates that the tunics are 'round' (περί) the
nature, thus stopping short of their mutual identification. Elsewhere
his use of phrases like 'mixture with evil'[125] and 'being together with
evil'[126] as well as the frequent 'medical' terminology[127] might be
thought to make the same point. Nevertheless, he has to admit (if
only on the basis of Ro 5 and 1 Cor 15) that, in the present life at

[121] So already Origen, *orat* 28,3 (376,22–377,16 Koetschau).
[122] *Or dom* V (GNO VII/2, 66,18–23). Cf. Walther (1914), 41–3.
[123] Cf. the varying interpretations at *virg* 13,1 (GNO VIII/1, 303,15–6); *or dom*
V (GNO VII/2, 65,3–9); *an et res* (PG 46, 148C); see also: Kees (1995), 231–5.
[124] At *or cat* (8) (GNO III/4, 30,9–12) the tunics are said to be mortality. Cf.
Kees (1995), 142.
[125] E.g. *cant* IV (GNO VI, 100,16–9); *or cat* (8,3) (GNO III/4, 29,15–6); *Eun* III/3
52 (GNO II,126,11–4).
[126] *Or dom* IV (GNO VII/2, 45,23–4).
[127] E.g. *ep* 3,17 (GNO VIII/2, 24,19–24).

least, death is 'natural' for human beings on account of Adam's Fall.[128] Yet, if this is granted, the consequence must be that human nature was indeed changed in Adam and as such a 'fallen' item passed on to later generations. It would appear, however, as has been argued above, that to explain such a theological given the derivative understanding of humankind's unity, identifying the first individual with the universal item, was specially suitable. There is thus some logic in Gregory's resorting to that theory in the present context.

There are indications that the same view underlies other passages dealing with fallen nature. Those would first of all include texts where reference is made to the descent (διαδοχή) as the principle of transmission since the latter term was found to be of central importance in Apollinarius' exposition of the derivative theory.[129] The same may be true of passages where Gregory cites the Pauline Adam-Christ typology.[130] However, in all those cases certainty cannot be reached.

I should thus conclude that at least in one passage, where Gregory uses human nature in a universal sense to argue for the universal impact of Adam's Fall, it seemed likely that he fell back to the otherwise rejected view that all human beings are Adam. While that text thus testifies that Gregory could make use of universal nature in connection with the Fall, it certainly does not support the systematic interpretation of Gregory's views on human nature, as there was no sign that he attempted an application of his own genuine theory to this doctrinal question. Other texts mentioning or implying universal nature as the principle of the fallen state may presuppose the same view, but do not make this explicit.

In summary, then, the following patterns employed for the explanation of the present, fallen and sinful state of humankind are to be discerned:

(i) At times Gregory seems to think in a quasi-Neoplatonic way of a necessary sequence inherent in the nature of evil itself. This view does not appear to employ universal human nature to explain the universality of the fallen state. For this and other reasons it seemed to fit best with Gregory's previously analysed understanding of human nature.

---

[128] *Or cat* (13) (GNO III/4, 41,9–10): γέννησίς τε καὶ θάνατος ἴδιον τῆς σαρκικῆς ἐστὶ φύσεως. Cf. *or cat* (16) (GNO III/4, 49,10–2).

[129] *Tunc et ipse* (GNO III/2, 11,16–9); *beat* VI (GNO VII/2, 145,6–10).

[130] E.g. *or cat* (16) (GNO III/4, 48,21–4).

(ii) Under the influence of Origenist views Gregory contrasts the present material state with an original state which often seems more or less clearly immaterial. Thus, the universality of the fallen state would be inferred from the universality of that material constitution.

(iii) Citing universal human nature as proof that human beings generally shared in the Fall of Adam, Gregory apparently draws on the otherwise rejected Apollinarian theory of a derivative unity of the descendants of Adam.

A further view might be identified in *De Hominis Opificio* 16 where Gregory all but says that God himself created the 'fallen' state in anticipation of the Fall.

From this it would appear that Gregory has strong views about the fallen state and its universality. However, only in one group of texts (the third in the above list) he clearly connects this with a theory of fallen, universal nature. In those texts, however, he appeared to draw on an understanding of this universal item which is otherwise alien to his thinking. It may be pointed out that he nowhere gets close to as explicit an exposition of this question as he would give in the context of creation.

I should thus conclude that the present survey has not shown a systematic use of universal human nature in Gregory's elaboration on the fallen state of man, that is such a use as would draw on the elaborate theory developed in the context of trinitarian theology and cosmology. This, I think, would most naturally indicate that Gregory felt that that theory could not be applied to the present doctrinal topic.

CHAPTER FIVE

HUMAN NATURE IN GREGORY'S
SOTERIOLOGY AND ESCHATOLOGY

Given the heterogeneous nature of Gregory's utterances concerning the fallen state of human nature, his teaching on soteriology should be expected to be similarly diverse. And this, I shall argue, is indeed the case. As in Gregory's doctrine of the Fall, so in his soteriology we find patterns indicating a variety of approaches to this question. Some of those seem to correspond more or less precisely to those patterns that were discerned in connection with the Fall: thus following his quasi-Neoplatonic theory of the Fall, Gregory is able to argue that on account of their retained faculty of free will, human beings can return to their original purity by means of ethical and ascetic endeavour. Christ, in this view, is the perfect human being, whom it is the task of Christians to imitate.

The influence of what I called the Origenist pattern can be perceived where Gregory's emphasis is primarily on the restoration of an initial, perfect state of creation which sometimes seems to imply incorporeality. Those two patterns occur together in soteriology even more often than in Gregory's treatment of the Fall.

The 'Apollinarian' theory of universal nature as fallen in Adam again seems to correspond to a soteriological view which treats of Christ as of the *arche* of a new humankind, equating the Church with his body.

In none of those patterns, however, does universal human nature seem to be conceptually relevant for Gregory's soteriological thinking. That is, neither the reality nor the universality of salvation depend in those views on the fact that human nature is ontologically a unity, except in the sense that, on account of its creation as a potential *pleroma*, its final *apokatastasis* is, strictly speaking, ontologically necessary. This latter fact, however, is part of, and will be discussed in connection with, Gregory's eschatological views. In texts echoing Apollinarius' views, again, universal human nature is used as an analogy for, not as the principle of, germinal origin and subsequent development of saved humankind, the Church.

Thus, I shall argue that, as far as these patterns are concerned, there is no reason to think that Gregory makes any conceptual use of universal human nature in his soteriology. What is more, the underlying approach to soteriology, an approach which I shall term 'humanistic', is often the same in all three patterns: they concur in seeing human salvation as a task primarily achieved by men's imitation of Christ's perfection. I shall thus feel entitled to treat all three patterns as closely connected in Gregory's mind.

There are, however, texts that appear to witness an altogether different approach to soteriology. In them Gregory seems to say that Christ, by mixing his divinity with universal human nature, has secured salvation for all human beings in so far as they all partake of universal human nature. He would thus have made the universality of human nature the principle of universal salvation. Those passages have attracted considerable scholarly attention in the past, earning Gregory some notoriety as featuring prominently in the development of a so-called 'physical doctrine of salvation'.[1]

For a start it may be useful to ask what kind of soteriology would qualify as 'physical' in this sense? The mere use of *phusis*-terminology would clearly not suffice. What Harnack and others found 'physical' about, for example, Irenaeus' and Athanasius' soteriology was the notion that God had to become *flesh* in order to save man's *phusis*, that is, man's bodily constitution: 'he became man in order that we might become divine' (Athanasius, *inc* 54,3). This soteriology is, in Harnack's neo-Kantian language, physical, not ethical, as the basis of human salvation is thought to be a change in physical constitution.[2]

This soteriology, it appears, was originally developed by Irenaeus to counter Gnostic docetism.[3] He cited the 'physical' need for human beings to be saved from corruption to support his insistence on a 'real' Incarnation of which all men are equally in need. It was not his intention, though, to argue on this basis for universal salvation. His 'physical' soteriology, then, emphasises the *universal* character of human nature only in as much as this universality is needed to maintain that all humanity is equally in need and capable of salvation through Christ. Neither Irenaeus nor, indeed, Athanasius or Apollinarius

---

[1] Harnack (1894) vol. III, 295–300; cf. Hübner (1974, 3–9) for an account of the history of this interpretation.
[2] Harnack (1894) vol. III, 164–5, n. 2.
[3] Cf. Meijering (1975), 39–51.

were interested in arguing that on account of Christ's Incarnation the *entirety* of humankind was actually saved, nor that it would be. None of them was a universalist,[4] they all saw, in principle, salvation as real only within the Church.[5] Salvation of human nature in this tradition, then, is a means of pressing home the soteriological need for a 'real', non-docetic Incarnation, not the universal effect of Incarnation.

It is to this latter effect, however, that the salvation of human nature is apparently employed in some of Gregory's writings. For while in a substantial proportion of his work Gregory seems largely independent of that 'physical' tradition, where he uses it, he appears especially interested in its universalist potential. His physical soteriology, then, cannot simply be equated with, let alone be derived from, Irenaeus, Athanasius, or Apollinarius. Two facts, then, have to be explained: first, Gregory's use of the 'physical' tradition in some writings; secondly, his universalist interpretation of that tradition.

For an explanation of the former, I shall start from chronological observations. It appears that the earliest relevant passages occur in writings belonging to the context of the Eunomian controversy. The topic recurs in Gregory's anti-Apollinarian *Antirrheticus* and in the apologetics of the *Catechetical Oration*. By way of a detailed analysis of the relevant passages I shall, then, attempt to demonstrate that and how the argumentative needs of those doctrinal contexts caused Gregory to fall back on the Irenaean and Athanasian tradition. As for the latter fact, I shall suggest that it was Gregory's own, genuine interest in universal salvation which seduced him to give that universalist twist to the 'physical' tradition.

I shall, therefore, argue that Gregory's 'physical' soteriology in some writings is to be understood as a combination of elements that are genuine to his thinking, universal resurrection and salvation that is, with the Irenaean and Athanasian tradition asserting that Christ had to become *flesh* in order to save humanity. It is not, however, the systematic consequence of his concept of universal human nature.

Accordingly, it will prove useful to structure the present chapter

---

[4] For Irenaeus see Ludlow (1996), 22–4; for Athanasius, Kelly (1958), 379. Cf. pp. 137–142 above.

[5] An exception may be found in Irenaeus' argument (against Tatian) that Adam is saved (*haer* III 23 [vol. III/2, 444–68 Rousseau/Doutreleau]) and, in Athanasius, at *inc* 9 (154 Thompson). But the latter text is, by any standard, not unequivocal: is it more than the *possibility* of universal salvation which Athanasius wishes to assert?

as follows: I shall deal first with Gregory's humanistic approach to soteriology, including elements of the three patterns sketched above. After this I shall expound the relevance, within the same framework, of universal human nature for Gregory's eschatology and his understanding of the *apokatastasis*. Finally, I shall turn to those passages which appear to employ physical concepts, starting from a chronological consideration ascertaining the probable order of the writings concerned and proceeding to an analysis of relevant texts.

5.1   *The 'humanistic' solution: salvation through imitation of Christ*

The 'Neoplatonic' pattern of the Fall seems to lead directly to a concept of salvation along the following lines: human beings can be saved if they recover the divine image which they still have within themselves. This they can achieve by means of imitating the divine for which they have the capacity on account of their retained faculty of free will and rational thinking. Thus Gregory, commenting on Ps 89,3 ('And you have said, Be converted sons of men'), writes:

> An utterance such as this is a precept, for the command takes our nature into account and proposes the cure for our evils. For, he says, since you fell away from the good because you are changeable, submit yourselves to the good again by means of change. Return again to the same thing from which you have fallen away, since the power of freely allotting to themselves whatever they wish, whether the good or the bad, lies in the power of human choice.[6]

God supports human beings towards that end by sending his Holy Spirit[7] and, first of all, by the Incarnation of Christ. The relevance of the latter event consists in this view primarily in the establishment of a sinless individual human being whose perfect imitation of the divine Christians are called to imitate.

Human nature as a universal does not appear to be of any immediate relevance in the context of this approach; this is not surprising: universal nature had not fallen and was thus not as such in need of salvation either.

This view of salvation has its proper place in Gregory's ascetic writings. To cite but one example from his writing *De Perfectione*:

---

[6] *Inscr* I 7 (GNO V, 46,22–47,1), ET: Heine (1995), 104.
[7] Cf. Jaeger (1954), 101–21.

Accordingly, this Person who is beyond knowledge and comprehension (sc. the second Person of the Trinity), the ineffable and the 'unspeakable' (1 Pet 1,8) and the 'inexpressible', (~ 2 Cor 9,15) in order that he might again make you an 'image of God', because of his love for man, *became* himself an 'image of the invisible God' so that he by his own form which he assumed be formed inside you and you through himself be again made like the beauty of the archetype, as you have been from the beginning. Therefore, if we also are to become an 'image of the invisible God', it is fitting that the form of our life be struck according to the 'example' (~ John 13,15) of the life set before us. But what is that? It is living in the flesh, but not 'according to the flesh'. (Ro 8,12) The archetypal 'image of the invisible God', born of the virgin, was tempted in all ways like human nature, except that unlike us he did not undertake any attempt to sin (cf. Hebr 4,15): 'Who did no sin, neither was deceit found in his mouth.' (1 Pet 2,22) Therefore, just as when we are learning the art of painting, the teacher puts before us on a panel a beautifully executed model, and it is necessary for each student to imitate in every way the beauty of that model on his own panel, so that panels of all will be adorned in accordance with the example of the beauty set before them; in the same way, since every person is the painter of his own life, and choice is the craftsman of the work, and the virtues are the paints for executing the image, there is no small danger that the imitation may change the prototype (. . .). But, *since it is possible*, one must prepare the pure colours of the virtues, (. . .) so that we become an image of the image, having achieved the beauty of the prototype through activity as a kind of imitation, as did Paul, who became an 'imitator of Christ' (1 Cor 4,16) through his life of virtue.[8]

This passage is not isolated. It is set within a writing dedicated to show on the basis of scriptural proof texts that to be a Christian means to imitate Christ and that, therefore, becoming like him ought to be the aim of every Christian. The present passage, then, applies this principle to Col 1,15 which is, strikingly but in line with Gregory's trinitarian views, understood to refer to Christ's humanity: in the Incarnation the Logos became an image of God in order to restore human beings to their original image character. It also seems plain that this restoration is contemplated here on the basis of imitation: like pupils, who learn to paint by looking at a well-drawn picture, human beings ought to learn perfection in the virtuous life from the perfect example set before them by Christ. That this result can possibly be reached is expressly stated and employed as a means of

---

[8] *Perf* (GNO VIII/1, 194,14–196,15), ET: Woods Callahan (1967), 110f. (amended; italics mine).

exhortation. This optimism is, I think, not primarily a result of Gregory's belief in human free will, but reveals the assumption of an undestroyed core of godlike human nature as underlying this argument: no 'substantial' change needs to be made to this nature; rather the 'mud', to use the language of *De Virginitate*, covering the nature and obscuring its image-character has to be cleansed.

With regard to the underlying christology it appears that Gregory's soteriology in this and similar passages is primarily based on the assumption of the saviour's perfect humanity. His divinity, on the other hand, does not seem to be of crucial importance. Gregory, it is true, formulates in the above text that God *becomes* an image of God. Yet, what does this mean? It does not mean, I think, that Christ's salvific function is based on the presence of divine substance in humanity. Humanity is always in need of divine assistance for achieving perfection, and thus Christ's humanity could not have reached that end without divine support. Yet, this support consists, in philosophical language, in participation (μετουσία), not in identity. If we ask which of these two notions Gregory's soteriology, as expressed in the above passage, presupposes, it would seem difficult to avoid the conclusion that it is the former. This, however, makes the relation between human and divine in Christ *in principle* the same as that in human beings in general. Gregory, to be sure, would point out that in Christ this participation reaches a degree which is un-equalled amongst human beings, nor can it be equalled. He might also insist that imitation of Christ means eventually imitation of God.

The latter point, however, does not really count against the present interpretation, for it is after all Christ's (the man's) imitation of God which we are called to imitate, thus becoming, in the language of the above passage, 'an image of an image'. As for the former, I should contend that, a gradual difference admitted, the principle is still the same. Gregory's christology, then, appears here inevitably 'divisive'.[9]

This finding may not be considered surprising. The 'humanistic' character of this soteriological approach, as I referred to it above, seems to be bound up with a view of the saviour along those lines. Gregory is here following in the footsteps of Origen, whom Chadwick has once called an (illiberal) humanist.[10] According to Origen, the

---

[9] For the term cf. Grillmeier (1975), 299 and passim.
[10] Chadwick (1966), 66.

Logos, the second Person of the Trinity, unites himself to one rational being that has not fallen alongside the others and, therefore, has retained a share of its original participation in the Logos.[11] This rational being then, united with the Logos on the basis of mutual love, descends into human beings. Like the philosopher in Plato's simile of the cave[12] it enters the realm of darkness in order to lead human beings, who are imprisoned there, back towards their original home in communion with God.

For Origen the principle of union between the Logos and the human soul of Christ is participation, the same principle that would exist between all rational beings and God had they all remained in their original state. The union itself is, of course, of an intensity surpassing any comprehension, like that of iron in a white-hot-fire,[13] but again this does not seem to impinge on the principal issue.[14]

It seems evident that the broad outlines of Gregory's views concur with those of Origen's. In particular, the coincidence of christological and soteriological views is remarkable: in both the perfect humanity of the saviour is crucial, since the process of salvation consists first of all in men's imitation of Christ. In both concepts, again, imitation of Christ is ultimately imitation of God, the latter imitation being thought of as ontological participation and as such the basis of the creatures' existence. In both, finally, we have a divisive christology; a real Incarnation is not achieved.

It is interesting then, to see that Origen himself was able to employ *phusis*-terminology in the context of soteriology:

> Christians see that with Jesus human and divine nature began to be woven together (συνυφαίνεσθαι), so that by fellowship with divinity human nature might become divine, not only in Jesus, but also in all those who believe and go on to undertake the life which Jesus taught, the life which leads everyone who lives according to Jesus' commandments to friendship with God and fellowship with Jesus.[15]

---

[11] *Princ* II 6 (139,3–147,19 Koetschau).

[12] See e.g. his *c Celsum* I 51 (vol. I, 102,11–6 Koetschau); also: IV 15 (vol. I, 285,16–22 Koetschau) with its 'verbal allusion to Plato, *Republic* 518A' (Chadwick's note on the passage [1953, 194]), and in general Meredith (1991), 53–6. For Gregory cf.: Daniélou (1966), 160–1.

[13] *Princ* III 6,6 (145,5–24 Koetschau).

[14] Cf. Grillmeier (1975), 146–7.

[15] *C Celsum* III 28 (vol. I, 226,13–8 Koetschau); ET: Chadwick (1953), 146.

If it is allowed (with Chadwick)[16] that salvation is here understood
as deification, it seems, nevertheless, evident that the deification of
human nature implied in this passage is altogether different from
the concept underlying the thought of, for example, Irenaeus and
Athanasius: it is 'by fellowship' that human nature becomes divine,
which undoubtedly means 'by fellowship with Jesus'. Deification,
then, is a name given to the change human beings undergo once
they decide to orient their lives towards the divine.

At the same time it seems clear that 'human nature' here does
not bear any universal sense; the text emphasises not the universality of salvation, but the real, quasi-substantial change made to human
beings (to their 'nature') in the process of salvation. Those changes
would probably not consist of any visible alterations, let alone of the
loss of corporeality; the respective person simply becomes different.

For a very similar approach in Gregory one may compare the
following passage from his second *Homily on Ecclesiastes*. Commenting
on Ecclesiastes 1,15b ('what is not there cannot be counted'), Gregory
writes:

> What does he mean by this sentence? He means that our humanity
> too was once counted within the totality of existence; for we too went
> to make up the sacred hundred sheep, the rational beings (cf. Lk 15,4).
> But when the one sheep—our nature—was led astray from the heav-
> enly way by evil, and was dragged down to this parched salty place,
> the flock which had not strayed did not add up to the same number
> as before, but are said to be ninety-nine. (...)
>   Therefore he came to seek and save what was lost (cf. Lk 19,10),
> and, taking it on his shoulders (cf. Lk 15,5), to restore (ἀποκαταστ-
> ῆναι) to those who are (τοῖς οὖσι) what was being lost throught the
> futility of unreal things, so that the totality of God's creation should
> be complete again, when the lost has been restored to those who are
> not lost.[17]

This text provides a good example of how Gregory could employ
the Origenist framework of salvation history without committing himself explicitly to pre-existent souls. As for its soteriology, it seems evident that Gregory embraces the 'humanistic' paradigm. It is by
imitation, by following the path of virtue, that human beings will

---

[16] Chadwick (1966), 92.
[17] *Eccl* II (GNO V, 304,23–305,13); ET: Hall/Moriarty (1993), 52–3, with slight
changes.

retain their original state, as he makes clear in what follows.[18] In particular, there is no hint that the interpretation of human nature as the lost sheep which Christ takes on his shoulders conditions any notion of 'physical' soteriology.

This latter point is somewhat different in some passages which otherwise appear to contain the very same Origenist notions. I shall first cite a text from Gregory's treatise *In illud: Tunc et ipse Filius*, which is entirely dedicated to the exegesis of 1 Cor 15,28. As will be seen later, this treatise shows traces of Origenist influence in more than one way:

> It was born in the mortal, perishable nature of men the pure and unmixed divinity of the Only-begotten. Out of the whole human nature with which the divine was mixed the man in Christ (ὁ κατὰ Χριστὸν ἄνθρωπος) came into being as a first fruits, as it were, of the common batch of dough. Through him the whole human item (πᾶν τὸ ἀνθρώπινον) has grown together (προσφύειν) with the Godhead. As now in him 'who did no sin' as the prophet says (Is 53,9) and 'in whose mouth there was found no guile' (1 Pet 2,22) the whole nature of evil has vanished, death, which follows sin, has vanished in him alongside sin— for there is no other origin of death but sin—and the disappearance of evil and the destruction of death took their beginning (ἀρχή) from him. Then something like an ordered sequence was imposed on the following events on account of a certain ἀκολουθία.[19]

In the present passage, the similarities to the 'Origenist' pattern are remarkable: Christ as the sinless human being has conquered death, which is only the consequence of sin, and thus restored human nature to its original state of sinless incorruptibility. The phrasing ('the human item has grown together with the Godhead') recalls, in fact, the above passage from *Contra Celsum*.

We find a similar reasoning at one place in *Contra Eunomium* III:

> As this now was the centre-piece of our misfortune, that the human item (τὸ ἀνθρώπινον) was alienated from the good Father and sepa- rated from the divine supervision and care, he who tends the whole rational creation left in the heights the unwavering and supermundane flock to follow the lost sheep, human nature I say, out of philanthropy. For human nature is a tiny and indeed the smallest part if judged with respect to the whole, and it is the only one that has deserted— in the parable's enigmatic language—the hundred (sc. sheep) of rational

---

[18] *Eccl* II (GNO V, 305,14–306,9).
[19] *Tunc et ipse* (GNO III/2, 14,8–15,1).

creation through evil. As it was impossible now for our life that was
alienated from God to be lifted up to the lofty and heavenly realm
on its own, therefore, as the apostle says (2 Cor 5,21), 'for our sake
he made him to be sin who knew no sin' and freed us from the curse
by making himself common with our curse and assuming our enmity
to God which is due to sin. And he killed it in himself, as the apostle
says (Eph 2,16),—for the enmity was sin—and became what we will
become through him and rejoined the human item with God.

For it is this new man who was created according to God, in whom
the fullness of the Godhead lived in the flesh (cf. Gal 2,9), whom
he (sc. Christ) has associated with kinship to the Father through purifica-
tion, drawing alongside with him to his own grace all who have community with his body and a nature akin (συγγενῆ). And this good news
he announces through this woman not only to those disciples, but to
all who have by now become disciples of the word as well, that man
is no more among the damned nor thrown out of God's kingdom, but
is again son, again formed by God, in so much as the batch of dough is
hallowed alongside the first fruits of humankind (cf. Ro 11,16). (...)

And the words are not a proof of the degradation of the Son, but
the good news of our reconciliation with God. For that which has
taken place in Christ's humanity is a common benefit bestowed upon
humankind generally.[20]

Here the traces of Gregory's Origenist background are, if anything,
even more visible: the suggestion that humanity is the one sheep
which has left the flock of rational beings recalls the text cited above
from Gregory's *Homilies on Ecclesiastes* and clearly belongs to the
Origenist pattern in Gregory's treatment of the Fall. As for restoration, on the other hand, it is again evident that it is 'by purity' in
the first place that the 'new man' leads human beings back to the
Father.

Yet, in spite of the apparent influence of Origenist thinking in
both those texts, it appears that Gregory's argument in them is not
fully explained referring to his Alexandrian forerunner. In fact, both
texts can be seen as giving a specific twist to that tradition. Origen,
as we have seen, had, in spite of his universalism, not used the notion
of human and divine *nature* being woven together to press home this
latter tenet; his use of *phusis*-terminology was solely a way of expressing the changes made to human beings once they follow Christ.
Gregory, however, in those two passages seems to move in precisely
that direction: he emphasises that Christ's divinity was mixed with

---

[20] *Eun* III/10 11–5 (GNO II, 293,13–294,26).

the 'whole human nature' the 'man in Christ' thus becoming the first fruits of the common batch of dough, i.e. humanity. Also, the mention, at the close of the text cited first, of a necessary sequence shows his interest in a connection of physical terminology with universalism. In the latter passage, again, it appears that the notion of Christ's 'drawing' everything connatural to the Father implies the same interest. It would thus appear that, by giving *phusis* a universal emphasis, Gregory in these texts attempts to give a *physical* foundation to universal salvation. Although this might appear a genuinely Origenist concern—Gregory, after all, employs Origen's *phusis*-terminology to argue for an Origenist tenet, the *apokatastasis*—it seems obvious that Gregory here moves towards an understanding which is ultimately alien to the Origenist, humanistic approach to soteriology.

There are a number of texts which underline the coherence between Christ and his followers drawing on the biblical notion of the Church as the body of Christ. As I noted above, those texts seem to employ the derivative understanding of *ousia*. As an example I shall cite another passage from *De Perfectione*:

> But learning that Christ is the 'head of the Church' (Eph 5,23), let this be considered before all else, that every head is of the same nature (ὁμοφυής) and *homoousios* with the underlying body, and there is a unity (συμφυΐα) of the individual parts with the whole, accomplishing by their common respiration (συμπνοία) a complete sympathy of all the parts. Therefore, if any part is divorced from the body, it also is altogether alienated from the head. Reason tells us that whatever the head is by nature, this the individual parts become, in order to be in communion with the head. But we are the parts who make up the body of Christ (cf. 1 Cor 12,27).[21]

This is perhaps the clearest piece of evidence for Gregory's use of the derivative theory. By combining Eph 5,23 and 1 Cor 12,27 Gregory equates Christ with both the head and the body as a whole. This corresponds to the 'Apollinarian' view, which has been analysed in *De incarnatione et contra Arianos*. It is remarkable that here this relationship is expressly termed *homoousios*, which again concurs with Apollinarius', but not with Gregory's view in the trinitarian context. Salvation, in this view, seems to be guaranteed by inclusion in this body, while at the same time that inclusion depends on individual

---

[21] *Perf* (GNO VIII/1, 197,19–198,4), ET: Woods Callahan (1967, with amendments), 111–2.

decisions. Thus there seems to be a balance of human action and divine support (the 'sympathy' of the parts with the whole) resembling that which was found in previously analysed texts and indicating that, in a sense, the present concept can be seen as part of Gregory's humanistic approach to soteriology.

It should be noted that the consubstantiality mentioned here is not assumed to exist between Christ's and our humanity as such. It is the relationship between Christ and the Christian, between Christ and his Church, which is thus characterised. As in Apollinarius, soteriology thus leads to ecclesiology, the basis of salvation being inclusion in this body. In this context Gregory can use language which is very similar to that of the ps.-Athanasian author of *De incarnatione et contra Arianos*:

> 'This is the day which the Lord made' (Ps 117,24), but different from the days made at the beginning of creation, by which time is measured, this is the beginning (ἀρχή) of another creation. For on this day God makes a new heaven and a new earth, as the prophet says. What heaven? The firmament of faith in Christ. What earth? I mean the good heart, as the Lord said, the earth which drinks the rain which comes on it and ripens plentiful grain. (. . .) In this is created also the true man who is made in the image and likeness of God.[22]

And, similarly, in his Homilies on the Song of Songs:

> For the foundation of the Church is the creation of a world. In that foundation, according to the word of the prophet (cf. Is 65,17), a new heaven is created—which is the firmament of faith in Christ, as Paul says (cf. Col 2,5)—and a new earth, which drinks the rain which comes on it (cf. Hebr 6,7), a new man is formed, who through his birth from above is renewed in the image of him who created him.[23]

The interpretation of the Church's foundation as a creation seems, although not derived from Prov 8,22, very likely to betray the influence of the conception that was found behind *De incarnatione et contra Arianos*.

This soteriological strand, then, seems to be more strongly represented in Gregory's thought than the corresponding notion of a universal Fall. This need not surprise us; after all, it could with ease be fitted into Gregory's humanistic approach. Thus, following the passage I quoted from the *Homilies on the Song of Songs*, he goes on

---

[22] *Trid spat* (GNO IX, 279,5–280,2), ET: Hall (1981), 34–5.
[23] *Cant* XIII (GNO VI, 384,13–385,6).

to describe the constitution of the body of Christ as based on imitation and individual virtues.[24]

While Gregory thus was able to integrate the Apollinarian view of the Church as new humanity into his humanistic approach, it is, on the other hand, plain that the same model *could* also be employed to quite a different end; after all, Apollinarius himself, following Athanasius, had employed it for what was not by any means a humanistic approach to soteriology, arguing that a deified *phusis* had to be passed on from Christ to his believers.

It appears now that in Gregory traces of this latter tendency emerge in some passages. This is, first of all, the case in his treatment of the Eucharist in his *Catechetical Oration*. Arguing that the human body too is in need of salvation Gregory writes there:

> What, then, is this remedy to be? Nothing else than the very body which has been shown to be superior to death, and has begun a (new) life for us. For, in the manner that, as the apostle says (1 Cor 5,6), a little leaven assimilates to itself the whole lump, so in like manner that body to which immortality has been given by God, when it is in ours, translates and transmutes the whole into itself. For as by the admixture of a poisonous liquid with a wholesome one the whole draught is deprived of its deadly effect, so too the immortal body, by being within that which receives it, changes the whole to its own nature.[25]

This text has often been seen as the climax of Gregory's physical soteriology.[26] Yet it seems evident that it is *not* physical in that it would imply the transmission of salvation on the basis of universal humanity. It certainly *is* physical in the sense in which Athanasius' and Apollinarius' thought was, prior to Gregory: the human body (which later in the text is equated with human *phusis*)[27] can only be saved by an injection of divine *phusis*.

While Gregory, if I understand him, does not imply an automatic transmission of salvation on the basis of the homogeneity of Christ's and our humanity,[28] he certainly forsakes his humanistic approach: salvation here is no longer primarily a matter of imitation,

---

[24] *Cant* XIII (GNO VI, 385,6–22).

[25] *Or cat* (37) (GNO III/4, 93,17–94,4); ET: Moore/Wilson (1893), 504–5 (with changes).

[26] Harnack (1894) vol. IV, 296; Hübner (1974), 176.

[27] Cf. GNO III/4, 95,26–96,1; 96,6–9.

[28] He repeatedly names the faith of those receiving the Eucharist (e.g. at GNO III/4, 96,1).

but happens on the basis of that participation in the divine which Christians gain in the sacraments. This conceptual shift cannot have happened by chance: Gregory goes on at some length to describe the exact 'physical', i.e. scientific, basis for this regeneration, thus making it clear that he really means what he writes.[29]

I should thus conclude that in one important strand of Gregory's theology universal human nature is of no conceptual importance for soteriology. Gregory here, in principle, takes over Origen's humanistic approach, arguing that human nature, equipped with freedom of will, enables human beings to decide for the good by following the example set by Christ's humanity. Where in such texts Gregory employs physical terminology it can often be understood as underlining the relevance of the changes made to human beings who decide to alter the course of their lives by modelling them on Jesus.

There have, however, been indications that at some point Gregory would forsake that humanistic approach. This happened in two ways: starting from an Origenist basis Gregory would seem to suggest that universal salvation has something to do with Christ's assumption of universal human nature. On the basis of the 'Apollinarian' model, on the other hand, Gregory was seen to fall back on the latter's emphasis on a salvation of man's corporeal *phusis*.

5.2   *The eschatological restoration of humankind*

With regard to that strand of Gregory's theology which has been analysed in the previous section of the present chapter, it can now be seen that universal human nature has relevance in the context of creation, but not in those of Fall and salvation. This, I have argued, was no coincidence: the very character of the thing created by God at the beginning did not allow for any substantial change to be made to it in the course of salvation history.

Would this, then, indicate that Gregory's attempt, as sketched in the context of his cosmology, to employ human nature in a sense consciously different from Apollinarius', but in line with the views he had developed in the trinitarian context, failed due to its inapplicability to salvation history at large? From the argument devel-

---

[29] *Or cat* (37) (GNO III/4, 94,5–98,7).

oped so far it would appear that this question has to be answered in the negative: Gregory, it is true, cannot show on the basis of 'his' theory of universal human nature that this item fell and was saved, but this, I have argued, was in line with his theological intention. His teaching on human nature as the image of God in *De Hominis Opificio* 16, as well as his frequent statements about the image as obscured, not destroyed, in fallen humanity, seemed into point into this very direction. Consequently, it was the recovery of this image, its cleansing from the mud of sinful passions rather than its reconstitution by a divine Incarnation, which dominated this one strand of his thinking.

The conclusion that can be reached at this point of our enquiry would thus appear to be that in a considerable part of his theological thinking Gregory employs one notion of universal human nature quite consistently and, secondly, that his approach to human nature in this context seems to condition a specific character of his theology.

This conclusion can be underscored, I think, by looking briefly at Gregory's eschatology, since it is here that Gregory's teaching on universal human nature resurfaces. That Gregory's eschatological thinking is founded on the notion of universal restoration (ἀποκατάστασις) is now, it seems, universally recognised.[30] It appears equally plain that this notion is Origenist heritage and that Gregory has preserved its full force including the much-condemned idea of an eventual salvation of the devil.[31] Moreover, as in Origen, restoration in Gregory seems to be based on principal, ontological considerations about God's goodness and the necessary limitation of evil.[32]

In the following I shall explore one strand only of Gregory's teaching on the *apokatastasis*, based on an interpretation of two pivotal passages from his *De Anima et Resurrectione* which seem to relate the notion of *apokatastasis* to that of human nature. I shall attempt to show that, in spite of the overall agreement between Origen and Gregory, the latter goes his own way in that he sees the *apokatastasis* in the strict sense as a restoration of the initial *state* of man only while the *pleroma* of humanity reached in the eschaton is thought of as the necessary result of the development of the germinal perfection of humanity which had been created in Adam.

---

[30] For a comprehensive treatment of this topic see now Ludlow (1996), 12–116.
[31] Ludlow (1996), 74–94.
[32] Holl (1904), 201; 207; Ludlow (1996), 79–83.

The context is Gregory's attempt to demonstrate that his own (or, in the dialogue, Macrina's) definition of the resurrection as 'the reconstitution of our nature in its original form' is perfectly consonant with Paul's celebrated words in 1 Cor 15,36–7. Thus he argues:

> In the beginning, we see, it was not an ear rising from a grain, but a grain coming from an ear (cf. Gen 1,11–2), and, after that, the ear grows round the grain: and so the order indicated in this (sc. Paul's) similitude clearly shows that all that blessed state which arises for us by means of the resurrection is only a return to our pristine state of grace. (. . .)
>
> The first man Adam, that is, was the first ear; but with the arrival of evil human nature was diminished into a mere multitude; and, as happens to the grain on the ear, each individual man was denuded of the form of that primal ear, and mouldered into the soil: but in the resurrection we are born again in our original splendour; only instead of that single primitive ear we become the countless myriads of ears in the cornfields.[33]

This passage illustrates quite well the difficulties Gregory incurs by adopting Origen's eschatological framework. For with Gregory the resurrection is a restoration of the initial state only in a limited and qualified sense: while it is supposed to return the blessings possessed by the first human beings ('their nature') it does not (or, at least, ought not) reconstitute the initial perfection of a *pleroma* of humanity.[34]

That Gregory is aware of this problem is, I think, indicated by the tension which exists between the two paragraphs of the quotation. Gregory starts from what appears to be a cyclic notion of salvation history: an ear at the beginning, an ear at the end; this is the logic of the *apokatastasis*. Where he mentions Adam, however, he changes the metaphor into that of an ear being first multiplied into single grains which in turn produce a multitude of ears. This, it appears, is no more a real *apokatastasis* since the outcome is not identical with the beginning.

Incidentally, this ambiguity in Gregory's present argument is indicative, in my view, of a more general ambiguity in his thinking: man's Fall from his initial state into 'a mere multitude' seems to hover between a fateful accident and an ontological necessity. It is true,

---

[33] *An et res* (PG 46, 256D–257B), ET: Moore/Wilson (1893), 467.
[34] Cf. Daniélou (1970, 205) '"La résurrection n'est rien d'autre que la restauration de l'état primitif" *au sense où elle est l'accomplissement du dessein de Dieu*' (italics mine).

and the present passage asserts this quite clearly, that ever since Adam human beings have been bereft of the original beauty of the image of God. At the same time it would appear that this development from the one ear into the multitude of the cornfield also has the momentum of necessity to it.

As regards the meaning of *phusis*, I should contend (as I have done in connection with the Fall, p. 181 above) that Nyssen consciously ignores its universal aspect where he employs this term in a quasi-Origenist context. The '*apokatastasis* of our *phusis* in its original form' would thus refer exclusively to the restoration of man's original state of communion with God with no universal implications whatever.[35]

That the universal character of human nature, nevertheless, is relevant for Gregory's eschatology is apparent in an earlier text from the same writing:

> Since every intellectual reality is fixed in a plenitude (πλήρωμα) of its own, it is reasonable to expect that humanity also will arrive at a goal (for in this respect also humanity is not to be parted from the intelligible world); so that we are to believe that it will not be visible for ever only in defect, as it is now: for this continual addition of after generations indicates that there is something deficient in our race.
>
> Whenever, then, humanity will have reached the plenitude that belongs to it, this on-streaming movement of production will altogether cease; it will have touched its destined bourn and a new order of things quite distinct from the present procession of births and deaths will carry on the life of humanity. If there is no birth, it follows necessarily that there will be nothing to die. (. . .) Therefore, if we are to go upon probabilities, the life after this is shown to us beforehand as something that is fixed and imperishable, with no birth and no decay to change it.[36]

This passage is interesting for a number of reasons. To begin with, Gregory here goes further than he normally would in all but asserting that the resurrection is a necessary consequence of the development of human nature into a *pleroma*. This is elsewhere clearly attributed to a further activity on the part of the Deity.[37]

It would appear that the link established here between the development of humankind into a *pleroma* and eschatology is in line with the notion of universal human nature that was detected in Gregory's

---

[35] That the phrase ἀποκατάστασις is with Gregory as yet no technical term has been shown by Ludlow (1996), 30–6.
[36] *An et res* (PG 46, 128C–D), ET: Moore/Wilson (1893), 459.
[37] *Op hom* 25 (PG 44, 221B–224B).

cosmology. There it had been stated that the creation of human nature implied the creation of 'man' who, *qua pleroma*, has his measure like the individual.[38] This *pleroma* had initially been visible to the foresight of God only, but this would imply (or so, at least, I have argued) that its quantitative development is actually determined by God. What we find here, then, seems to be no more than an eschatological application of that theory: since humankind was created as a germinal *pleroma*, its development is bound to stop at some point.

At the same time, this framework also helps us understand why Gregory apparently thinks he can quasi-deduce the reconstitution of the original *state* of blessedness from that *physical* necessity: *pleroma* is, after all, a heavily charged term implying more than mere numerical fulfilment.[39] If the development into a *pleroma* is a law of our *phusis*, then, we may understand, this ultimately includes perfection in every sense; the *pleroma* simply would not be a *pleroma* without a restoration of man's initial state including incorruptibility.

I should thus conclude that in his eschatology, unlike in his teaching on Fall and salvation, Gregory resumes that view of universal human nature which he had developed in his cosmological writings and which had been shown to be in principal agreement with his line of argument in the trinitarian context. It would, then, appear that, as I indicated above, Gregory's application to the economy of this (his genuine) view of universal nature is indicative of a theology strongly emphasising creation, eschatology and the universal presence of the divine more than strict notions of universal sin and salvation through Incarnation.

5.3   *Gregory's use of soteriological theories based on universal human nature*

It remains, then, to submit to somewhat closer scrutiny those texts which have given rise to the charge of a physical soteriology. Since they are to be found in one group of Gregory's writings only, it may be appropriate to start from a brief consideration of chronology.

The writings concerned are the following: *In illud: Tunc et ipse Filius, Contra Eunomium* III, *Refutatio confessionis Eunomii, Antirrheticus adversus*

---

[38] *Op hom* 16 (PG 44, 185B).
[39] About its background see Gregorios (1980), 185–6.

Apolinarium, and *Oratio Catechetica*. Of those writings only one can be dated with a high degree of certainty: the *Refutatio* was written by Gregory as a reply to the creed Eunomius had forwarded to the emperor at the 383 synod in Constantinople.[40] It seems evident, then, that it was written soon after that synod, in the latter half of the same year.

The third volume of Gregory's great anti-Eunomian work is usually assumed to be of an earlier date. At the same time we have a *terminus post quem* in the Constantinopolitan Council of 381 if Jerome's note about Nyssen's reading from his books against Eunomius to him there[41] is understood to refer to the first two books only.[42] If it is, then, likely that Gregory resumed his anti-Eunomian polemic as soon as he could after the council, we may assume that the third book was written in 381/2.

The brief treatise *In illud: Tunc et ipse Filius* was, apparently, prompted by the Eunomian controversy too. At *Contra Eunomium* I 193 (GNO I, 83,13–4) Gregory remarks that a more detailed investigation of 1 Cor 15,28 would be desirable. *Tunc et ipse*, then, which carries out this intent, would have *Contra Eunomium* I as a *terminus post quem*. It would, on the other hand, appear likely that Gregory carried out his plan fairly soon after the completion of the anti-Eunomian writing. I should tend to place *Tunc et ipse* prior to *Contra Eunomium* III in 381,[43] but there is, of course, no knowing about its exact date.

As for Gregory's anti-Apollinarian *Antirrheticus*, scholarly opinion is divided. Lietzmann argued in his seminal study on Apollinarius that Gregory would probably not have written his extensive *Antirrheticus* prior to his anti-Apollinarian letter to Theophilus which betrays, in his view, only superficial knowledge of the Apollinarian heresy. As the latter, however, presupposes Theophilus' episcopate, which commenced only in 385, the latter date has to be regarded as a *terminus post quem* for the *Antirrheticus* which would thus fall into the latter half of the 380s.[44]

It seems to me, however, that Lietzmann's argument does not hold. The letter to Theophilus and the *Antirrheticus* are quite different

---

[40] Cf. Jaeger (1954), 83–4.
[41] Jerome, *vir ill* 128 (*PL* 23, 713B).
[42] Jaeger (1954), 81–2.
[43] So also Hübner (1974), 31.
[44] Lietzmann (1904), 83–4; accepted by Mühlenberg (1968), 90–1 and May (1966), 125–6; (1971), 61.

in both purpose and form; the former is about 'Apollinarians', who are regarded as a dangerous, schismatic group. The *Antirrheticus*, on the other hand, does not mention Apollinarians at all; indeed the writing does not seem to be concerned about Apollinarius as a schismatic in the first place but treats him rather as a uniquely wayward individual, a wolf in sheep's clothing, as Basil had done before.[45] Gregory had no reason, I think, to indicate to Theophilus any detailed knowledge he may have had about Apollinarian theology.

While there is thus no compelling reason to assign to the *Antirrheticus* a date after 385, some observations seem to make a date prior to the *Refutatio* likely. This is first of all the case with Lebourlier's comparison of some texts referring to the state of Christ between death and resurrection.[46] Following hints by Daniélou,[47] Lebourlier argued, convincingly in my view, that the use made of this notion in those texts would indicate their chronological order, thus arriving at a relative chronology of the respective works. Interestingly, most of the writings discussed by Lebourlier are amongst those which are at present relevant:[48] their chronological order is, according to him,[49] as follows: *Contra Eunomium* III, *Antirrheticus adversus Apolinarium*, *Refutatio confessionis Eunomii*, *Oratio Catechetica*. Applying the fixed dates reached above the *Antirrheticus* would thus fall into 382/3.

As for the *Oratio Catechetica* there is not much to assist its dating. A very full consideration of this question in a recent monograph has not yielded strikingly new results.[50] At one place Gregory refers to doctrinal works of both a controversial and an uncontroversial nature which he says he has written on the Trinity.[51] This would indicate a date after his anti-Eunomian writings. If those include the *Refutatio*, the *Oratio* might be placed in the vicinity of the year 385, not too long, I think, after the *Refutatio*.

The chronology at which we thus arrive would be as follows: 381 *In illud*, 381/2 *Contra Eunomium* III, 382/3 *Antirrheticus*, 383 *Refutatio*,

---

[45] Cf. Basil, *ep* 263,4 (vol. III, 124–5 Courtonne); *ep* 265,2 (vol. III, 128–31 Courtonne); 244,3 (vol. III, 76–7 Courtonne).

[46] Lebourlier (1962/63); accepted by Hübner (1974, 135–6, n. 166); Wickham (1981, 279–82); now also Mühlenberg (1978, 364,44–50). Critical: Maraval (1987).

[47] Daniélou (1958).

[48] Lebourlier's account also includes Gregory's *ep* 3 and his Easter sermon *trid spat*.

[49] Lebourlier (1963), 178–80.

[50] Kees (1995), 201–8.

[51] *Or cat* (38) (GNO III/4, 98,8–16).

after 383 *Oratio Catechetica*. All those writings thus seem to have been written in a comparatively brief time span of perhaps not much more than three years.

In those years, I believe, we see Gregory develop a specific kind of physical soteriology which is chiefly characterised by a combination of the Irenaean and Athanasian 'physical' tradition with his own, Origenist universalism on the basis of universal human nature. I shall thus attempt to show that Gregory adopted elements of the 'physical' soteriology, modifying them by the application of *universal* human nature.

The results of the previous section provide some useful presuppositions for the present enquiry: thus it has emerged that Gregory in his humanistic approach adopted elements of both the Origenist and the 'Apollinarian' soteriology of *De incarnatione et contra Arianos*. It further became clear that within both these traditions there were elements which Gregory could develop into a view making universal human nature the principle of universal salvation, while, at the same time, this latter view in itself was alien to both of them. What needs to be shown, then, is how, and under what conditions, influences of both these traditions co-operated towards the formation of Gregory's specific physical views.

5.3.1 *Physical soteriology and universalism in* Tunc et ipse

A convenient starting point may be Gregory's treatise *Tunc et ipse*. It is Gregory's purpose in that writing to demonstrate that this Pauline verse is not evidence of the Son's ontological inferiority to the Father, thus tackling a problem which had arisen for him as part of the Eunomian controversy.[52]

For a number of reasons this writing is of particular interest here. The first of them is its apparent dependence on *De incarnatione et contra Arianos*.[53] It can be shown, I think, how Gregory, while drawing on that treatise, shifts its argument in a clearly different direction. The second point of interest is the writing's obvious Origenism. It is here that Gregory commits himself most explicitly to the doctrine

---

[52] Cf. *Eun* I 191–6 (GNO I, 82,19–84,10) and *ref Eun* 198–201 (GNO II, 396,1–397,20). For the Arian and Eunomian interpration of this verse see: Theodoret, *in 1 Cor* (PG 82, 357).

[53] Cf. Hübner (1974), 53; 288.

of universal salvation, that main stumbling block in Origen's teaching for later orthodoxy. For this very reason also the work's authenticity has been doubted, but scholarship has been able to disperse those doubts convincingly.[54] Finally, the ultimately anti-Eunomian background has to be borne in mind and may help elucidate Gregory's specific concerns.

I have argued above that the view of salvation to be found in one passage of this treatise[55] owes much to Origen, while at the same time it seems to deviate from his approach in one important regard. It is interesting to see, then, that in the same treatise Gregory is able to draw heavily on *De incarnatione et contra Arianos*, whose author apparently is no Origenist whatever. That Gregory resorted to the ps.-Athanasian writing in the first place may well be due to the fact that it contains an anti-Arian exegesis of 1 Cor 15,28.

To the exegetical problem presented by this verse the ps.-Athanasian author had presented the following solution:[56] the subjection mentioned by Paul is the subjection of the world which occurs in the flesh of Christ. This subjection, however, will take place only when 'we all' have been subjected to Christ, that is, have become his members. Then he himself will be subjected as the head for his own members.

It seems clear that, in the context of that writing (see pp. 139–41 above), the process envisaged here is the growth of the Church; the more human beings are included in this 'body' the more are subject to Christ, and the ultimate completion of that process would be reached when there are no more people left outside that body. The author does not seem to be interested in this latter, apparently universalist, aspect of the problem though; it is important to note this as with Gregory it will be different. Ps.-Athanasius' exegesis of the verse simply extends his soteriological views in a cosmic perspective: the incorporation of human beings into Christ's body will eventually result in the 'subjection' of the world to God. Ultimately, his exegesis is defensive against a (neo)-Arian abuse of the verse; he does not express any positive, theological interest in the Pauline text.[57]

For Gregory's solution to the problem it is characteristic that, first

---

[54] Cf. Downing in: GNO III/2, xxxix–li.
[55] GNO III/2, 14,8–15,1; see p. 195 above.
[56] *D inc et c Ar* 20 (PG 26, 1020A–1021A).
[57] *Pace* Tetz (1964), 257–8.

of all, he accepts in principle ps.-Athanasius' exegesis of the subjection as the final stage of salvation history, although the process leading to that stage is described in Gregory's own 'humanistic' terminology:

> When, then, we all will be outside evil on account of our imitation of the first fruits, the entire batch of dough will have been assimilated to that first fruit and become one continuous body. Then it will accept for itself dominion by the good only. Thus, when the whole body of our nature will have been mingled with the divine and unmixed nature, the aforesaid subjection of the Son occurs *in us*. This subjection, which is carried out in his body, is said of him who in us has effected the grace of subjection.[58]

At the same time it is evident that for him the universalist aspect of the verse is equally crucial. That is, *he*, unlike ps.-Athanasius, has a positive interest in the verse; *he* is not content merely to defend it against a heretical interpretation, but wants to recapture it for the orthodox cause, that is for his own interest in the *apokatastasis*. Thus, he states right from the outset:

> ... that once the nature of evil will pass over into non-existence, having been made to disappear completely from being. Then the divine and unmixed goodness will contain all rational nature within itself, and nothing which came into evil will fall short of God's dominion. When all evil that is mixed with beings has been destroyed, like some base substance through the refinery of purifying fire, everything which had its being through God will be such as it was from the beginning when as yet it had not received evil.[59]

Up to this point it would not appear that Gregory might face any particular difficulty in his attempt. Although ps.-Athanasius had not shown any interest in a universalist exegesis of the verse, such a conclusion could easily be drawn from his elaboration. By adding some reasoning that, on account of certain principles (Gregory's celebrated *akolouthia*, for example), the process initiated by the Incarnation would necessarily lead to an eventual subjection of *all* creatures, Gregory could, one would think, have achieved his point with relative ease.

He proceeds, however, in a different way. It may be worthwhile to recall at this point the observation, made in the 'Origenist' passage analysed above (pp. 195–7), that Gregory seems to twist Origen's

---

[58] *Tunc et ipse* (GNO III/2, 16,13–22).

[59] *Tunc et ipse* (GNO III/2, 13,22–14,7), ET: Ludlow (1996), 79–80 (with amendments).

soteriological use of *phusis*-terminology in a direction which allows it to be applied to the issue of universalism. Christ, Gregory wrote, assumed 'the whole human nature' and has thus become 'the first fruits' of the common lump of humanity. A similar shift can be observed in his use of ps.-Athanasian arguments.

To begin with, in some places he seems clearly influenced by the 'derivative' soteriology of *De incarnatione et contra Arianos.* Thus he cites Col 1,24–5; 1 Cor 12,27; and Eph 4,15–6 to support the notion that the body of Christ is the Church.[60] The argument in those lines seems to correspond perfectly with what we have found in the ps.-Athanasian writing, except for the strong universalist emphasis.

Elsewhere, however, Gregory introduces a further notion which seems in principle to be at odds with that view:

> His body is, as has often been said, *the whole human nature* with which he was mixed.[61]

At first sight one might think that this statement once more emphasises Gregory's universalist interpretation of ps.-Athanasius' argument: the growth of the body leads necessarily to its eventual inclusion of the entire human race (= human 'nature'). Upon close examination, however, it appears that it says more than this: the phrasing ('mixture' of the divine with human nature) indicates that Gregory thinks of *phusis* here not in the looser sense of 'all humankind',[62] but has something more technical in mind, some item which, through Incarnation, Christ has assumed so that now it can be equated with his body. There cannot be much doubt, I think, that this must be some sort of universal item, the assumption of which is thought to guarantee the universality of salvation. This would agree with a tendency that was seen in that quasi-Origenist passage, which mentioned the union of divine and the 'whole human nature' to proceed with claims about the necessary universality of the salvific process.[63]

The consequences seem plain: if the body of Christ is human nature, not the Church, then the building up of his body is not primarily conditioned by an ever-further integration of human beings

---

[60] *Tunc et ipse* (GNO III/2, 18,19–19,12).
[61] *Tunc et ipse* (GNO III/2, 21,10–1).
[62] See pp. 174–5 above.
[63] *Tunc et ipse* (GNO III/2, 14,10–1): 'the whole human nature with which the divine was mixed.'

into the Church but by a physical penetration of divine nature through universal human nature on account of their mutual penetration in Christ.

The present writing thus shows how Gregory uses elements from two soteriological traditions towards the establishment of a doctrine which is ultimately alien to both of them: drawing on both Origenist and Apollinarian views he introduces universal human nature to press home the universality of salvation on the basis of the physical homogeneity of Christ and human beings. This, then, is the fateful physical doctrine of salvation in a form which, I think, is owed to Gregory himself.

At the same time it must not pass unnoticed that in the same writing Gregory is still much indebted to his humanistic approach. One might even argue that this approach still dominates his argument. Repeatedly, Gregory emphasises the constitutive import of human acts like imitation, virtues and cleansing for the fulfilment of salvation history; Christ himself, as we have seen, is said to have conquered death on account of his sinless life.[64]

Yet, it would be wrong, I think, to deny the above analysis of Gregory's physical *tendency* on account of those statements. Rather, this latter observation would seem to support the idea that here we see Gregory develop. There is no rupture which would indicate that Gregory had, from one moment to another, altogether changed his mind on this issue. Still, there is a new idea which cannot easily be integrated into his original approach, and we shall see that in the course of the years immediately following the writing of the present treatise this new notion becomes much more dominant in Gregory's doctrinal thinking.

Two questions, I think, ought to be addressed with regard to that new doctrine: first, can it at all be explained why Gregory resorted to this theory and, secondly, what understanding of universal human nature underlies it?

To begin with the first one, it seems evident that, while ps.-Athanasius does not make the physical unity of humanity the basis for any sort of universalist speculation, he certainly does stand in the 'physical' tradition in the Athanasian sense. That is, he employs the notion of physical union between human and divine nature which

---

[64] *Tunc et ipse* (GNO III/2, 14,13-8).

is, at first sight, very similar to the view employed by Gregory. The former view, I have argued, was developed and became relevant wherever the reality of the Incarnation had to be defended on soteriological grounds. That is, it became important wherever the christological issue itself became controversial.

Now it seems that precisely this occurred to Gregory in the course of the Eunomian controversy: his insistence on the Son's full divinity could easily be charged with neglecting the necessity, or even practically preventing the possibility, of Incarnation thus ending, in Eunomius' words, with 'two Lords and two Christs'.[65] It would thus seem natural to assume that Gregory in this situation resorted to christological patterns inherent in the 'physical' tradition and found, *en passant* as it were (perhaps when he tried to work out the orthodox exegesis of 1 Cor 15,28), that, on the basis of a universal interpretation of *phusis*, he could at the same time use that tradition for his own universalist claims.

This hypothesis can only be argued for on the basis of Gregory's *Contra Eunomium* itself. I shall thus, starting from some more general considerations of the way the Eunomian controversy made christology controversial, proceed to an elucidation of some key passages showing especially the interaction of soteriological and christological arguments.

5.3.2   *Soteriology and christology in the Eunomian controversy*

Scholarship has given little consideration to the christological implications of the trinitarian debates of the fourth century. Yet it seems evident that, as soteriological concerns were at the heart of that controversy, the christological issue could not be left apart. As for the Cappadocians it is perhaps not too much to say that they, with the exception of Nazianzen,[66] did not genuinely have strong christological concerns. They were content to emphasise, in the Origenist tradition, the full humanity of the saviour as a presupposition for their humanistic soteriology, while at the same time stressing the salvific necessity of the Son's full divinity. Indeed with regard to that latter point, or so, at least, I have argued in the first part of this study, they went beyond the position of Athanasius by asserting the com-

---

[65] Ap. Gregory, *Eun* III/3,15 (GNO II, 112,10–6).
[66] Holl (1904), 178–96.

plete co-ordination of the Trinitarian Persons. They did not, however, feel the need to address the resulting christological problem of
how the union of human and divine could be conceived of under
those conditions. And this, I think, not by coincidence, but rather
as a consequence of their 'humanistic' soteriology which could work
without a precise christological framework.

It would appear that the sharp mind of Eunomius had not failed
to perceive this conceptual weakness. In a passage dealing with Basil's
exegesis of Phil 2,6ff. he complains that Basil's interpretation would
make this text treat of 'a man humbled into a man'.[67] Basil, in his
attempt to deny that this theologically important pericope could be
used to prove the Son's subordination, had adopted the frequent
exegetical 'trick' of applying such texts to Christ's humanity, thus
giving Eunomius occasion to score a point: surely, the subject of
those verses must be the Logos and his descent into human nature.

Apart from the fact that Basil's exegesis apparently makes nonsense
of the Pauline argument, it also sheds some light on his soteriological approach: Basil *could* forsake such a text so easily because he
was ultimately not in need of the concept of *kenosis* for his theology.

It would appear that Gregory in his defence of his brother had
become aware of this problem. He certainly does not concede to
Eunomius the justification of the latter's criticism; rather he tries to
prove that Eunomius' own, subordinate Christ could not have saved
humankind. This, of course, is a genuinely Athanasian argument.
Yet it is interesting that and how Gregory here follows in the footsteps of the Alexandrian patriarch:

> We say that the only begotten Son through himself led all things into
> existence and rules all things in himself. One of the things generated
> by him is human nature which, having slid into evil and therefore
> become [subject to] death's corruptibility, is again drawn towards
> immortal life through him. Through the man in whom he dwelt
> (κατεσκήνωσεν: cf. John 1,14) he assumed the whole human item to
> himself, mixing his own life-giving power with the mortal and perish-
> able nature and changing our mortality into living grace and power
> through the amalgamation with himself. And this we call the mystery
> of the Lord's Incarnation that the unchangeable was in the change-
> able in order that, having changed to the better and turned away from
> the worse, he consumed from the nature the evil mixed with the

---

[67] *Apol apol*, ap. Gregory, *Eun* III/3,17 (GNO II, 113,19–20).

changeable condition (διάθεσις), having destroyed the evil in himself.
For our God is a consuming fire (Hebr 12,29) by whom the entire
matter of evil is consumed.[68]

Creator and saviour are identical; this is the first and central point
Gregory makes. The Son is both origin of all things and origin of
human salvation. This is the foremost purpose of his polemical attack:
salvation could be enacted only by the same divinity which also had
been active in creation.

A second point that emerges is that for the precise characterisation of the salvific import of the Incarnation Gregory here employs
the physical terminology of the Irenaean-Athanasian tradition. In
comparison, the terminological agreement with some passages from
Tunc et ipse is striking; had his source there been shown to be *De
incarnatione et contra Arianos*, it could well be the same here, although
Gregory would certainly have known the main Irenaean and Athanasian writings also.

The underlying idea is that due to sin human nature has fallen
into mortality, a process which is reversed only by the Incarnation.
Salvation here is clearly deification; human mortality is gradually
overcome by mixture with the divine.

With regard to Gregory's soteriology the consequences are remarkable. The shift away from the humanistic approach is practically
complete. The subject of salvation and the focus of attention in the
present passage is the Logos. 'The man in whom he dwelt' appears
to be scarcely more than an instrument that was used by the Godhead
for its universal purpose of salvation. At the same time, not surprisingly, the relevance of the consummation of evil has shifted alongside. It is no more the unique achievement of one human being
which we are called to imitate, but the almost inevitable consequence
of the dwelling of divine in human nature. There is certainly nothing remarkable in the fact that God is sinless.

This change of emphasis seems most easily understood as following from the argumentative need in the present context, Gregory's
task to prove that only the consubstantial Logos could possibly have
saved humanity.

A further observation concerns the universal property of human
nature. It would appear that, as in similarly worded passages from

---

[68] *Eun* III/3, 51–2 (GNO II, 125,28–126,15).

Tunc et ipse, Gregory envisages the salvation of human nature as a universal act based on the community of *phusis*. While there is no special emphasis on this universality in the present passage, it would appear that the present context indicates a further incentive which could have influenced Gregory's adoption of this kind of speculation: if salvation, like creation, is after all an activity of the Logos, is it, then, not appropriate to think of it as done on the level of *phusis*? The Logos, as we have seen, creates on that level, should he not also save on that plane?

Elsewhere in the same work Gregory's argument seems to move in the same direction, albeit from a different starting point. This occurs where he attempts to defend Paul's use of the term πρωτότοκος for Christ. Not surprisingly, his claim is that all those texts refer to Christ's humanity, not his divinity. With regard especially to Col 1,15, where Christ is called the 'first-born of all created things', Gregory argues:

> We recognise a twofold creation of our nature, the first that whereby we are made, the second that whereby we are made anew. But there would have been no need of the second creation had we not made the first unavailing by our disobedience. Accordingly, when the first creation had waxed old and vanished away, it was needful that there should be a new creation in Christ (. . .) for the maker of human nature at the first and afterwards is one and the same.[69]

To begin with, the notion of a new creation in this context is, of course, biblical (2 Cor 5,17; Gal 6,15). It also has been shown that Gregory elsewhere could make use of the Church as a new humankind, thus drawing on the analogous application of derivative humanity by Apollinarius. In the present passage, however, the emphasis is on the Logos, who is active in both creations; this text seems primarily interested in drawing an exact parallel between both *qua* his involvement. It thus appears consequent that, in order to demonstrate the need for direct divine intervention, man's fallen state is strongly underlined.

More important at present seems a further corollary: the parallel drawn here between creation and salvation could again be seen to provide for additional justification for the use of universal human nature in the context of soteriology. For with regard to creation we

---

[69] *Eun* III/2, 52–3 (GNO II, 69,22–70,7), ET: Moore/Wilson (1893), 158.

saw Gregory consciously employ *phusis*-terminology to express the universality of the divine act; could, then, not the same be said with regard to soteriology?

That Gregory, in spite of his adoption of the language of the Irenaean-Athanasian tradition, was far from a consistent christology is made clear by the lines immediately following this last quotation:

> Then he took dust from the earth and formed man, again he took dust from the virgin and not only formed man, but formed him around himself; then he created, afterwards he was created; then the word made flesh, afterwards the word became flesh in order to transform our flesh into spirit by partaking of our flesh and blood.[70]

Here Gregory all but repeats Athanasius' deification formula: the Logos had to become flesh in order to transform our flesh. At the same time, I believe, this passage makes it quite clear that this kind of thinking had not become genuine to Gregory. The text exposes, as distinctly as one could wish, the lack in his thought of a christo-logical concept capable of maintaining the personal unity and iden-tity of the saviour, the lack that is, of the very notion that was of vital importance for the 'physical' soteriology.

The ambiguity is obvious: on the one hand, Gregory wishes to make a clear-cut distinction between human and divine in Christ, making the divine the creator of the human. On the other hand, he says of the same subject that 'he created' and 'he was created'. This ambiguity comes out even more clearly in comparison with a text from Irenaeus' *Adversus Haereses* which may well stand behind Gregory's statement:

> As the protoplast himself, Adam, had his substance from untilled and as yet virgin soil (. . .), and was formed by the hand of God, that is, by the word of God, for 'all things were made by him,' and the Lord took dust from the earth and formed man; so did he who is the Word (i.e. the Logos), recapitulating Adam in himself, rightly receive a birth, enabling him to gather up Adam [into himself] from Mary, who was as yet a virgin.[71]

The crucial difference is that Irenaeus quite plainly asserts that it is the Logos himself who is born from the virgin, while Gregory seems

---

[70] *Eun* III/2, 54 (GNO II, 70,7–13).
[71] Irenaeus, *haer* III 21,10 (vol. III/2, 426–8 Rousseau/Doutreleau); ET: Roberts/ Rambaut, 358.

to introduce a difference between the 'man' who was created and the Logos who created: it is not difficult to see how opponents, Eunomius and Apollinarians alike, could charge him with teaching 'two Lords and two Christs'.[72]

In summary, then, it appears that Gregory, under the pressure of maintaining, against Eunomius, the salvific necessity of Christ's full divinity, shifted the emphasis of his soteriology away from the humanistic approach of the Origenist tradition towards an approach stressing the salvific activity of the Logos.

With regard to his use of *phusis*-terminology in soteriology this was seen to have two consequences. First, he adopts the 'monophysite' deification language of the Irenaean and Athanasian tradition which, as I have argued, could account for his soteriological *use* of *phusis*-terminology in the first place. Secondly, his emphasis on the divine activity in man's salvation would seem to call for a universal approach: after all, the Logos deals with the world, not with individuals. This seemed, in particular, implied by the way Gregory here draws a parallel between creation and salvation; it would seem easy to take this reasoning one step further by arguing that, as in creation so in salvation, the Logos acts on the level of *phusis*.

Ultimately, Gregory's speculations about the Logos' activity in salvation expose, in my view, the absence from his thought of a proper grasp of the Irenaean or Athanasian Incarnation theology: his Logos does not really *become* flesh, he 'creates it around himself'; there apparently remain two subjects. One might go so far as to argue that the saving Logos is still the cosmic principle; a real Incarnation is not achieved.

While Gregory's *Contra Eunomium* shows, more strongly than his treatise on 1 Cor 15,28, indications of a shift away from the humanistic approach to soteriology, it is at the same time evident that the work still contains passages whose argument appears to be based on this very approach. It might be sufficient to recall here that text from *Contra Eunomium* III/10 which was discussed in connection with Gregory's Origenist heritage (pp. 195–7 above) and found to betray only slight indications of a departure from that humanistic view.

---

[72] For Eunomius see e.g.: *Eun* III/3, 15 (GNO II, 112,10–6), for Apollinarians: *Theoph* (GNO III/1, 120,15–9); cf. also: *antirrh* (GNO III/1, 185,1).

5.3.3 *Human nature in Gregory's anti-Apollinarian* Antirrheticus

5.3.3.1 *Gregory's* Third Epistle *and its historical setting*

The historical details of Gregory's involvement in the Apollinarian controversy have not as yet been eventually explained. It appears that in most of his writings he does not see the christological issue as a prominent theological topic. At the same time it would seem that, if the findings of the present study have any claim to be accurate, Gregory must have been acquainted with Apollinarius' theology to a considerable degree and, while not admitting it as such, drawn on it all the same. These two observations need not be in contradiction: on the contrary, the very fact that Gregory seems largely untouched by the intricacies of the christological problem could make understandable his use of Apollinarius, whom he thus had no reason to regard as a heretic. They would, however, make it difficult to accept the assumption of Gregory's chancing on one of Apollinarius' books and finding its teaching so abhorrent that he at once decided he had to combat it. Rather it would appear likely that Gregory was pushed into that controversy by some external force.

The most obvious occasion for this to have happened would seem to be Gregory's fateful stay in Jerusalem which, I think, must be placed in 381 or, more likely, 382.[73] From the account he gives of those events in his *Third Epistle* it appears that he was accused by people, with whom he shared the same Nicene faith, of heterodox teachings. In strong words he expresses his bewilderment at this fact:

> I affirm that it is a lawful thing to hate God's enemies, and that this hatred is pleasing to our Lord: and by God's enemies I mean those who in any way deny the glory of our Lord, be they Jews, or downright idolaters, or those who through Arius' teaching idolise the creature, and so adapt the error of the Jews. Now when the Father, the Son, and the Holy Ghost, are with orthodox devotion being glorified and adored by those who believe that in a distinct and unconfused Trinity there is one nature, glory, kingship, power, pious service, and

---

[73] The common assumption that Gregory must have visited Jerusalem *immediately* after either the 379 or the 381 synod is, I think, due to a misreading of *ep* 2,12 (GNO VIII/2, 17,1–10). In fact, from *vit Macr* (GNO VIII/1, 370,6–371,1) it would appear that Gregory's main purpose *was* a pilgrimage to Jerusalem (*pace* his statement at *ep* 2,12 loc. cit.). Could *ep* 3,1 (GNO VIII/2, 20,3–4) be understood as saying that Gregory spent Easter at Jerusalem? This, I think, would most likely be Easter 382; so also Lebourlier (1963), 178–9.

universal rule, in such a case as this what good excuse for fighting
can there be?[74]

Unfortunately, Gregory does not relate the precise nature of those
accusations, but from his defence it becomes clear that they must
have been directed at his christology. Now, from what has been
found about Gregory's christology on the basis of his *Contra Eunomium*
III, it would not seem surprising that somebody should have taken
exception to it. Indeed, both Apollinarians and anti-Apollinarians, if
for the sake of convenience I may thus simplify the possible camps,
could be thought to object to the conceptions expressly stated in, or
implied by, Gregory's elaboration.

   Who, then, were the opponents in Jerusalem? It would appear
that the key to this question is to be found in the final paragraph
of Gregory's letter where he writes as follows:

> Have any of ourselves dared to say 'mother of man' (ἀνθρωποτόκος)
> of the holy virgin, the mother of God (θεοτόκος): which is what we
> hear that some of them say without restraint.[75]

From this it would appear that his opponents cannot have been
Apollinarians of any kind, since for them the virgin birth was of
such central importance that Gregory could scarcely have been mistaken about this point. Yet, if the opponents themselves cannot have
been Apollinarians, it would seem likely that, where Gregory in the
same context refers to Apollinarian doctrines, he really defends *himself*:

> Do we romance about three resurrections? Do we promise the glut-
> tony of the millenium? Do we declare that the Jewish animal-sacrifices
> shall be restored? Do we lower men's hopes again to the Jerusalem
> below, imagining its rebuilding with stones of a more brilliant material?[76]

It has sometimes been thought that with these words Gregory
characterises his opponents as Apollinarians, but this interpretation
is not inevitable, for Gregory here does not claim that this is what
his opponents believe, but simply states that he does *not* hold those
views. While this *could* be read as implying that his opponents do,
this inference is not by any means necessary. Incidentally, the present enumeration of Apollinarian doctrines shows that Gregory was

---

[74] *Ep* 3,8 (GNO VIII/2, 22,1–12); ET: Moore/Wilson (1893), 542 (with amendments).
[75] *Ep* 3,24 (GNO VIII/2, 26,18–20); ET: Moore/Wilson (1893), 544.
[76] *Ep* 3,24 (GNO VIII/2, 26,20–25); ET: Moore/Wilson (1893), 544.

well-acquainted with Apollinarius' teaching, which confirms the above suggestion that he could not have thought that the Laodicene called Mary ἀνθρωποτόκος.

It would, then, appear from the present passage that in Jerusalem Gregory was himself accused of being an Apollinarian:[77] he claims that 'some' of his accusers think of Mary as bearer of a man and gives a list of Apollinarian doctrines to which he asserts that he does not subscribe.

I shall not go into a detailed enquiry here of the question what, in particular, those opponents found 'Apollinarian' about Gregory's teaching, since this would require a detailed analysis of the *Third Epistle* which is beyond the scope of the present investigation. Suffice it to say that it certainly cannot have been any express rejection of a human soul or mind in Christ as this is a view Gregory never held. Rather, it would appear that, on the basis of the 'physical' language in *Contra Eunomium* III, one could argue that to use this kind of terminology would presuppose a word-flesh christology which ultimately could not steer clear of the Apollinarian heresy.

Be this as it may, for the present purpose the following two points are, I think, important: first, the fact that Gregory was accused of being an Apollinarian could explain that he wrote his *Antirrheticus* in order to clear himself of those charges. Secondly, as regards his use of human nature in soteriology, it would seem natural to expect that Gregory, under the impact of those charges, modified the position of *Contra Eunomium* III by dropping its 'monophysite' element while at the same time increasing the emphasis on the duality of human and divine which, as has been shown, was already present in the anti-Eunomian work. That this shift will not increase the consistency of his christology may be expected.

5.3.3.2   *The position of the* Antirrheticus

It is not easy to find in Gregory's wordy anti-Apollinarian *Antirrheticus* many passages devoted to positive doctrinal elaboration. If Gregory in his anti-Eunomian writings was not a fair polemicist, he is considerably less so in his anti-Apollinarian treatise. What is more, had the former writing given him occassion to develop the wealth of his own trinitarian thinking, the latter does not seem to inspire him in

---

[77] So already Lietzmann (1904), 36 and May (1966), 120.

a similar way. Only rarely is the flux of rhetorical arguments and slander interrupted by a passage containing positive teaching. If the above explanation of the historical background is accepted, the poor quality of the writing could perhaps be explained alongside, since Gregory would have had little interest in the subject beyond his current, practical purpose.

One of those few, rather constructive texts is the following, which I shall quote slightly abridged:

> (. . .) the Logos, who was in the beginning and was with God, became flesh in the last days by his community with the lowliness of our nature out of philanthropy. Therefore he was mixed with man and received in himself the whole of our nature in order to divinise the human item (τὸ ἀνθρώπινον) by means of amalgamation with the divine: through that first fruit the whole batch of dough of our nature is sanctified alongside. (. . .) For who does not know the divine mystery that the prince of our salvation took, like a shepherd, the lost sheep upon himself. We men are that sheep; by sin we have been led astray from the hundred (sheep), the rational beings. And he takes the whole sheep upon his own shoulders. For the aberration was not in part of the sheep, but as the whole has fallen away so also is the whole led upwards again. For it is not the skin that is carried while the entrails are left as Apollinarius would have it.
>
> This now having happened in the shoulders of the shepherd, that is the divinity of the Lord, it (sc. the sheep) becomes one with him because of the assumption. Therefore he, who came to seek and save the lost (Lk 19,10), once he had found what he had been looking for, assumed to himself what he had found. For the sheep was not carried any more by its own feet, which had once been led astray, but it was taken care of by the Godhead. Therefore what appears to be a sheep, which is man, did not recognise its traces as is written (Ps 76,20). For he, who carries with himself that sheep, has not imprinted a trace of sin or fault on human life: but, as it was likely that traces of God would be imprinted due to his way of life, so it actually happened in what were his teachings, healings, and resuscitations of dead people, and the other miracles. Thus the shepherd, who took upon himself the sheep, became one with it. Therefore also he calls the flock with the voice of the sheep. For how could human weakness have coped with the impact of the divine voice? But humanly or—if one should like to say so—'ovinely', he speaks to us saying (John 10,27): 'My sheep hear my voice.' Now the shepherd, who assumes to himself the sheep and talks to us through it, is both sheep and shepherd: sheep in what is assumed, shepherd in what assumes.[78]

---

[78] *Antirrh* (GNO III/1, 151,14–152,29).

The main tendency of this very full exposition of the salvific impact of the Incarnation seems to be characterised by the attempt to maintain, within the soteriological framework developed in the course of the Eunomian controversy, the salvific necessity of, so to speak, two natures. To begin with, it is evident that in the first part of the text Gregory reiterates the kind of soteriological summary which we have encountered before in *Contra Eunomium* III/3 and in the treatise on 1 Cor 15,28: the Logos, his descent, his 'assumption' of human nature, their mutual mixture, the deification of humanity, all these elements have been related elsewhere in a very similar way.

The same is true for the ensuing reference to the parable of the lost sheep, but only up to a point: the exegesis of this parable, which similarly has been found in Gregory's *Homilies on Ecclesiastes*, had there had a very Origenist and humanistic, *soteriological* emphasis: Christ came to call human nature back to its original home. Not only has at the present place this humanistic emphasis vanished and been practically reversed—the sheep is now unable to walk and has to be carried by the shepherd!—, but the ultimate interest here is not in soteriology at all but in christology. The 'whole sheep', which the text insists was carried by the shepherd, is not the entirety of humanity, that is all human beings, but the entire human nature, that is body and soul.

This latter twist might not be considered surprising: after all, it was Gregory's task to rebut Apollinarius' claim that Christ did not have a human soul, or, at least, not a rational soul, and he may thus have felt that, by giving 'the whole of human nature' a slightly different emphasis, he could conveniently score that point.

What follows, then, is more interesting. Gregory must have felt that with his christological exegesis of the parable the charge of a divisive christology would inevitably return in full force; and this, I think, with perfect legitimacy. The notion of the incarnate Christ as shepherd and lamb expresses much of Gregory's christological dilemma. As in *Contra Eunomium* III, Gregory here ends with two subjects. The present passage, at least, shows his awareness of this problem. Still, his attempt at a solution—sheep and shepherd become one—is too forceful to convince.

While thus the present passage demonstrates how Gregory tried, without much success, to overcome the divisive christology of the *Contra Eunomium* on the basis of the very soteriological framework which had been developed in the latter work, the immediate sequence produces a new argument for Christ's full humanity:

Now, as it is necessary that the good shepherd gives his soul for his sheep in order to destroy death through his own death, the prince of our salvation became both for human nature: physician and lamb effecting death in what was capable of receiving the community of suffering. But, since death is nothing other than the separation of body and soul, he, who had united himself to both—to soul I say and body—, was not separated from either ('For the gifts of God are irrevocable,' as the apostle says [Ro 11,29]) but giving himself partially to both, body and soul, he opens the paradise for the robber through the soul (cf. Lk 23,46) and checks the activity of corruption through the body. And this is the destruction of death that corruption, which had befallen the vivifying power, is undone. For what has happened to them becomes the new blessing and grace of our nature. And so he, who was in both, rejoins through resurrection all that has been separated. He, who voluntarily gave his body to the heart of the earth as is written (Mt 12,40) and handed over his soul, as he says to the Father: 'Into thy hands I commit my spirit,' and to the robber (Luk 23,46): <'Tomorrow you will be with me in paradise,'>[79] is true in both (. . .).

Thus he has been in death, but not been dominated by death. For the composite is divided, but the uncomposite does not suffer dissolution, but the uncomposite nature remains in the partition of the composite and, while body is separated from soul, it is not separated from either. (. . .) For the simple and uncomposite is not split up alongside that division. (. . .)

For in him who dies and rises for us, the Only-begotten God has reconciled the world with himself (2 Cor 5,19) redeeming us like prisoners, as it were, through our related blood, all who are in community with his flesh and blood. This seems to be what the words of the apostle are looking at which say (Eph 1,7) that we have salvation through his blood and forgiveness of sins through his flesh.[80]

At the core of this passage is an argument which, in an interesting way, combines the salvific necessity of Christ's death and resurrection with the salvific necessity of his full humanity. If Lebourlier is to be believed, and I think that he is right, then the present text is not the *first* use by Gregory of this argument. In his aforementioned article Lebourlier discerns this very argument five times in Nyssen's works, and dates two of these occurrences prior to the *Antirrheticus*.[81] One of the former, incidentally, is to be found in the *Third Epistle*. Typical of this argument is its dual emphasis: on the one hand it has a clearly anti-Apollinarian, christological point, underlining the

---

[79] <> add. Mueller.
[80] *Antirrh* (GNO III/1, 152,30–154,21).
[81] Lebourlier (1963).

soteriological need for human body and soul in Christ, on the other, it argues for a very specific 'physical' soteriology which, however, is again un-Apollinarian: the human *phusis*, consisting of body and soul, could only be saved by death and resurrection of Christ, the Logos, in so far as he was united to both parts of the human compound. It seems as though this latter idea was produced especially to counter the soteriological force behind the Logos-flesh christology of Apollinarius. In spite of similar terminology, the intent of the two is very different: where, in Athanasius and Apollinarius, human flesh had been in need of transformation by an infusion of divinity, here it is the composite nature of man that needs Incarnation to overcome its inherent tendency towards dissolution.

Clearly, in the present passage the emphasis is on the first aspect. Gregory practically presupposes the second, soteriological assumption to press home the need for Christ to have both, human body and soul. Yet it is equally evident that this soteriological schema provides precisely what Gregory was argued to be in need of: a 'physical' formula which, nevertheless, avoids any suspicion of Apollinarian 'monophysitism'.

At the same time this schema can hardly be thought to constitute the result of an organic development in Gregory's thought: several of its elements, for example the notion of death as the separation of body and soul, and that of resurrection as effected by Christ's resurrection, are in plain contradiction to positions at which Gregory seemed to have arrived after careful consideration.[82] It would therefore appear likely that Gregory adopted the present argument not as part of an overall theological paradigm shift, but rather *ad hoc* for the purpose of warding off charges of Apollinarianism while maintaining the advantages gained from the 'physical' approach.

It is worthy of mention also that in the present context Gregory makes no use of *universal* human nature. Quite generally in the *Antirrheticus*, his emphasis being on christology, he is primarily concerned to secure that Christ was fully human; indeed it can be observed that frequently he now gives his favourite phrase 'the whole human nature' a new meaning as signifying Christ's complete manhood, consisting of body and soul.[83]

---

[82] Ludlow (1996), 38–48.
[83] E.g. at *antirrh* (GNO III/1, 214,24–6); cf. also the reinterpretation of the 'lost sheep'.

The anti-Apollinarian writing would thus witness, not a renewed interest on the part of Gregory in universal salvation, but a need to modify his christology to clarify its commitment to both human body and soul in Christ. This means that one element that is present already in *Contra Eunomium* III, a tendency towards 'divisive christology', is additionally emphasised at the expense of the other element pointing towards monophysitism, which had been equally present in the anti-Eunomian treatise.

5.3.4 *The re-emergence of universal human nature in the* Refutatio Confessionis Eunomii

Gregory's *Refutation of Eunomius' Creed* which, I have argued, was written after his anti-Apollinarian *Antirrheticus*, bears witness to a renewed interest in universal salvation, based now on the new christological insights Gregory had gained during the anti-Apollinarian interlude. This is especially distinct in a lengthy passage dealing with Eunomius' apparent denial of a human soul in Christ.[84] There several features from the anti-Apollinarian writing recur, including the christological exegesis of the parable of the lost sheep. The same could be said about the argument, related above, concerning the salvific necessity of Christ's death; although here we see Gregory give this argument a slightly different emphasis:

> For the Godhead is always the same, before the Incarnation, in the flesh and after the suffering. Being by nature (φύσει) always what it was and remaining (the same) in eternity, the Godhead fulfilled the dispensation for our benefit in the passions of human nature. By separating for a time the soul from the body without, however, detaching itself from either of those with which it had earlier been blended, it finally reunited the divided parts thus providing a necessary sequence (ἀκολουθία) and the beginning (ἀρχή) of the resurrection of the dead for the whole of human nature so that the perishable will put on the imperishable and the mortal immortality (1 Cor 15,53) as our first fruits has been changed into divine nature through amalgamation with God.[85]

Besides retaining its christological emphasis the present use of this argument points, more expressly than the one in the *Antirrheticus*, to its soteriological implications.

---

[84] *Ref Eun* 173–81 (GNO II, 385,2–389,4).
[85] *Ref Eun* 179 (GNO II, 387,14–25).

To begin with, the references to the universal effect of the Incarnation recall remarks from *Tunc et ipse*: Christ's humanity as the first fruits which, by amalgamation with the divine, constitutes the beginning (ἀρχή) of a necessary sequence, is employed in both texts to the same end. As for the precise content, however, of that sequence, it seems that the two texts are quite different. In both of them, it is true, the final purpose of salvation is said to be the abolition of human mortality. Yet in *Tunc et ipse* Gregory does not mention Christ's death and resurrection in this connection but says, explicitly, that sinlessness would suffice, 'since there is no origin of death except sin'.[86] Nor would he appear to see the eschatological resurrection as a prominent feature of salvation history.

The present passage, then, witnesses a new approach to universal salvation which is based on the anti-Apollinarian argument, which we have seen Gregory employ in his *Antirrheticus* to a christological end. This approach is characterised first of all by an understanding of salvation that primarily emphasises the universality of the resurrection. This event now seems to be something like the epitome of universal salvation, which is remarkable as there is little or no evidence that Gregory, prior to, and indeed outside of, his use of this particular argument, developed any speculation in this direction although he had, quite recently, devoted an entire book, *De Anima et Resurrectione*, to the topic of eschatology.

While, then, Gregory's use of this argument at the present place can still be explained by its christological implications, one may wonder why he stresses its soteriological impact given that this implied notions which were rather alien to his thought? For this fact, it seems, an explanation could be advanced if it could be shown that the universalist interpretation, in which Gregory certainly had a genuine interest, was originally part of that argument; in this case, its universalism could be thought to have lured Gregory into its soteriological application.

That the argument did indeed contain a universalist element, inferring universal resurrection from Christ's resurrection, seems to be suggested by its apparent dependence on Irenaeus:

> Therefore, then, the Lord himself gave us a sign in the depth and in the heights (cf. Is 7,11) which a man had not asked for, since they

---

[86] *Tunc et ipse* (GNO III/2, 14,17–8).

had not hoped that a virgin could conceive whilst remaining a virgin and give birth to a child. This child, then, is 'God for us' (Is 7,14); he descended unto those who are down below on earth, seeking the lamb that had perished, that is, his very creature. He then ascended into the heights taking with himself and offering to the Father the man whom he had thus found, effecting in himself the first fruits of the resurrection of man in order that, if the head is raised from the dead so also the remaining body of every human being, who will be found in life, is going to be resuscitated in his turn, once the time of their condemnation on account of their trespass is fulfilled.[87]

It would appear most likely that whoever first devised that anti-Apollinarian argument, would have had this text in mind. Indeed, it is likely that Gregory, whether or not he himself is its originator,[88] recalled that Irenaean passage both when he wrote against Apollinarius and in the present context. This, at least, is suggested by the coexistence of allusions to the parable of the lost sheep with the argument about Christ's and our resurrection.

Be this as it may, if it is accepted that Irenaeus in the present passage infers universal resurrection from Christ's resurrection, then this universalist element should be regarded as a genuine part of the anti-Apollinarian argument discussed above. This, then, could account also for Gregory's soteriological application of it.

It may be worthwhile to pause briefly at this point to review the observations which have so far been made concerning Gregory's use of universal human nature in soteriology. From his writing *Tunc et ipse* it appeared that Gregory combined the 'physical' terminology of the Athanasian tradition with the Origenist tenet of universal salvation, thus arguing, by giving *phusis* a universal interpretation, that on account of the mixture of the Logos with our *phusis* the whole of humanity would eventually be saved. Gregory's adoption of that Athanasian soteriology was then explained as being due to a need he had encountered in the course of the Eunomian controversy, as Eunomius had levelled against Basil the charge of a 'divisive' christology.

This development, I suggested, was given a further twist when Gregory was subsequently suspected of Apollinaranism. In order to combat this charge he increased the 'diphysite' element of his

---

[87] Irenaeus, *haer* III 19,3 (vol. III/2, 380–2 Rousseau/Doutreleau).
[88] This he disclaims at *trid spat* (GNO IX, 291,11), but cf. Wickham (1981), 282.

christology. In particular, he adopted an argument designed to show
the salvific necessity of Christ's human body and soul. This latter
argument, finally, was employed with a soteriological emphasis in
Gregory's *Refutatio*, stating that Christ's resurrection would lead to
universal resurrection.

Two principal models, then, the Athanasian 'physical' soteriology
and the anti-Apollinarian argument about the effect of Christ's death
and resurrection, are developed by Gregory to support his interest
in universal salvation. Only with regard to the latter could it be
shown that Gregory's universalist interpretation is inherited from the
theological tradition he is drawing on.

While Gregory's reasons for adopting this kind of speculation could
be thus elucidated, we have as yet not found any substantial hint
concerning a specific understanding of universal human nature which
would be required for it. To this end we now have to turn to the
Catechetical Oration, which is the only writing where Gregory develops such a theory.

5.3.5 *The universality of salvation in the* Catechetical Oration

Gregory's *Catechetical Oration* contains his most explicit treatment of
the universality of salvation and of the relevance for it of a particular understanding of human nature. In this treatise, which Gregory
wrote—although indirectly[89]—for the teaching of catechumens, he is
more than elsewhere concerned to explain the exact details of
Incarnation and salvation. This it is important to notice; here it is
not, as in *Contra Eunomium*, the problem that truly *God* was incarnate, nor, as in the *Antirrheticus*, the notion of Christ's full humanity
which is at issue. The background rather is traditional Christian
apologetics. The ultimate addressees of the treatise were non-Christians
who would take exception to the doctrine of Incarnation more than
to other Christian views, as Gregory himself admits.[90] That Gregory
in the *Catechetical Oration* is particularly influenced by the apologetic
tradition is thus not surprising and is revealed by even a brief comparison with, for example, Athanasius's book *On the Incarnation*.[91]

Gregory would thus have dealt in this book with what he considered to be basics of Christian belief, which we may safely assume

---

[89] Cf. *or cat* (1) (GNO III/4, 5,1–5).
[90] *Or cat* (9) (GNO III/4, 36,17–37,5).
[91] Cf. the *index fontium* at GNO III/4, 109 and Kees (1995), 78–90.

to hold for Christians in general, not only for beginners. At the same time, however, there is no reason to discard the views he expresses in other writings in favour of those put forth here. By some, it is true, the *Catechetical Oration* has been seen as something like Gregory's *Dogmatic Theology*,[92] and, consequently, the views expressed here have crucially influenced their perception of Gregory's theology as a whole. Yet, while the work certainly has to be taken seriously as representing Gregory's considered opinion on a number of issues, I could not convince myself of the perspicuity of that view.

Twice in this treatise Gregory treats explicitly of the universality of salvation as effected through the Incarnation of Christ. In both these passages it is the problem of Christ's death, a major stumbling block for any Christian apologist, which Gregory has to account for.

In the first of them Gregory starts from a consideration of how the doctrine of Incarnation can be reconciled with the notion of divine impassibility.[93] He argues that passions in the strict sense of the word are only sexual lust and ethical faults;[94] as Christ has not been prone to either—not even his birth was due the exertion of sexuality[95]—he was *qua* man passionless. In fact, the so-called passions of human life, growth, eating, drinking, birth and even death, are really only motions (κινήσεις)[96] of human nature.[97] There is therefore nothing wrong in saying that God, in the Incarnation, was subject to them, but, on the contrary, this confirms that God actually *was* man. This is true for death as well as for birth for both are, as it were, corresponding motions of human nature.[98]

After these assertions Gregory continues with an account of the precise relevance of the death and resurrection of Christ for salvation. He writes there:

> For we say that God was in both motions of our nature, in that by which the soul is linked to the body and in that by which body is

---

[92] See for this opinion Ueberweg's summary, quoted by Srawley (1903), xvi–xvii, Harnack's judgment (1894, vol. IV, 334) and most recently Kees (1995, *passim*).

[93] *Or cat* (15) (GNO III/4, 44,4ff.).

[94] *Or cat* (16) (GNO III/4, 46,2–12).

[95] *Or cat* (16) (GNO III/4, 47,3–7).

[96] *Or cat* (16) (GNO III/4, 47,15).

[97] Note the striking contradiction to, e.g., *an et res* (PG 46, 137B–140B).

[98] At this point Gregory seems to entangle himself in difficulties: he compares death as the 'separation' (διάζευξις) of body and soul to their connection (συνδρομή, συνάφεια) at birth: that would entail an existence of the soul prior to its earthly 'incarnation' which Gregory elsewhere sharply repudiates.

separated from soul, being mixed with both of them (with the sensible, I say, and the intelligible [part] of the human compound) through
that ineffable and inexpressible amalgamation, effecting that of those
who had once been united (of soul, I say, and body) the unity remains
in eternity. For, as in him also our nature according to its own law
(ἀκολουθία) was moved towards the separation of body and soul, he
joined the separated together again as with a kind of glue (the divine
power, I say) connecting the divided elements into an unbreakable
unity. And this is the resurrection, the re-junction of the separated elements after their dissolution into an unresolvable oneness of parts that
are grown together (ἀλλήλοις συμφυομένον) in order that the first grace
of humanity be called back and that we may again enter into eternal
life, once the evil that is mixed with our nature has flown out through
our dissolution (. . .).

   As the principle of death was in one and went through the entire
human nature, in the same way also the principle of resurrection
extends from one into the whole of humanity. For he who again united
the soul, which had been assumed by himself, with its proper body
by means of his power which had been mixed with both of those at
their first constitution, mixed, in a more general way, the intelligible
substance with the sensible so that the beginning (ἀρχή) is with consequence led to its perfection (πέρας). For when in that man, who was
assumed by himself, the soul re-entered the body after the dissolution,
the same kind of junction of the separated passed over from it as from
a starting point (ἀρχή), as it were, potentially (τῇ δυνάμει) to the entire
human nature. And this is the mystery of God's plan (οἰκονομία) with
regard to his death and his resurrection from the dead: that, rather
than preventing the separation of his soul and body by death according to nature's necessary development (ἀκολουθία), both would be
reunited with each other in the resurrection; so that he might become
in himself the meeting-ground both of life and death, having re-estab-
lished in himself that nature which death had divided, and being himself the originating principle of the uniting of those separated portions.[99]

It seems immediately clear that this is yet another use by Gregory
of the aforementioned, originally anti-Apollinarian argument. At the
present place it is employed to emphasise the soteriological need for
Christ's death. In comparison with previously analysed texts it appears
that here the equation between universal resurrection and salvation
is complete. Gregory appears no longer to have any doubts about
this fact. Further, this salvific activity is unequivocally attributed to
Christ *qua* Logos. He is the one who is said to reunite the separated
parts which he had assumed. Gregory's christology is thus as divi-

---

[99]   *Or cat* (16) (GNO III/4, 48,2–49,16).

sive as ever. As for the underlying anthropology, it is remarkable that Gregory here calls death, the separation of human body and soul, an ἀκολουθία of human nature. He rarely goes thus far in allowing a change of the *phusis* which now makes death 'natural'.[100]

More important for the present enquiry than any of those observations, however, is what Gregory writes in the second paragraph. Although again he does not dwell on any specific notion of universal human nature, he makes it quite clear that he here thinks of a quasi-scientific process: the resurrection-principle, generated by the Logos in *one* man, contains at the same time the potential for the resurrection of the entire human race.

Hübner was the first to suggest, comparing similar phrasing elsewhere in Gregory's writings, that Gregory's use here of τῇ δυνάμει could be understood as referring to his doctrine of creation.[101] There, we have seen, the initial, germinal creation had been said to constitute the entire world *potentially*. In a similar way, then, the deification of the man in Christ would be the germinal deification of humankind.

It appears, however, that there is not much evidence to be found in the present passage to support the view that Gregory here has cosmological theories in mind. Elsewhere, of course, we have seen him treat of salvation as of a new creation,[102] but there is no trace of such an argument at the present place. There remains the mention of potentiality; yet this notion in itself is too wide-spread in ancient philosophy to allow an easy identification with one particular topic. I should thus suggest discarding any obvious connection of the present argument with Gregory's cosmology.

A parallel, of course, exists: as in cosmology, Gregory in the present passage envisages the development of a principle from its germinal origin into its fully developed form, apparently seeing this development as a strictly necessary process. This, I think, must be the relevance of the 'potentiality' mentioned here; Christ's resurrection is as yet not the universal resurrection in actuality, but it guarantees universal resurrection as surely as the creation of the initial principles *is* the creation of the whole world.

Why does this development take place? In the first place, it is true, the change of the nature is attributed to the influence of a

---

[100] Cf. p. 275 with n. 86 above.
[101] Hübner (1974), 107–11.
[102] *Eun* III/2 52–3 (GNO II, 69,22–70,13); see p. 215 above.

force transcending it, that is the Logos. Yet the Logos, according to
these lines, carried out a change in one human individual. This,
then, is supposed to constitute a potential change to the entire nature.

How precisely the unfolding from 'potential' into 'actual' deification
of the nature is thought to function is not related here. At a later point
in the same work, however, Gregory is more explicit on this issue:

> Since, then, there was needed a lifting up from death for the whole
> of our nature, he stretches forth a hand as it were to prostrate man,
> and stooping down to our dead corpse he came so far within the grasp
> of death as to touch a state of deadness, and then in his own body
> to bestow on our nature the principle of resurrection, raising as he
> did potentially (τῇ δυνάμει or: by his power) along with himself the
> whole man. For since from no other source than from the concrete
> lump of our nature had come that man, who was the receptacle of
> the Godhead and in the resurrection was raised up together with the
> Godhead, therefore just in the same way as, in the instance of this
> body of ours, the operation of one of the organs of sense is felt at
> once by the whole system, as one with that member, so also the res-
> urrection principle of this member, as though the whole of mankind
> (πάσῃ φύσις) was a single living being, passes through the entire race
> (τὸ πᾶν), being imparted from the member to the whole by virtue of
> the continuity and oneness of the nature.[103]

More distinct than in the previously analysed text, the death and
(by implication) resurrection of Christ are the topic of the present
elaboration. In the paragraph preceding the text quoted Gregory
first says[104] that Christ's death occurred as a necessary consequence
of his birth; then, however, as if correcting himself, he adds that it
might be better to say that the birth in a way occurred in order
that Christ could die. Thus his death becomes the real climax of
the Incarnation. It has been observed that Gregory's theology is—
unlike, for example, that of his Nazianzen namesake—not centred
around the mystery of Christ's death.[105] This is true even here, for
our Gregory, saying that Christ's death is the objective of the Incarnation, ultimately thinks of the resurrection for which his death
is only the necessary condition.[106]

---

[103] GNO III/4, 78,3–17, ET: Moore/Wilson (1893), 499 (with amendments).
[104] *Or cat* (32) (GNO III/4, 77,15–21).
[105] So, e.g., Holl (1904), 178–96 (for Nazianzen); 232–5 for Nyssen and the difference between the two.
[106] On importance and understanding of the resurrection in the *or cat* see: Winling
(1989).

In its description of the way this restoration is supposed to work, the present text resembles the previously analysed one. Once more we have the notion of an *arche* functioning as both a beginning and a principle for universal resurrection. Interesting also are two other formulations in the same sentence: τῇ δυνάμει, which as signifying the relationship of Christ's individual and universal resurrection is recurrent, could here also refer to Christ's power.[107] This ambiguity, I think, is not unimportant for a proper understanding of the present passage. Secondly, we have the phrase τὸν ὅπου ἄνθρωπον as an equivalent for 'human nature' in its extensive sense.

To this line of reasoning Gregory then adds the metaphor, already known from elsewhere,[108] of first fruits and dough. This metaphor, employed by Irenaeus in connection with universal resurrection,[109] is (generally, it appears) used by Gregory to emphasise the community of human nature as the principle of universal salvation.

At the present place, this approach is backed up by a further comparison which is apparently meant to illustrate how this community can explain the transmission of salvation: in our body the sense-perception of one part is transmitted throughout the whole in so far as it is united to the part; so also in the case of our nature, which is, in a way, like a single living organism, what is done to a part is transmitted to the whole of it.

To find out how this is meant to illustrate the point Gregory wishes to make, it should first be explained how Gregory would have understood the analogy between a body and human nature. In *De hominis opificio* 16 this analogy is employed to argue that both are in a similar way limited.[110] Here the idea is that both have an organic constitution. What is the ontological basis of this constitution? It has been pointed out that the organic constitution of the individual was compared to that of the world by the Stoics.[111] We read in one of their fragments:

> In the case of unified bodies (σώματα ἡνωμένα) there exists a certain 'sympathy,' since, when the finger is cut, the whole body shares in its condition. So then, the universe also is a unified body.[112]

---

[107] This is the interpretation of Moore/Wilson (1893), loc. cit.
[108] *Tunc et ipse* (GNO III/2, 14,11); *ref Eun* 143 (GNO II, 374,9–12).
[109] *Haer* III 19,3 (vol. III/2, 380 Rousseau/Doutreleau).
[110] *Op hom* 16 (PG 44, 185B).
[111] Hübner (1974), 150–5; 246–9.
[112] Sextus Empiricus, *adv math* IX 80 (= SVF II, 302, 34–6); ET: Bury (Loeb III, 45–6). Cf. also: Plato, *Tim* 30D–31A and Origen, *princ* II 1,2 (107,19–28 Koetschau).

It has, therefore, been argued that Gregory uses a Stoic model here
to illustrate his understanding of the universality of salvation.[113]
However, this inference is not necessary as by Gregory's time the
same view could be maintained on Platonic principles.[114] In fact, it
is rather unlikely that Gregory understood it the Stoic way. We know
from other writings that his anthropology was completely un-Stoic:[115]
for Gregory the organic constitution of the body would hint at the
existence of an intelligible soul.[116]

Perhaps it is of ultimately secondary importance whether the analogy here is understood in a Stoic or a Neoplatonic way; the decisive point is that humanity constitutes a kind of reality enabling a
transmission from one part to the whole. The differences between
the two philosophical approaches with regard to this question, however, seem to be all but negligible. From our sources it seems indubitable that the point of the Stoic doctrine was *not* that one part
could be able to change the whole, but that the whole would determine each single part.[117] Thus Platonists using their language only
had to insist that this 'whole' was properly understood to be an intelligible item transcending the parts.[118] In either interpretation, then, the
principle of this assumed interaction of the parts is their determination by an entity which is ontologically prior to them.

In our case, it would appear, this entity must be universal human
nature. Ultimately, it is true, the transcendent entity determining the
fate of human beings is the Logos himself. By means of his *dunamis*,
which is present in human nature, the creature is changed. It is
for this reason that, as I noted above, the *potential* salvation of all
humankind can also be understood to be a salvation 'by the power',
the power, that is, of the Logos. Yet this power is mediated, and
the subject of this mediation is most properly thought to be universal *phusis*. It seems to be precisely this mediation which Gregory
has in mind when he explains, in the *Refutatio*, Paul's use of the term
μεσίτης at 1 Tim 2,5 as follows:

---

[113] Hübner (1974), ibid.
[114] Cf. Plotinus, *Enn* IV 4,32; IV 7,7.
[115] See e.g. *op hom* 12 (PG 44, 156Cff.) against the notion of a ἡ γεμονικόν; *op
hom* 6 (PG 44, 140A), 11 (PG 44, 153C–D) for the intelligible character of the
human mind.
[116] This is Gregory's way of using the microcosm analogy: *an et res* (PG 46,
28B–D); *inscr* I 3 (GNO V, 30,24–12).
[117] E.g. SVF II, 269,10–18; cf. Gregory's own account at *fat* (GNO III/2, 37,12–22).
[118] Cf. Plotinus' argument at *Enn* IV 7,7,16–28.

By the distinction implied in the word 'mediator' he reveals to us the whole aim of the mystery of godliness. Now the aim is this: the human item once revolted through the malice of the enemy, and, brought into bondage to sin, was also alienated from the true life. Afterwards, the Lord of the creature calls back to himself his own creature, and becomes man while still remaining God, entirely being the latter, entirely becoming the former, and thus the human item was indissolubly united to God, the man that is in Christ conducting the work of mediation, to whom, by the first fruits assumed from us, all the lump is potentially (τῇ δυνάμει) united.[119]

What kind of entity, then, would human nature have to be in order to function like this? Could it be the item envisaged by Gregory in the context of trinitarian theology and cosmology? This seems all but impossible. There as here, it is true, he employs the notion of universal *phusis* to mediate between God's simplicity and the world's multiplicity. There is also agreement on the notion that, in the realm of sensible reality, this *phusis develops* towards its perfection. Yet otherwise the two theories are clearly different. In particular it is noteworthy that in both cosmology and trinitarian theology the transmission of the nature depended on a precise immanent mechanism: it is no coincidence that the Father is the Father, nor that Adam is the progenitor of all humanity. We have seen Gregory expressly assert[120] that human nature is transmitted from Adam by sexual generation to posterity. It seems plain that Christ *qua* man cannot pass on a deified nature to the entire human race on the basis of such a principle. Incidentally, it appears that an inevitable logical presupposition of the present theory, the assumption of universal *phusis* as fallen, cannot be argued for in the same conceptual framework (see pp. 185f. above).

It would appear that Gregory here gets closest to a Neoplatonic notion of the universal. This statement I hasten to qualify, for two central features of this view are not Platonic at all. First, the notion of a Logos changing a *phusis* to whatever precise purpose is alien to Platonism in general; secondly, as I noted before (p. 128 above), Neoplatonists were often careful to give room in their ontology to human individuality more than the present theory of *phusis* seems to do. The present theory seems to be Neoplatonic, then, in that it

---

[119] *Ref Eun* 142–3 (GNO II, 374,2–12).
[120] *Eun* III/1 74–5 (GNO II, 30,7–24), see p. 99 above.

draws on a concept like the following, developed by Plotinus to explain how Mind, the second hypostasis *is* the entirety of its genera:

> And [we can say] the great Intellect (νοῦς) exists by itself, and so do the particular intellects (sc. the genera) which are in themselves, and again that the partial intellects are comprehended in the whole and the whole in the partial; the particular ones are on their own and in another, and that great Intellect is on its own and in those particular; and all are potentially in that Intellect which is on its own, which is actually all things at once, but potentially each particular separately, and the particular intellects are actually what they are, but potentially the whole.[121]

The following features agree in both Plotinus and Gregory. First, the whole *is*, in a sense, the sum of its parts. In Gregory this is the implication of the analogy with an organism, while Plotinus explicitly states that the whole is all particulars at once and each of them separately. Secondly, each part is said to be potentially the whole. This, perhaps, is the most striking agreement. While in Plotinus this is again expressly asserted, in Gregory it is implied by his mention of the potential salvation in Christ.

It would, then, appear that the notion of human nature underlying Gregory's soteriological argument from *Catechetical Oration* 32 is that of a universal unity in multiplicity in which the whole is at once with each part in order that the transmission of salvation from Christ to all humanity can be explained. From this, however, it follows that the present soteriological theory cannot be thought to form a system together with applications by Gregory of human nature in other theological subjects, which confirms a suggestion made at the outset of this chapter.

Ultimately, I think, it is most likely that the present theory of universal nature was devised by Gregory to account for a specific soteriological interest rather than *vice versa*. It is possible, not proven, that the same theory stands behind other passages employing universal *phusis* in the soteriological context. It appears certain that it is not part of an overarching system in the sense underlying the 'systematic interpretation' of Gregory's use of *phusis*-terminology.[122]

---

[121] Plotinus, *Enn* VI 2,20,16–23; ET: Armstrong (1966) vol. VI, 167.
[122] See pp. 125–6 above.

In summary, then, it could, I hope, be shown that the use Gregory makes of universal human nature in soteriology cannot be seen as a systematic feature of his theological thinking. Rather, it was argued that in one particular situation Gregory was prompted to develop speculations in this direction. Their motivation could reasonably be explained by his involvement in doctrinal controversies combined with his interest in universal salvation.

In most of the relevant passages Gregory gives no indication that a precise concept of universal human nature would underlie his argument. Where he does, this concept is clearly different from his, largely consistent, use of this concept in other parts of his theology.

I should thus draw the following conclusions:

(i) Gregory clearly employs universal human nature in soteriology.
(ii) This use is not as incidental as some wish to have it.
(iii) It was Gregory's genuine interest in the Origenist *apokatastasis*, combined with the need to develop a more consistent christology that lured him into this kind of argument.
(iv) A concept of universal human nature answering to this soteriological view is to be found only in the *Oratio Catechetica*.
(v) The theory laid out there is clearly different from that underlying Gregory's argument in the context of cosmology and trinitarian theology.
(vi) This theory would, then, appear to follow from Gregory's soteriological speculations rather than *vice versa* and should thus not be regarded as their philosophical foundation.

CONCLUSION

It was defined as the primary object of this study to elucidate the use Gregory of Nyssa makes of universal human nature. With regard to this aim several conclusions can now be drawn immediately. To begin with, Gregory's strong inclination towards this kind of thinking, which had been surmised at the outset, has been carried beyond doubt. In many passages he was seen employing *phusis*-terminology to precisely this end; those passages extend virtually throughout his entire work. *Phusis*-terminology is applied to practically all doctrinal topics, notably to trinitarian theology, the doctrine of creation, and soteriology, a variety of occurrences was also detected in connection with Gregory's treatment of the Fall, of christology and of eschatology.

It seems, furthermore, indubitable that Gregory's utterances do not all point towards one defined philosophical theory. He often employed *phusis*-terminology more or less loosely in order to indicate either the total of properties characteristic of human beings or the totality of the human race. This result can hardly be thought to be surprising. Few people, probably, would expect to find in an author like Gregory a worked-out terminology which is applied universally in all cases.

At the same time, however, it has become clear that in many places Gregory does aim at a concept of *phusis* as a universal. It could be shown not only that Gregory finds it convenient to apply universal *phusis* to a variety of theological subjects, but that he strove to develop philosophical concepts capable of accounting for those applications. His theological interest was predominant in so far as it provided, as far as we are able to make out, for a starting point for his philosophical thinking: there is no evidence that Gregory ever ventured on an elucidation of 'the problem of universals' independently of theology. Within this framework, however, his philosophical interest was considerable. It only needed an occasion for this to be roused.

This occasion first arose, it appeared, in the area of trinitarian theology. The problem there was this: one of the most frequent objections to the use of *homoousios* for the Trinity was that it allegedly required co-ordination *qua* substance, thus necessitating the imposition of the common *ousia* as an independent entity above the Persons to guarantee their unity. This difficulty was elegantly avoided by Apollinarius of Laodicaea, who argued that universal humanity could be an analogy for the Godhead if it was understood as a derivative genus. In this interpretation, the first instantiation of the genus, Adam or the Father, would also be the common *ousia*. This theory, it appeared, was capable of reconciling the term *homoousios* with a slight notion of subordination *qua* substance and, at the same time, avoided the introduction of *ousia* as a further entity into the Godhead, thus removing major *aporiae* of Nicene theology.

In the Cappadocians' view, however, this application by Apollinarius of human nature, ingenious though it may have been, could no longer be upheld. Eunomius' provocative claim that the Son was *anhomoios*, positing in its consequence the alternative of either equal or dissimilar, meant the demise of the derivative interpretation of the Trinity and thus, by implication, that of the analogy of human-ity as a derivative genus. Still, the Cappadocians decided to retain that analogy in principle; it thus became necessary to reinterpret it in order to make it fit their new understanding of the Trinitarian Godhead.

This task we have seen first Basil, then Gregory undertake; it was a complicated one and their result was found to be deficient in cru-cial aspects. At the same time it appeared, or so at least I have argued, that it would be difficult to think of a better solution they could have reached given the doctrinal and philosophical require-ments they found themselves subject to.

Their solution was an attempted reconstruction of the Apollinarian theory on the basis of co-ordinated *hupostasis*. To explain how the common *ousia* could be conceived of in this model they employed two concepts, precisely the aforementioned notions of human nature as the total of properties characteristic of humanity and as the total-ity of human beings. While these two views could be used loosely by Gregory at times, it appeared that they were often applied in a systematic way. In this latter case, the two notions were distinct but complementary to each other. In the former, the properties would be indicative of an entity that is the same in all human individuals and is the cause of their being as well as of their being humans. The latter notion would indicate that this immanent item occurs in so many individuals and nowhere else; the existence of the human race as such would thus be due to one property of that former entity and would, indeed, be one aspect of it. On account of that fact, then, it was permissible to refer to the entirety of humankind as to 'one man'.

This theory was found to be present in Gregory's works in quite an elaborate form. In the context of trinitarian theology it appeared that both Basil's and his interest were primarily in its logical features, first of all the notion that, due to the presence of the same nature or substance in each individual of the race, they are ontologically co-ordinate. Also, they emphasised that the immanent *phusis* or *ousia* was indicated by a *logos*, a definitional formula, which is the same with all the Persons of the Godhead, thus guaranteeing their equality *qua* substance. The universal name is understood, consistently it appears, as indicating the extension, the entire nature.

This same theory was then detected in Gregory's treatment of subjects pertaining to the divine economy. His treatment of creation, in particular, could be shown to be based on identical principles. Thus, he sees human nature on the one hand as a thing created completely prior to the existence of Adam, yet seen in him and his descendants only. This entity, which was learned to be passed down immanently by means of sexual generation, appeared to be identical with the aforementioned, former notion of *phusis* or *ousia* in trinitarian theology as a kind of immanent form. To this again corresponded the idea that, on account of this continuum, all humanity is one man and as such was foreseen by God at the creation. This is how Gregory expounds Gen 1,27: that God is said to create 'man' means that he creates the entire human race, their *pleroma*) at once—but potentially, by creating its immanent *phusis* which in a necessary process develops into actual humanity.

This process, Gregory would argue, is an essential aspect of that immanent *phusis*, and it will come to a close only when the entire number of human beings has been generated. Their whole number, their entire *phusis*, is germinally provided at the creation of man already and, at that point, seen by God's foresight. Thus the whole history of humankind from creation to the eschaton is the development of human nature from potential to actual completion.

The philosophical background of this theory is multiple. In its primarily logical use in trinitarian theology its author could be shown to draw on late ancient interpretations of the problem of universals in Aristotle's *Categories*. While its interpretation integrated Stoic and Neoplatonic ingredients, it should not, I think, be called eclectic, as it aims at one consistent interpretation of that problem.

Gregory's cosmological use of universal nature, on the other hand, revealed substantial parallels to Neoplatonic theories of *phusis*. In neither case, however, was Gregory seen to copy slavishly or to reproduce philosophical lore which he was ultimately unable to comprehend. He rather emerged as a creative Christian theologian well versed in the arts and attempting to apply the tools provided by the Greek intellectual tradition to further the cause of Christianity. As a rule, I think, inconsistencies should be seen as resulting from difficulties inherent in this attempt rather than from basic limitations of Gregory's abilities.

For Gregory's theology it proved important that he equated human nature as an entity immanent in all human beings with 'godlikeness' (cf. esp. *De Hominis Opificio* 16). Thus, God's creation of man in his own image is the foremost proof of divine grace. A consequence of this view is that, within this framework, Gregory could not account for a Fall of the nature; man's image character is blurred, not destroyed. Where Gregory employed *phusis*-terminology in connection with the fallen state of man, he often neglected its universal aspect, emphasising, in the Origenist tradition, the quasi-substantial changes human beings suffered on account of their trespass. In a few passages, though, he claimed that universal nature has fallen, and in one passage apparently embraces a derivative understanding of men's unity.

A similar picture emerged with regard to man's salvation. In one important strand of Gregory's utterances on soteriology he took what I termed a humanistic approach emphasising men's potential for salvation on account of their retained faculties of rational thinking and free will, which are indicative of the continuing presence, albeit obscured, of the divine image in human beings. This view, while not drawing expressly on universal human nature, seemed in perfect harmony with the interpretation of it as of an immanent universal equally present in all human beings.

Within this humanistic approach patterns could be discerned which more or less precisely corresponded to those that were observed in Gregory's treatment of the Fall. While Gregory could use *phusis*-terminology, he nowhere in those texts made universal human nature the conceptual basis of his soteriology.

A number of texts, admittedly, argued for universal salvation on the basis of universal humanity. It could, however, be rendered likely that those passages represent one, rather limited, strand in Gregory's thinking, conditioned above all by needs he encountered in the context of doctrinal controversies. The occurrence of those passages was limited to a number of dogmatic writings written in a comparatively brief time span. Their understanding of universal humanity, where Gregory makes this explicit, differed from that encountered elsewhere in his writings. While details may remain controversial, it seems appropriate to conclude, then, that those passages cannot be regarded as the genuine application of Gregory's conception of universal human nature to soteriology.

It is in eschatology, then, that the topic of universal human nature becomes once more conceptually relevant. The *apokatastasis* of our nature is in Gregory's view the ultimate realisation of the complete number germinally embraced by the initial creation of the nature. *Apokatastasis* is thus, unlike in Origen, a return only in the sense that it restores the lost, perfect state of man; the complete number of men is constituted, not restituted, in the final restoration.

It thus emerged that what I termed the 'systematic' interpretation of Gregory's application of human nature to the economy should, in its traditional form, no longer be upheld. Gregory's understanding of universal human nature does not lend itself to a systematic exposition of what was to become the classical framework of salvation history. It also became clear that Gregory had at his disposal a theory of universal nature, that of Apollinarius, which would have suited that purpose much better. It is therefore difficult to argue that he aimed at, but fell short of, such a systematic application.

At the same time it would appear that Gregory's application of human nature to the economy is quite systematic, albeit in a different sense. It is systematic, first, in that Gregory normally strives to stick with one model of universal nature, the same one he had employed in trinitarian theology. It is systematic, further, in that many of Gregory's various applications of human nature to the economy seem to support one particular understanding of salvation history. It might, then, appear the best conclusion to say that the traditional systematic interpretation is not to be totally abandoned, but to be modified.

What is this particular understanding of salvation history? Answering this question it may be convenient to refer, once more, to Apollinarius and his application of universal human nature. In Apollinarius we encountered a very systematic use of this theory serving a theology that is essentially pessimistic about man in his present state. Apollinarius apparently had, more than many Greek theologians—an obvious exception being Athanasius—, grasped the essence of Paul's teaching about man's present alienation from God and the exclusive role of divine grace in the process of his salvation. Had it not been for his christological extravagances, he might have become an Augustine of the East.

In contrast, it appears that Gregory's teaching on universal human nature is indicative of a view at the opposite end of the theological spectrum. Equating human nature with godlikeness, he sees the divine grace active primarily in creation; consequently, his outlook on the present world and on human beings in it is characterised by a deep-rooted optimism; the notion of *apokatastasis* is, therefore, an essential part of his theology. The divine is present in this world as in its creation; divine grace is seen in all human beings on account of their possession of mind (*De Hominis Opificio* 16). If human beings are, at present, unaware of it, if their appearance even, at times, makes it difficult to perceive of them in such a way, it is the more important to remind them of the truth that is fundamental to their existence: that they are created in the image of God.

It would be wrong to deny that the elements that are typical of Apollinarius' approach are to be found in Gregory and *vice versa*. The former holds man to be God's image as well as the latter knows of man's present alienation from God. This is not surprising as both base their teaching on the same biblical foundation. Looking, however, at the emphasis and frequency of their use of those notions, the above considerations are confirmed. Characteristic and, of course, central for the present study is their interpretation of universal human nature. In this, it appears now, they are both of the same calibre. It is fascinating to observe how what might at first seem like the adoption of alternative philosophical models only is then pressed into the service of two fundamentally different approaches to Christian theology. Human nature as identified with Adam on the basis of Paul's Adam-Christ typology allows humanity to be seen as alienated from God on account of their progenitor's trespass; it then needs the second Adam to redeem them. Human nature as identified with the godlike item created by God according to Gen 1,27 would, on the other hand, be precisely what Gregory needed to guarantee continuity in the world's development from creation to restoration according to God's plan.

This, then, is the modified version of the aforesaid systematic interpretation of Gregory's application of human nature to salvation

history: for Gregory, human nature as the creation of God is responsible for the continuity of God's presence in this world. It is the
bond that ties together God and man. It exhorts the latter in his
present state of alienation from God to cleanse himself in order to
restore what is an image of the divine within himself to its original
splendour. It guarantees the *apokatastasis* as the restoration of human
nature.

At this point one ultimate question arises with regard to the subject of the present enquiry which, it seems to me, is not easily
answered on any count. It was shown in the first part of this study
how the 'Aristotelian' model of a co-ordinate human nature was chosen by Basil and his theological allies for reasons emerging directly
from the course of the trinitarian controversy. It was in order to
avoid any notion of subordination, or so at least I have argued, that
the Cappadocians modified the derivative interpretation of humanity offered to Basil by Apollinarius.

Gregory's application of the same notion to subjects pertaining to
the economy could then be supposed to result from an attempt to
be consistent with Basil's and, indeed, his own use of human nature
in the trinitarian context. It has turned out, however, that Gregory's
application of 'his' theory of universal human nature to those subjects is equally indicative of genuine theological concerns of his. This,
then, raises the question of priority: was there, initially, Basil's adoption of human nature for his trinitarian theology which was then
taken over by Gregory, who employed it in this area as well as in
other theological fields; or was there from the very beginning an
overarching theory, modelled on the Apollinarian one and intended
to apply an alternative understanding of the human *phusis* to the
entirety of theology? This overarching theory would, in all likelihood, have had Gregory of Nyssa as its originator, and thus a corollary of the latter alternative would be the questioning of Basil's
priority in the development of the Cappadocian approach to the
trinitarian problem.

The results reached in the course of this study do not, I think,
allow for an unequivocal answer to this question. The fact that the
'Aristotelian' model was seen as standing, in principle, even behind
Basil's earliest pronouncements on the trinitarian issue may be regarded
as an indicator of some weight for the priority of this application.
Gregory may have discovered later that his brother's modification

of the Apollinarian model was useful way beyond its limited application to the single *ousia* of the Godhead.

At the same time, this consideration does not seem sufficient to decide finally on this issue. It must not be forgotten that Nyssen did not come into existence all of a sudden after Basil's death. While we are virtually ignorant about his intellectual activities in, say, the early 360s, it is by no means impossible that his later ideas were already taking shape at that time, and that he was in exchange with Basil about them would not be unlikely, to say the least. It would seem conceivable, then, that Gregory should be credited with considerable influence on the shaping of Cappadocian theology in general. This influence would certainly go beyond anything that could be inferred directly from his or Basil's writings and must thus remain speculative.

If Gregory was not involved in Basil's early theological decisions, however, it would be the more impressive that his theology of universal humanity offers such an admirable integration of his brother's trinitarian approach into a systematic whole. Gregory, then, would have been—as he himself might have wished to be seen—his brother's perfect pupil, capable of understanding his teacher better than the latter had understood himself and bringing into full form the seeds that lay dormant in his teaching. The words Gregory himself used of the relation between Moses' and Basil's accounts of creation could thus perhaps be applied analogously to his brother's and his own teaching on human nature (*hex*; PG 44, 61D–64A):

Ὃν γὰρ ἔχει λόγον πρὸς τὸν κόκκον ὁ ἄσταχυς, καὶ ἐξ ἐκείνου ὢν, κἀκεῖνο μὴ ὢν, μᾶλλον δὲ ἐκεῖνο μὲν ὢν τῇ δυνάμει, παρηλλαγμένος δὲ μεγέθει, καὶ ποικιλίᾳ καὶ σχήματι· τὸν αὐτὸν εἴποι τις ἂν ἐπέχειν λόγον, πρὸς τὴν τοῦ μεγάλου Μωϋσέως φωνὴν, τὰ παρὰ τοῦ μεγάλου Βασιλείου διὰ φιλοπονωτέρας θεωρίας ἐξεργασθέντα νοήματα.

BIBLIOGRAPHY

This bibliography has no claim to be comprehensive; it contains in principle only works mentioned or otherwise referred to in the book.

1. Ancient authors

Where the edition forms part of a work that is listed in the second part of this bibliography, the editor is cited with year only, for example Lietzmann (1904).

Alcinous, *Didascalicus*, ed. Whittaker, Paris 1990: *didasc*
Alexander of Aphrodisias, *Quaestiones* I, ed. Bruns, *Supplementum Aristotelicum* II/2, Berlin 1892, 1–43: *quaest*
——, *In Aristotelis Metaphysica*, ed. Hayduck, CAG I: *in Met*
Ammonius Hermiae, *In Aristotelis Categorias*, ed. Busse, CAG IV/4: *in Cat*
Apollinarius of Laodicea, *Epistula ad Basilium Caesariensis* (= Basil, *ep* 362), ed. de Riedmatten (1956), 203–4 (= vol. III, 222–4 Courtonne): (Basil), *ep* 362
——, *Ad episcopos Diocaesarienses*, ed. Lietzmann (1904), 255–6: *ad Diocaes*
——, *Fides secundum partem* (Ἡ κατὰ μέρος πίστις), ed. Lietzmann (1904), 167–84: *KMP*
——, *De unione corporis et divinitatis in Christo*, ed. Lietzmann (1904), 185–93: *de unione*
——, *Ad Diodorum* (fragments), ed. Lietzmann (1904), 237–42
——, *Fragmenta in Octateuchum*, ed. Devreesse (1959), 128–54: *in Gen* etc.
——, *Fragmenta in Psalmos*, ed. Mühlenberg (1975), vol. I, 1–118: *in Ps*
——, *Fragmenta in Ezechielem*, ed. Mai (1852), vol. VII/2, 82–91
——, *Fragmenta in Matthaeum*, ed. Reuss (1957), 1–54: *in Mat*
——, *Fragmenta in Iohannem*, ed. Reuss (1966), 3–64: *in Ioh*
——, *Fragmenta in Epistulam ad Romanos*, ed. Staab (1933), 57–82: *in Rom*
Apollinarius (?), *Quod unus sit Christus*, ed. Lietzmann (1904), 294–302
Apollonius Dyscolus, *De nomine*, ed. Schneider, *Grammatici Graeci* II/3, Leipzig 1910, 38–69: *nom*
Aristotle, *Categoriae*, ed. Minio-Paluello, Oxford 1949: *cat*
——, *Ethica Nicomachea*, ed. Bywater, Oxford 1894: *EN*
——, *Liber de interpretatione*, ed. Minio-Paluello, Oxford 1949: *de int*
——, *Physica*, ed. Ross, Oxford 1950: *phys*
——, *Politica*, ed. Ross, Oxford 1957: *pol*
——, *Metaphysica*, ed. Jaeger, Oxford 1957: *met*
Athanasius of Alexandria, *De incarnatione*, ed. Thomson, Oxford 1971: *inc*
——, *Orationes adversus Arianos* I–II, ed. Tetz, Athanasius Werke I/1, Berlin 1998, 109–260: *c Arian*
——, *Oratio III adversus Arianos*, ed. Migne, PG 26, 321–468: *c Arian*
——, *De decretis Nicaenae synodi*, ed. Opitz, Athanasius Werke II/1, Berlin 1935ff., 1–45: *decr Nicaen*
——, *De sententia Dionysii*, ed. Opitz, op. cit., 46–67: *sent Dion*
——, *De synodis*, ed. Opitz, op. cit., 231–78: *syn*
——, *Epistulae ad Serapionem*, ed. Migne, PG 26, 530–676: *ad Serap*
——, *Tomus ad Antiochenos*, ed. Migne, PG 26, 796–809: *tom ad Ant*

(ps.)-Athanasius, *De incarnatione et contra Arianos*, ed. Migne, PG 26, 984–1028: *d inc et c Ar*

———, *Contra Apollinarium* I–II, ed. Migne, PG 26, 1093–1165: *c Apoll*

Atticus, *Fragmenta*, ed. des Places, Paris 1977: *fr*

Basil of Caesarea, *Epistulae*, ed. Courtonne, 3 vols., Paris 1957–66: *ep*

———, *Adversus Eunomium* I–III, ed. Migne, PG 29, 497–669: *adv Eun*

———, *De spiritu sancto*, ed. Johnson, Oxford 1898: *d spir sanct*

———, *Homiliae in Hexaëmeron*, edd. Amand de Mendieta/Rudberg, GCS, n.F. 2: *hom in hex*

Boethius, *In librum Aristotelis* Περὶ Ἑρμηνείας, ed. Meiser, 2 vols., Leipzig 1877–80: *in de Int*

———, *Liber de divisione*, ed. Migne, PL 64, 875–92 (= Porphyry, *fr* 169F Smith): *div*

Dexippus, *In Aristotelis Categorias*, ed. Busse, CAG IV/2: *in Cat*

Didymus the Blind, *In Genesim*, 2 vols., ed. Nautin, SC 233/244: *in Gen*

———, *Fragmenta in Psalmos*, ed. Mühlenberg (1975), vol. I, 119–375; II: *in Ps*

Diogenes Laërtius, *Vitae philosophorum*, 2 vols., ed. Long, Oxford 1964

Dionysius Thrax, *Ars grammatica*, ed. Uhlig, *Grammatici Graeci* I/1, Leipzig 1883: *ars gramm*

———, *Scholia Vaticana in artem Dionysii*, ed. Hilgard, *Grammatici Graeci* I/2, Leipzig 1901: *in art Dion*

Epiphanius of Salamis, *Panarion*, edd. Holl/Dummer, GCS 25/31/37: *haer*

Eunomius of Cyzicus, *Liber Apologeticus*, ed. Vaggione (1987), 34–74: *apol*

———, *Apologia apologiae* (fragments), in: Gregory of Nyssa, *Eun*, passim: *apol apol*

Eusebius of Caesarea, *Historia ecclesiastica*, ed. Schwartz, GCS 9: *hist eccl*

Eustathius of Antioch, *Fragmenta*, ed. Spanneut (1948): *fr*

———, *Adversus Photinum* (fragment), ed. Lorenz (1980), 125–8 (Syriac), 112–4 (German)

Galen, *Definitiones medicae*, ed. Kühn, *Claudii Galeni opera omnia*, vol. XIX, Leipzig 1830, 346–462: *def med*

Gregory of Nazianzus, *Epistulae*, ed. Gallay, GCS 53: *ep*

———, *Orationes: or*
  or 20–23, ed. Mossay, SC 270
  or 27–31, edd. Gallay/Jourjon, SC 250
  or 38–41, edd. Moreschini/Galley, SC 358

Gregory of Nyssa, *Contra Eunomium* I–III, ed. Jaeger, GNO I–II: *Eun*

———, *Refutatio confessionis Eunomii*, ed. Jaeger, GNO II, 312–410: *ref Eun*

———, *Ad Eustathium de Sancta Trinitate*, ed. Mueller, GNO III/1, 1–16: *Eust*

———, *Ad Graecos ex communibus notionibus*, ed. Mueller, GNO III/1, 17–33: *graec*

———, *Ad Ablabium quod not sint tres dii*, ed. Mueller, GNO III/1, 35–57: *Abl*

———, *Ad Theophilum adversus Apollinaristas*, ed. Mueller, GNO III/1, 119–128: *Theoph*

———, *Antirrheticus adversus Apollinarium*, ed. Mueller, GNO III/1, 131–233: *antirrh*

———, *In illud: Tunc et ipse filius*, ed. Downing, GNO III/2, 1–28: *tunc et ipse*

———, *Contra fatum*, ed. McDonough, GNO III/2, 29–63: *fat*

———, *De infantibus premature abreptis*, ed. Hörner, GNO III/2, 65–97: *infant*

———, *Oratio Catechetica*, ed. Mühlenberg, GNO III/4: *or cat*

———, *Apologia in Hexaëmeron*, ed. Migne, PG 44, 61–124: *hex*

———, *De hominis opificio*, ed. Migne, PG 44, 125–256: *op hom*

———, *De anima et resurrectione*, ed. Migne, PG 46, 12–160: *an et res*

———, *In inscriptiones Psalmorum*, ed. McDonough, GNO V, 24–175: *inscr*

———, *In Ecclesiasten*, ed. Alexander, GNO V, 277–442: *eccl*

———, *In Canticum Canticorum Homiliae*, ed. Langerbeck, GNO VI: *cant*

———, *De Beatitudinibus*, ed. Callahan, GNO VII/2, 75–171: *beat*

————, *De Oratione Dominica*, ed. Callahan, GNO VII/2, 1–74: *or dom*
————, *De Virginitate*, ed. Calvarnos, GNO VIII/1, 215–346: *virg*
————, *De Perfectione*, ed. Jaeger, GNO VIII/1, 173–214: *perf*
————, *De vita santae Macrinae*, ed. Woods Callahan, GNO VIII/1, 370–414: *vit Macr*
————, *Epistulae*, ed. Pasquali, GNO VIII/2: *ep*
————, *De tridui inter mortium et resurrectionem domini nostri Jesu Christi spatio*, ed. Gebhardt, GNO IX, 273–306: *trid spat*
Hilary of Poitiers, *De synodis*, ed. Migne, PL 10, 471–546: *syn*
Irenaeus, *Adversus haereses*, edd. Rousseau/Doutreleau, 10 vols., SC 100/152/153/210/211/263/264/293/294: *haer*
John Philoponus, *In Aristotelis Categorias*, ed. Busse, CAG XIII/1: *in Cat*
Jerome, *Epistulae I–LXX*, ed. Hilberg, CSEL 54: *ep*
————, *De viris illustribus*, ed. Migne, PL 23, 602–720: *vir ill*
Justin Martyr, *Dialogus*, ed. Goodspeed, *Die ältesten christlichen Apologeten*, Göttingen 1915, 90–265: *dial*
Marcellus of Ancyra, *Fragmenta*, edd. Klostermann/Hansen, GCS 14, 185–215: *fr*
Marius Victorinus, *Contra Arium*, edd. Henry/Hadot; CSEL 83: *c Arium*
Methodius of Olympus, *De autexousio*, ed. Bonwetsch, GCS 27, 143–206: *autex*
Nemesius of Emesa, *De natura hominis*, ed. Morani, Leipzig 1987: *nat hom*
Olympiodorus, *Commentarium in Alcibiadem I*, ed. Westerink, Amsterdam 1956: *in Alcib I*
Origen, *In Leuiticum Homiliae XVI*, ed. Baehrens, GCS 29, 280–507: *in Lev hom*
————, *In Numeros homiliae*, ed. Baehrens, GCS 30, 3–285: *hom in Num*
————, *Commentarii in Iohannem*, ed. Preuschen, GCS 10: *in Ioh*
————, *Commentarii in Epistulam ad Romanos*, ed. Migne, PG 14, 833–1292: *in Rom*
————, *De principiis*, ed. Koetschau, GCS 22: *princ*
————, *De Oratione*, ed. Koetschau, GCS 3: *orat*
————, *Contra Celsum*, ed. Koetschau, GCS 2/3: *c Celsum*
————, *Philocalia*, ed. Robinson, Cambridge 1893
Philo of Alexandria, *De opificio mundi*, ed. Arnaldez, Paris 1967: *op mun*
Philostorgius, *Historia Ecclesiastica*, edd. Bidez/Winckelmann, GCS 21: *hist eccl*
Plato, *Timaeus*, ed. Rivaud, Paris 1956: *Tim*
Plotinus, *Enneades*, edd. Henry/Schwyzer, 3 vols., Oxford 1964–82: *Enn*
Porphyry, *Fragmenta*, ed. Smith, Leipzig 1993: *fr*
————, *Sententiae ad intelligibilia ducentes*, ed. Lamberz, Leipzig 1975: *sent*
————, *Isagoge sive quinque voces*, ed. Busse, CAG IV/1, 1–22: *Isagoge*
————, *In Aristotelis Categorias expositio per interrogationem et responsionem*, ed. Busse, CAG IV/1, 55–142: *in Cat*
————, *Vita Plotini*, edd. Henry/Schwyzer, *Plotini Opera*, vol. I, 1–38: *vit Plot*
————, *Fragmenta in Platonis Timaeum*, ed. Sodano, Naples 1964: *in Tim*
————, *De abstinentia*, ed. Bouffartigue, 3 vols., Paris 1977ff.: *abst*
Proclus, *In Platonis Timaeum*, 3 vols., ed. Diehl, Leipzig 1903–1906: *in Tim*
Simplicius, *In Aristotelis Categorias*, ed. Kalbfleisch, CAG VIII: *in Cat*
Simplicius (?), *In Aristotelis De Anima*, ed. Hayduck, CAG XI: *in d An*
Socrates, *Historia Ecclesiastica*, ed. Hansen, GCS, n.F. 1: *hist eccl*
Sozomen, *Historia Ecclesiastica*, ed. Bidez/Hansen, GCS 50: *hist eccl*
Stoicorum Veterum Fragmenta, ed. v. Arnim, 4 vols., Leipzig 1903–1924: SVF
Themistius, *In libris Aristotelis De Anima paraphrasis*, ed. Heinze, CAG V/3: *in d An*
(ps.)-Themistius, *Anonymi Paraphrasis Themistiana*, ed. Minio-Paluello, *Aristoteles Latinus* I 1–5, Bruges/Paris, 129–75: *paraphr Themist*
Theodoretus, *Interpretatio in I epistulam ad Corinthos*, ed. Minge, PG 82, 225–376

2. *Modern authors*

Abramowski, L. (1966), 'Eunomius' in: *RAC* 6, 936–47
——— (1979), 'Theologische und Christologische Hypostasenformeln' in: *ThPh* 54 (1979), 38–49
——— (1982), 'Dionys von Rom († 268) und Dionys von Alexandrien († 264/5) in den arianischen Streitigkeiten des 4. Jahrhunderts' in: *ZKG* 93 (1982), 240–72
Ackrill, J.L. (1963), *Aristotle's* Categories *and* De Interpretatione. *Translated with Notes*, Oxford 1963
Alt, K. (1993), *Weltflucht und Weltbejahung. Zur Frage des Dualismus bei Plutarch, Numenios, Plotin*, Mainz 1993 (AAWLM.G)
Altenburger, M., Mann, F. (1988), *Bibliographie zu Gregor von Nyssa*, Leiden 1988
Andresen, C. (1961), 'Zur Entstehung und Geschichte des trinitarischen Personbegriffes' in: *ZNW* 52 (1961), 1–39
Armstrong, A.H. (1948), 'Platonic Elements in Gregory of Nyssa's Doctrine of Man' in: *DomSt* 1 (1948), 113–26
——— (1954), 'The Plotinian Doctrine of ΝΟΥΣ in Patristic Theology' in: *VigChr* 8 (1954), 234–238
——— (1962), 'The Theory of the Non-Existence of Matter in Plotinus and the Cappadocians' in: *StPatr* 5 (1962), 427–429 (= id., *Plotinian and Christian Studies*, London 1979)
——— (1966), *Plotinus. With an English Translation*, 7 vols., London/New York, 1966–88 (LCL)
Aubineau, M. (1959), 'Le Thème du "Bourbier" dans la littérature grecque profane et chrétienne' in: *RSR* 47 (1959), 185–214
——— (1966), *Grégoire de Nysse. Traité de la Virginité. Introduction, Texte Critique, Traduction et Index*, Paris 1966 (SC 119)
Balás, D.L. (1966), ΜΕΤΟΥΣΙΑ ΘΕΟΥ. *Man's Participation in God's Perfections according to Saint Gregory of Nyssa*, Rome 1966 (StAns 55)
——— (1969), 'Participation in the Specific Nature according to Gregory of Nyssa: Aristotelian Logic or Platonic Ontology?' in: *Arts Libéraux et Philosophie au Moyen Age, Actes du Quatrième Congrès International de Philosophie Mediévale, Montreal Canada, 27 août–2 septembre, 1967*, Paris 1969, 1079–85
——— (1976), 'The Unity of Human Nature in Basil's and Gregory of Nyssa's Polemics against Eunomius' in: *StPatr* XIV (= TU 117), Berlin 1976, 275–281
——— (1979), '*Plenitudo humanitatis*. The Unity of Human Nature in the Theology of Gregory of Nyssa' in: *Disciplina Nostra. Essays in Memory of Robert F. Evans*, ed. Donald F. Winslow, Cambridge (Mass.) 1979, 115–131 (PatMS 6)
——— (1985), 'Gregor von Nyssa' in: *TRE* 14, 173–81
Balthasar, H.Urs von (1995), *Présence et Pensée: essay sur la philosophie religieuse de Grégoire de Nysse*, Paris 1942 (ET: *Presence and Thought*, 1995)
Bammel, C.P. (1989), 'Adam in Origen' in: R.Williams (ed.), *The Making of Orthodoxy: Essays in Homour of Henry Chadwick*, Cambridge 1989, 62–93 = Bammel (1995), N° XII
——— (1995), *Tradition and Exegesis in Early Christian Writers*, London 1995 (Variorum)
Barnes, M.R. (1985), 'Δύναμις and the Anti-Monistic Ontology of Nyssens' *Contra Eunomium*' in: Gregg (1985), 327–34
———, Williams, D.H. (1993), *Arianism after Arius. Essays on the Development of the Fourth Century Trinitarian Conflict*, Edinburgh 1993
Bates, W.H. (1961), 'The Background of Apollinaris's Eucharistic Teaching' in: *JEH* 11 (1961), 139–54
Bethune-Baker, J.F. (1901), *The Meaning of* Homoousios *in the 'Constantinopolitan' Creed*, Cambridge 1901 (TaS 7/1)

———— (1929), *An Introduction to the Early History of Christian Doctrine to the Time of the Council of Chalcedon*, London ⁴1929

Bianchi, U. (1978), 'Presupposti platonici e dualistici nell' antropogonia di Gregorio di Nissa' in: id. (ed.), *La 'doppia creazione' dell'uomo negli Alessandrini, nei Cappadoci e nella gnosi*, Rome 1978, 83–115

Bigg, C. (1913), *The Christian Platonists of Alexandria. The 1886 Bampton Lectures*, Oxford 1913

Blank, D.L. (1995), *Ammonius. On Aristotle on Interpretation 1–8. Translated*, London 1995

Brennecke, H.Chr. (1984), *Hilarius von Poitiers und die Bischofsopposition gegen Konstantius II. Untersuchungen zur dritten Phase des arianischen Streites (337–361)*, Berlin/New York 1984 (PTS 26)

———— (1984ᵃ), 'Zum Prozeß gegen Paul von Samosata: Die Frage nach der Verurteilung des Homoousios' in: *ZNW* 75 (1984), 270–90

———— (1988), *Studien zur Geschichte der Homöer*, Tübingen 1988 (BHTh 73)

———— (1989), 'Erwägungen zu den Anfängen des Neunizänismus' in: Bienert, W., Papandreou, D., Schäferdieck, K. (eds.), *Oecumenica et Patristica: Festschrift für Wilhelm Schneemelcher zum 75. Geburtstag*, Chambisy-Geneva 1989, 241–57

Bury, R.G., *Sextus Empiricus. With an English Translation*, 4 vols., London/ Cambridge Mass. 1933–49 (LCL)

Butterworth, G.W., *Origen. On First Principles. Being Koetschau's text of the* De Principiis *Translated into English, Together with an Introduction and Notes*, Gloucester, Mass. 1973

Cattaneo, E. (1981), *Trois homélies pseudo-Chrysostomiennes sur la Pâque comme œuvre d'Apollinaire de Laodicée*, Paris 1981 (ThH 58)

Cavallin, A. (1944), *Studien zu den Briefen des hl. Basilius*, Lund 1944

Chadwick, H. (1953), *Origen*: Contra Celsum. *Translated with an Introduction and Notes*, Cambridge 1953

———— (1966), *Early Christian Thought and the Classical Tradition. Studies in Justin, Clement, and Origen*, Oxford 1966

Cherniss, H. (1930), 'The Platonism of Gregory of Nyssa' in: *UCPCP* XI (1930), 1–92

Clark, E.A. (1992), *The Origenist Controversy*, Princeton 1992

Colson, F.H., Whitaker, G.H. (1929), *Philo. With an English Translation*, 10 vols., London/New York 1929–62 (LCL)

Corsini, E. (1957), 'Nouvelles perspectives sur le problème des sources de l'Hexaëméron de Grégoire de Nysse' in: *StPatr* 1 (1957), 94–103

———— (1971), 'Plérôme humain et plérôme cosmique chez Grégoire de Nysse' in: Harl (1971), 111–26

Courcelle, P. (1967), 'Grégoire de Nysse. Lecteur de Porphyre' in: *REG* 80 (1967), 402–6

Cowper, R. (1861), *Syriac Miscellanies*, London 1861

Daniélou, J. (1953), 'Akolouthia chez Grégoire de Nysse' in: *RevSR* 27 (1953), 219–49

———— (1955), 'La chronologie des sermons de Grégoire de Nysse' in: *RevSR* 29 (1955), 346–72

———— (1958), 'L'état du Christ dans la mort d'après Grégoire de Nysse' in: *HJ* 77 (1958), 63–72

———— (1966), 'La chronologie des œuvres de Grégoire de Nysse' in: *StPatr* 7 (1966), 159–69

———— (1967), 'Philon et Grégoire de Nysse' in: *Philon d'Alexandrie. Lyon 11–15–Septembre 1966: colloques nationaux du Centre National de la Recherche Scientifique*, Paris 1967, 333–45

———— (1970), *L'être et le temps chez Grégoire de Nysse*, Leiden 1970

Devreesse, R. (1959), *Les ancien commentateurs grecs de l'Octateuque et des Rois (fragments tirés des chaînes)*, Vatican City 1959 (StT 201)

Dinsen, F. (1976), *Homoousios: Die Geschichte des Begriffs bis zum Konzil von Konstantinopel (381)*, D.Phil. dissertation (unpublished), Kiel 1976

Dooley, W.I. (1993), *Alexander of Aphrodisias. On Aristotle, Metaphysics 5. Translated*, London 1993

Dörrie, H. (1955), 'Ὑπόστασις, Wort- und Bedeutungsgeschichte' in: *NGWG.PH* 1955, 35–92

———, Altenberger, M., Schramm, U. (eds.) (1976), *Gregor von Nyssa und die Philosophie*, Leiden 1976

——— (1976ᵃ), 'Gregors Theologie auf dem Hintergrunde der Neuplatonischen Metaphysik' in: Dörrie (1976), 21–39

——— (1983), 'Gregor von Nyssa' in: *RAC* 12, 863–95

Dörries, H. (1956), *De Spiritu Sancto. Der Beitrag des Basilius zum Abschluß des trinitarischen Dogmas*, Göttingen 1956 (AAWG.PH 39)

Dorner, J.A. (1862), *History of the Development of the Doctrine of the Person of Christ. Division First. First Four Centuries*, vol. II, Edinburgh 1862

Drecoll, V.H. (1996), *Die Entwicklung der Trinitätslehre des Basilius von Cäsarea: Sein Weg vom Homöusianer zum Neunizäner*, Göttingen 1996 (FKDG 66)

Dünzl, F. (1993), 'Die Canticum-Exegese des Gregor von Nyssa und des Origenes im Vergleich' in: *JAC* 36 (1993), 94–109

——— (1994), 'Formen der Kirchenväter-Rezeption am Beispiel der sogenannten physischen Erlösungslehre des Gregor von Nyssa' in *ThPh* 69 (1994), 161–81

——— (1994ᵃ), *Gregor von Nyssa. In Canticum Canticorum Homiliae. Homilien zum Hohenlied. Griechisch-Deutsch. Übersetzt und eingeleitet*, 3 vols. Freiburg 1994

Fedwick, P.W. (1978), 'A Commentary of Gregory of Nyssa or the 38ᵗʰ Letter of Basil of Caesarea' in: *OCP* 44 (1978), 31–51

Frede, M. (1978), 'Individuen bei Aristoteles' in: *AuA* 24 (1978), 16–39

——— (1987), *Essays in Ancient Philosophy*, Minneapolis 1987

——— (1987ᵃ), 'Substance in Aristotle's Metaphysics' in: Frede (1987), 72–80

——— (1987ᵇ), 'The Origins of Traditional Grammar' in: Frede (1987), 338–59

——— (1997), 'Der Begriff des Individuums bei den Kirchenvätern' in: *JAC* 40 (1997), 38–54

Fremantle, W.H. (1893), *The Principal Works of Jerome. Translated*, Oxford/New York 1893 (NPNF, Second Series, vol. VI)

Früchtel, U. (1968), *Die kosmologischen Vorstellungen bei Philo von Alexandrien. Ein Beitrag zur Geschichte der Genesisexegese*, Leiden 1968

Geyer, B. (ed.) (1919), *Peter Abaelards Philosophische Schriften*, I.1, Münster 1919 (BGPhMA XXI,1)

Graef, H.C. (1954), *St. Gregory of Nyssa. The Lord's Prayer. The Beatitudes. Translated and Annotated*, Westminster/London 1954 (ACW 18)

Graeser, A. (1983), 'Aspekte der Ontologie in der Kategorienschrift' in: P. Moraux/ J. Wiesner (eds.), *Zweifelhaftes im Corpus Aristotelicum*, Berlin/New York 1983, 30–56

Gregg, R.C. (ed.) (1985), *Arianism. Historical and Theological Reassessment*, Philadelphia 1985 (PatMS 11)

Gregorios, P., *Cosmic Man. The Divine Presence*, New Dehli 1980

Grillmeier, A. (1975), *Christ in Christian Tradition*, London ²1975

Gronau, K. (1914), *Poseidonius und die jüdisch-christliche Genesisexegese*, Berlin-Leipzig 1914

Gummerus, J. (1900), *Die homöusianische Partei bis zum Tode des Konstantius*, Leipzig 1900

Gwatkin, H.M. (1900), *Studies of Arianism*, Cambridge ²1900

Haers, J.R.H. (1992), *Creation Theology in Origen*, D.Phil. dissertation (unpublished), Oxford 1992

Hahn, A. (1897), *Bibliothek der Symbole und Glaubensregeln der Alten Kirche*, Breslau ³1897

Hall, S.G. (1981), 'On the Three-Day Period' in: Spira/Klock (1981), 31–50

——— (1988), 'Gregory Bishop of Nyssa. A refutation of the first book of the two published by Eunomius after the decease of holy Basil' in: Mateo-Seco (1988), 35–135

——— (ed.) (1993), *Gregory of Nyssa. Homilies on Ecclesiastes. An English Version with Supporting Studies*, Berlin/New York 1993

———/Moriarty, R. (1993), 'Gregory, Bishop of Nyssa: Homilies on Ecclesiastes. Translation' in: Hall (1993), 31–144

Hammerstaedt, J. (1991), 'Zur Echtheit von Basiliusbrief 38' in: E. Dassmann (ed.), *Tesserae. Festschrift für J.Endemann*, Münster 1991 (JAC.E 18), 416–9

——— (1994), 'Hypostasis' in: *RAC* 16, 986–1035

Hanson, R.P.C. (1988), *The Search for the Christian Doctrine of God*, Edinburgh 1988

Harl, M. (ed.) (1971), *Écriture et culture philosophique dans la pensée de Grégoire de Nysse*, Leiden 1971

Harnack, A. von (1894), *History of Dogma* (ET: N. Buchanan et alii), 6 vols., 1894–99

Hauke, M. (1993), *Heilsverlust in Adam. Stationen griechischer Erbsündenlehre: Irenäus-Origenes-Kappadozier*, Paderborn 1993

Hauschild, W.-D. (1967), *Die Pneumatomachen*, D.Phil. dissertation (unpublished), Hamburg 1967

——— (1970), 'Die antinizänische Synodalaktensammlung des Sabinus von Herakles' in: *VigChr* 24 (1970), 105–26

——— (1973), *Basilius von Cäsarea, Briefe. Eingeleitet, übersetzt und erläutert*, Stuttgart 1973–93 (BGrL 3, 32, 37)

Heine, R.E. (1995), *Gregory of Nyssa's Treatise on the Inscriptions of the Psalms*, Oxford 1995

Holl, K. (1904), *Amphilochius von Ikonium in seinem Verhältnis zu den großen Kappadoziern*, Tübingen/Leipzig 1904

Hübner, R.M. (1971), 'Gregor von Nyssa und Markell von Ankyra' in: Harl (1971), 199–229

——— (1972), 'Gregor von Nyssa als Verfasser der sog. ep. 38 des Basilius' in: J. Fontaine, Ch. Kannengiesser (eds.), *Epektasis. Mélanges patristiques offerts au Cardinal Jean Daniélou*, Paris 1972, 463–90

——— (1974), *Die Einheit des Leibes Christi bei Gregor von Nyssa. Untersuchungen zum Ursprung der 'physischen' Erlösungslehre*, Leiden 1974

——— (1989), *Die Schrift des Apolinarius von Laodicea gegen Photin (Pseudo-Athanasius, contra Sabellianos) und Basilius von Caesarea*, Berlin/New York 1989 (PTS 30)

——— (1993), 'Basilius von Cäsarea und das Homoousios' in: Wickham/Bammel (1993), 70–91

Jaeger, W. (1914), *Nemesius von Emesa: Quellenforschung zum Neuplatonismus und seinen Anfängen bei Poseidonius*, Berlin 1914

——— (1954), *Two Rediscovered Works of Ancient Christian Literature Gregory of Nyssa and Macarius*, Leiden 1954

——— (1966), *Gregor von Nyssa's Lehre vom Heiligen Geist* (ed. H. Dörries), Leiden 1966

Kees, R.J. (1995), *Die Lehre von der Oikonomia Gottes in der Oratio Catechetica des Gregor von Nyssa*, Leiden 1995 (SVigChr 30)

Kelly, J.N.D. (1958), *Early Christian Doctrines*, London 1958

——— (1972), *Early Christian Creeds*, ³London 1972

——— (1975), *Jerome. His Life, Writings, and Controversies*, London 1975

Kopecek, Th.A. (1979), *A History of Neo-Arianism*, 2 vols., Cambridge, Mass. 1979 (PatMS 8)

Krämer, H.J. (1973), 'Aristoteles und die akademische Eidoslehre. Zur Geschichte des Universalienproblems im Platonismus' in: *AGP* 55 (1973), 119–90

Kraft, H. (1954), 'ΟΜΟΟΥΣΙΟΣ' in: *ZKG* 66 (1954/55), 1–24

Ladner, G.B. (1958) 'The Philosophical Anthropology of Saint Gregory of Nyssa' in: *DOP* 12 (1958), 59–94

Laplace, J. (1944), *Grégoire de Nysse. La création de l'homme. Introduction et traduction.* Notes de Jean Daniélou, Paris-Lyon 1944 (SC 6)

Lebon, J. (1952/1953), 'Le sort du "consubstantiel" nicéen' in: *RHE* 47 (1952), 485–529, 48 (1953), 632–82 (quotations are given the year of the part from which they are taken)

Lebourlier, J. (1962/1963), 'A propos l'état de Christ dans la mort' in: *RSPhTh* 46 (1962), 629–49, 47 (1963), 161–80 (quotations are given the year of the part from which they are taken)

Leisegang, H., 'Physis' in: RE XX/1, 129–64

Leÿs, R. (1951), *L'image de Dieu chez Grégoire de Nysse. Esquisse d'une doctrine,* Brussels 1951

Lietzmann, H. (1904), *Apollinaris von Laodicea und seine Schule,* Tübingen 1904

——— (1950), *From Constantine to Julian (A History of the Early Church,* vol. III; ET: B.L. Woolf), London 1950

Lloyd, A.C. (1955), 'Aristotelian Logic and Neoplatonic Logic' in *Phronesis* 1 (1955), 58–79, 146–60

——— (1970), 'Aristotle's Principle of Individuation' in: *Mind* 79 (1970), 519–29

——— (1990), *The Anatomy of Neoplatonism,* Oxford 1990

Löhr, W.A. (1993), 'A Sense of Tradition. The Homoiousian Church Party' in: Barnes (1993), 81–100

Loofs, F. (1922), 'Das Nicänum' in: O. Scheel (ed.), *Festgabe für K. Müller,* Tübingen 1922, 62–82

——— (1924), *Paulus von Samosata,* Leipzig 1924 (TU 44)

——— (1950), *Leitfaden zum Studium der Dogmengeschichte,* 2 vols. (ed. K. Aland), Halle (Saale) 1950–3

Lorenz, R. (1980), 'Die Eustathius von Antiochien zugeschriebene Schrift gegen Photin' in: *ZNW* 71 (1980), 109–128

——— (1982), 'Eustathius von Antiochien' in: *TRE* 10, 543–6

Ludlow, M.A. (1996), *Restoration and Consummation: The Interpretation of Universalistic Eschatology by Gregory of Nyssa and Karl Rahner,* D.Phil. dissertation (unpublished), Oxford 1996

Mai, A. (1852), *Patrum Nova Bibliotheca,* 10 vols., Rome 1852–1910

Maraval, P. (1987), 'La lettre 3 de Grégoire de Nysse dans le débat christologique' in: *RevSR* 61 (1987), 74–89

——— (1990), *Grégoire de Nysse. Lettres. Introduction, Texte Critique, Traduction, Notes et Index,* Paris 1990 (SC 363)

Mateo-Seco, L.F., Bastero, J.L. (eds.) (1988), *El 'Contra Eunomium I' en la producción literaria de Gregorio de Nisa,* Navarra 1988

May, G. (1966), 'Gregor von Nyssa in der Kirchenpolitik seiner Zeit' in: *JÖBG* 15 (1966), 105–132

——— (1971), 'Die Chronologie des Lebens und der Werke des Gregor von Nyssa' in: Harl (1971), 51–66

——— (1978), *Schöpfung aus dem Nichts: Die Entstehung der Lehre von der creatio ex nihilo,* Berlin/New York 1978 (AKG 48)

McCarthy Spoerl, K. (1993), 'The Antiochene Schism since Cavallera' in: Barnes (1993), 101–26

Meijering, E.P. (1975), *God Being History,* Amsterdam 1975

Meredith, A. (1972), *Studies in the Contra Eunomium of Gregory of Nyssa,* D.Phil. dissertation (unpublished), Oxford 1972

——— (1988) 'The divine simplicity: Contra Eunomium I 223–241' in: Mateo-Seco (1988), 339–51.

——— (1991) 'Plato's 'cave' (*Republic* vii 514a–517e) in Origen, Plotinus, and Gregory of Nyssa' in: *StPatr* 27 (1991), 49–61

——— (1995), *The Cappadocians,* London 1995

Moore, W., Wilson, H.-A. (eds.) (1893), *Select Writings and Letters of Gregory, Bishop of Nyssa. Translated, with Prolegomena, Notes and Indices*, New York/Oxford/London 1893 (NPNF. Second Series, vol. V)

Moraux, P. (1973), *Der Aristotelismus bei den Griechen*, 2 vols., Berlin/New York 1973ff.

Mosshammer, A.A. (1988), 'The Created and the Uncreated in Gregory of Nyssa' in: Mateo-Seco (1988), 353–79

———— (1990), 'Non-Being as Evil in Gregory of Nyssa' in: *VigChr* 44 (1990), 136–67

Mühlenberg, E. (1966), *Die Unendlichkeit Gottes bei Gregor von Nyssa. Gregors Kritik am Gottesbegriff der klassischen Metaphysik*, Göttingen 1966 (FKDG 16)

———— (1968), *Apollinaris von Laodicea*, Göttingen 1968 (FKDG 23)

———— (1975), *Psalmenkommentare aus der Katenenüberlieferung*, 3 vols., Berlin/New York 1975ff. (PTS 15, 16, 19)

———— (1977), 'Synergism in Gregory of Nyssa' in: *ZNW* 68 (1977), 93–122

———— (1978), 'Apollinaris von Laodiaea' in: *TRE* 3, 362–71

Norris, R.A. (1963), *Manhood and Christ. A Study in the Christology of Theodore of Mopsuestia*, Oxford 1963

Oesterle, H.-J. (1985), 'Probleme der Anthropologie bei Gregor von Nyssa. Zur Interpretation seiner Schrift "De hominis opificio"' in: *Hermes* 113 (1985), 101–14

Otis, B. (1958), 'Cappadocian Thought as a Coherent System' in: *DOP* 12 (1958), 97–124

———— (1976), 'Gregory of Nyssa and the Cappadocian Concept of Time' in: *StPatr* XIV.3 (1976), 327–357

Prestige, G.L. (1936), *God in Patristic Thought*, London/Toronto 1936

———— (1956), *St. Basil the Great and Apollinaris of Laodicea* (ed. H. Chadwick), London 1956

Quasten, J. (1960), *Patrology*, vol. III: *The Golden Age of Greek Patristic Literature. From the Council of Nicaea to the Council of Chalcedon*, Utrecht/Antwerp 1960

Raven, C.E. (1923), *Apollinarianism. An Essay on the Christology of the Early Church*, Cambridge 1923

Reuss, J. (1957), *Matthäuskommentare aus der griechischen Kirche. Aus Katenenhandschriften gesammelt und herausgegeben*, Berlin 1956 (TU 61)

———— (1966), *Johannes-Kommentare aus der Griechischen Kirche. Aus Katenenhandschriften gesammelt und herausgegeben*, Berlin 1966 (TU 89)

Richard, M. (1945), 'L'introduction du mot "hypostase" dans la théologie de l'Incarnation' in *MSR* 2 (1945), 5–32, 243–70

Ricken, F. (1969), 'Nikaia als Krise des altkirchlichen Platonismus' in: *ThPh* 44 (1969), 321–41

Riedmatten, H. de (1948), 'Some neglected aspects of Apollinarist Christology' in: *DomSt* 1 (1948), 239–60

———— (1956), 'La correspondance entre Basile de Césarée et Apollinaire de Laodicée' in: *JTS* 7 (1956), 199–210; 8 (1957), 53–70

———— (1957), 'La Christologie d'Apollinaire de Laodicée' in *StPatr* 2 (1957), 208–34

Risch, F.X. (1992), *Pseudo-Basilius. Adversus Eunomium IV–V. Einleitung, Übersetzung und Kommentar*, Leiden 1992 (SVigChr 16)

Rist, J.M. (1967), *Plotinus: The Road to Reality*, Cambridge (1967)

———— (1971), 'Categories and their Uses' in: A.A. Long (ed.), *Problems in Stoicism*, London 1971, 38–57

———— (1981), 'Basil's "Neoplatonism". Its Background and Nature' in: J.P. Fedwick (ed.), *Basil of Caesarea. Christian, Humanist, Ascetic*, Toronto 1981, vol. I, 137–220

Ritter, A.M. (1965), *Das Konzil von Konstantinopel und sein Symbol. Studien zur Geschichte und Theologie des 2. Ökumenischen Konzils*, Göttingen 1965 (FKDG 15)

Roeder, J.-A. (1993), *Gregor von Nyssa, Contra Eunomium* I, 1–146, eingeleitet, übersetzt und kommentiert, Frankfurt 1993

Ross, W.D. (ed.) (1928), *The Works of Aristotle Translated into English*, vol. VIII, *Metaphysica*, Oxford ²1928

Rousseau, Ph. (1994), *Basil of Caesarea*, Berkeley (. . .) 1994
Runia, D.T. (1986), *Philo of Alexandria and the* Timaeus *of Plato*, Leiden 1986 (PhAnt 44)
Schoemann, J.B. (1943), 'Gregor von Nyssa's Anthropologie als Bildtheologie' in: *Scholastik* 18 (1943), 31–53; 175–200
Schwartz, E. (1904), 'Zur Geschichte des Athanasius' in: *NGWG.PH* 1904, 333–401 = Schwartz (1938), vol. IV, 1–85
——— (1925), 'Der sog. Sermo maior de fide des Athanasius' in: *SBAW.PH* 1924, 6, Munich 1925
——— (1935), 'Zur Kirchengeschichtsschreibung des vierten Jahrhunderts' in: *ZNW* 34 (1935), 129–213 = Schwartz (1938), vol. IV, 1–110
——— (1938), *Gesammelte Schriften*, 4 vols., Berlin 1938–1960
Sellers, R.V. (1928), *Eustathius of Antioch and his Place in the Early History of Christian Doctrine*, Cambridge 1928
——— (1940), *Two Ancient Christologies*, London 1940 (repr. 1954)
Sharples, R.W. (1992), *Alexander of Aphrodisias. Quaestiones 1.1–2.15. Translated*, London 1992
Simonetti, M. (1973), 'Su alcune opere attribuite di recente a Marcello d'Ancira' in: *Rivista di Storia e Litteratura Religiosa* 9 (1973), 313–29
Skouteris, K.V. (Σκουτερης, K.B.) (1969), Ἡ ἑνότης τῆς ἀνθρωπίνης φύσεως ὡς πραγματικὴ προυπόθεσις τῆς σωτηρίας. Ἐκ τῆς ἀνθρωπολογίας τοῦ ἁγίου Γρηγορίου Νύσσης, Athens 1969
Spanneut, M. (1948), Recherches sur les écrits d'Eustathe d'Antioche, Lille 1948
——— (1954), 'La position théologique d'Eustathe d'Antioche' in: *JTS* 5 (1954), 220–4
——— (1967), 'Eustathe d'Antioche' in: *DHGE* 16, 13–23
Spira, A./Klock, C. (eds.) (1981), *The Easter Sermons of Gregory of Nyssa. Proceedings of the Fourth International Colloquium on Gregory of Nyssa*, Philadelphia 1981 (PatMS 9)
Sorabji, R. (1983), *Time, Creation and the Continuum*, London 1983
——— (1988), *Matter, Space and Motion*, Ithaca New York 1988
Srawley, J.H. (1903), *The Catechetical Oration of Gregory of Nyssa*, Cambridge 1903
Staab, K. (1933), *Pauluskommentare aus der griechischen Kirche*, Münster 1933 (NTA 15)
Stead, G.C. (1961), 'The Significance of the *Homoousios*' in: *StudPatr* 3 (1961), 397–412 = Stead (1985), No. I
——— (1974), '"Homoousios" dans la pensée de Saint Athanase' in: C. Kannengiesser (ed.), *Politique et théologie chez Athanase d'Alexandrie*, Paris 1974, 231–53
——— (1976), 'Ontology and Terminology in Gregory of Nyssa' in: Dörrie (1976), 107–119 = Stead (1985), No. IX
——— (1977), *Divine Substance*, Oxford 1977
——— (1985), *Substance and Illusion in the Christian Fathers*, London 1985 (Variorum)
——— (1990), 'Why Not Three Gods?' in: H.R. Drobner/Chr. Klock (eds.), *Studien zu Gregor von Nyssa und der christlichen Spätantike*, Leiden 1990 (SVigChr 12), 149–63
——— (1994), 'Homousios' in: *RAC* 16, 364–433
Steenson, J.N. (1983), *Basil of Ancyra and the Course of Nicene Orthodoxy*, D.Phil. dissertation (unpublished), Oxford 1983
——— (1985), 'Basil of Ancyra on the Meaning of Homoousios' in: Gregg (1985), 267–79
Strange, S.K. (1992), *Porphyry. On Aristotle's Categories*, London 1992 (English translation with introduction and notes)
Tennant, F.R. (1903), *The Sources of the Doctrine of the Fall and Original Sin*, Cambridge 1903
Tetz, M. (1964), 'Zur Theologie des Markell von Ankyra I. Eine Markellische Schrift "De incarnatione et contra Arianos"' in: *ZKG* 75 (1964), 217–70
Tobin, T.H. (1983), *The Creation of Man: Philo and the History of Interpretation*, Washington 1983 (CBQ.MS 14)

Ulrich, J. (1994), *Die Anfänge der abendländischen Rezeption des Nizänums*, Berlin/New York 1994 (PTS 39)

Urmson, J.O./Lautner, P. (1995), *Simplicius*. On Aristotle, On the Soul 1.1–2.4, London 1995 (English translation with introduction and notes)

Uthemann, K.-H. (1993), 'Die Sprache der Theologie nach Eunomius von Cyzicus' in: *ZKG* 104 (1993), 143–75

Vaggione, R.P. (1987), *Eunomius. The Extant Work*, Oxford 1987

Verghese, T.P. (1976), 'Διάστημα and διάστασις in Gregory of Nyssa. Introduction to a Concept and the Posing of a Problem' in: Dörrie (1976), 243–58

Walther, G. (1914), *Untersuchungen zur Geschichte der griechischen Vaterunser-Exegese*, Leipzig 1914 (TU 40,3)

Wickham, L.R. (1968), 'The *Syntagmation* of Aetius the Anomean' in: *JTS* 19 (1968), 532–69

———— (1969), 'The Date of Eunomius' *Apology*: A Reconsideration' in: *JTS* 20 (1969), 231–40

———— (1981), 'Soul and Body. Christ's Omnipresence (De Tridui Spatio 290, 18–294,13)' in: Spira/Klock (1981), 279–92

———— (1990), 'Translation Techniques Greek/Syriac and Syriac/English' in: *V Symposium Syriacum. 1988*, Rome 1990 (OCA 236), 345–53

————/Bammel, C.P. (eds.) (1993), *Christian Faith and Greek Philosophy in Late Antiquity. Essays in Tribute to George Christopher Stead*, Leiden 1993 (SVigChr 19)

Widdicombe, P. (1994), *The Fatherhood of God from Origen to Athanasius*, Oxford 1994

Williams, N.P. (1929), *The Ideas of the Fall and of Original Sin. A Historical and Critical Study*, London (. . .) 1929

Williams, R.D. (1983), 'The Logic of Arianism' in: *JTS* 34 (1983), 56–81

———— (1993), 'Macrina's Deathbed Revisited: Gregory of Nyssa on Mind and Passion' in: Wickham/Bammel (1993), 227–46

Winden, J.C.M. van (1988), 'Hexaemeron' in: *RAC* 14, 1250–69

———— (1991), 'Notiz über ΔΥΝΑΜΙΣ bei Gregor von Nyssa' in: *EPMHNEYMATA. Festschrift für Hadwig Hörner zum sechzigsten Geburtstag*, Frankfurt 1991, 147–50 (= id., *Arché. A Collection of Patristic Studies*, Leiden 1997 [SVigChr 41], 146–50)

Winling, R. (1989), 'La résurrection comme principe explicatif et comme élément structurant dans le Discour catéchetique de Grégoire de Nysse' in: *StPatr* 22 (1989), 74–80

Wolfson, H.A. (1947), *Philo, Foundations of Religious Philosophy in Judaism, Christianity and Islam*, 2 vols., Cambridge, Mass. 1947

———— (1970), 'The Identification of *ex nihilo* with Emanation in Gregory of Nyssa' in: *HThR* 63 (1970), 53–60

Woods Callahan, V. (1967), *Saint Gregory of Nyssa. Ascetical Works. Translated*, Washington 1967 (FaCh 58)

Zahn, Th. (1867), *Marcellus von Ancyra*, Gotha 1867

Zgusta, L. (1984), *Kleinasiatische Ortsnamen*, Heidelberg 1984

INDEX OF BIBLICAL REFERENCES

INDEX OF ANCIENT AUTHORS

INDEX OF MODERN AUTHORS

GENERAL INDEX

SUPPLEMENTS TO VIGILIAE CHRISTIANAE

1. Tertullianus. *De idololatria.* Critical Text, Translation and Commentary by J.H. Waszink and J.C.M. van Winden. Partly based on a Manuscript left behind by P.G. van der Nat. 1987. ISBN 90 04 08105 4

2. Springer, C.P.E. *The Gospel as Epic in Late Antiquity.* The *Paschale Carmen* of Sedulius. 1988. ISBN 90 04 08691 9

3. Hoek, A. van den. *Clement of Alexandria and His Use of Philo in the* Stromateis. An Early Christian Reshaping of a Jewish Model. 1988.
ISBN 90 04 08756 7

4. Neymeyr, U. *Die christlichen Lehrer im zweiten Jahrhundert.* Ihre Lehrtätigkeit, ihr Selbstverständnis und ihre Geschichte. 1989.
ISBN 90 04 08773 7

5. Hellemo, G. *Adventus Domini.* Eschatological Thought in 4th-century Apses and Catecheses. 1989. ISBN 90 04 08836 9

6. Rufin von Aquileia. *De ieiunio* I, II. Zwei Predigten über das Fasten nach Basileios von Kaisareia. Ausgabe mit Einleitung, Übersetzung und Anmerkungen von H. Marti. 1989. ISBN 90 04 08897 0

7. Rouwhorst, G.A.M. *Les hymnes pascales d'Éphrem de Nisibe.* Analyse théologique et recherche sur l'évolution de la fête pascale chrétienne à Nisibe et à Édesse et dans quelques Églises voisines au quatrième siècle.
2 vols: I. Étude; II. Textes. 1989. ISBN 90 04 08839 3

8. Radice, R. and D.T. Runia. *Philo of Alexandria.* An Annotated Bibliography 1937–1986. In Collaboration with R.A. Bitter, N.G. Cohen, M. Mach, A.P. Runia, D. Satran and D.R. Schwartz. 1988. repr. 1992.
ISBN 90 04 08986 1

9. Gordon, B. *The Economic Problem in Biblical and Patristic Thought.* 1989.
ISBN 90 04 09048 7

10. Prosper of Aquitaine. *De Providentia Dei.* Text, Translation and Commentary by M. Marcovich. 1989. ISBN 90 04 09090 8

11. Jefford, C.N. *The Sayings of Jesus in the Teaching of the Twelve Apostles.* 1989.
ISBN 90 04 09127 0

12. Drobner, H.R. and Klock, Ch. *Studien zu Gregor von Nyssa und der christlichen Spätantike.* 1990. ISBN 90 04 09222 6

13. Norris, F.W. *Faith Gives Fullness to Reasoning.* The Five Theological Orations of Gregory Nazianzen. Introduction and Commentary by F.W. Norris and Translation by Lionel Wickham and Frederick Williams. 1990. ISBN 90 04 09253 6

14. Oort, J. van. *Jerusalem and Babylon.* A Study into Augustine's *City of God* and the Sources of his Doctrine of the Two Cities. 1991.
ISBN 90 04 09323 0

15. Lardet, P. *L'Apologie de Jérôme contre Rufin.* Un Commentaire. 1993.
ISBN 90 04 09457 1

16. Risch, F.X. *Pseudo-Basilius: Adversus Eunomium IV-V.* Einleitung, Übersetzung und Kommentar. 1992. ISBN 90 04 09558 6

17. Klijn, A.F.J. *Jewish-Christian Gospel Tradition*. 1992. ISBN 90 04 09453 9
18. Elanskaya, A.I. *The Literary Coptic Manuscri pts in the A.S. Pushkin State Fine Arts Museum in Moscow*. ISBN 90 04 09528 4
19. Wickham, L.R. and Bammel, C.P. (eds.). *Christian Faith and Greek Philosophy in Late Antiquity*. Essays in Tribute to George Christopher Stead. 1993. ISBN 90 04 09605 1
20. Asterius von Kappadokien. *Die theologischen Fragmente*. Einleitung, kritischer Text, Übersetzung und Kommentar von Markus Vinzent. 1993. ISBN 90 04 09841 0
21. Hennings, R. *Der Briefwechsel zwischen Augustinus und Hieronymus und ihr Streit um den Kanon des Alten Testaments und die Auslegung von Gal. 2,11-14*. 1994. ISBN 90 04 09840 2
22. Boeft, J. den & Hilhorst, A. (eds.). *Early Christian Poetry*. A Collection of Essays. 1993. ISBN 90 04 09939 5
23. McGuckin, J.A. *St. Cyril of Alexandria: The Christological Controversy*. Its History, Theology, and Texts. 1994. ISBN 90 04 09990 5
24. Reynolds, Ph.L. *Marriage in the Western Church*. The Christianization of Marriage during the Patristic and Early Medieval Periods. 1994. ISBN 90 04 10022 9
25. Petersen, W.L. *Tatian's Diatessaron*. Its Creation, Dissemination, Significance, and History in Scholarship. 1994. ISBN 90 04 09469 5
26. Grünbeck, E. *Christologische Schriftargumentation und Bildersprache*. Zum Konflikt zwischen Metapherninterpretation und dogmatischen Schriftbeweistraditionen in der patristischen Auslegung des 44. (45.) Psalms. 1994. ISBN 90 04 10021 0
27. Haykin, M.A.G. *The Spirit of God*. The Exegesis of 1 and 2 Corinthians in the Pneumatomachian Controversy of the Fourth Century. 1994. ISBN 90 04 09947 6
28. Benjamins, H.S. *Eingeordnete Freiheit*. Freiheit und Vorsehung bei Origenes. 1994. ISBN 90 04 10117 9
29. Smulders s.j., P. (tr. & comm.). *Hilary of Poitiers' Preface to his* Opus historicum. 1995. ISBN 90 04 10191 8
30. Kees, R.J. *Die Lehre von der* Oikonomia Gottes in der Oratio catechetica *Gregors von Nyssa*. 1995. ISBN 90 04 10200 0
31. Brent, A. *Hippolytus and the Roman Church in the Third Century*. Communities in Tension before the Emergence of a Monarch-Bishop. 1995. ISBN 90 04 10245 0
32. Runia, D.T. *Philo and the Church Fathers*. A Collection of Papers. 1995. ISBN 90 04 10355 4
33. De Coninck, A.D. *Seek to See Him*. Ascent and Vision Mysticism in the Gospel of Thomas. 1996. ISBN 90 04 10401 1
34. Clemens Alexandrinus. *Protrepticus*. Edidit M. Marcovich. 1995. ISBN 90 04 10449 6
35. Böhm, T. *Theoria – Unendlichkeit – Aufstieg*. Philosophische Implikationen zu *De vita Moysis* von Gregor von Nyssa. 1996. ISBN 90 04 10560 3

36. Vinzent, M. *Pseudo-Athanasius, Contra Arianos IV*. Eine Schrift gegen Asterius von Kappadokien, Eusebius von Cäsarea, Markell von Ankyra und Photin von Sirmium. 1996. ISBN 90 04 10686 3

37. Knipp, P.D.E. *'Christus Medicus' in der frühchristlichen Sarkophagskulptur*. Ikonographische Studien zur Sepulkralkunst des späten vierten Jahrhunderts. *In Preparation*.

38. Lössl, J. *Intellectus gratiae*. Die erkenntnistheoretische und hermeneutische Dimension der Gnadenlehre Augustins von Hippo. 1997. ISBN 90 04 10849 1

39. Markell von Ankyra. *Die Fragmente. Der Brief an Julius von Rom*. Herausgegeben, eingeleitet und übersetzt von Markus Vinzent. 1997. ISBN 90 04 10907 2

40. Merkt, A. *Maximus I. von Turin*. Die Verkündigung eines Bischofs der frühen Reichskirche im zeitgeschichtlichen, gesellschaftlichen und liturgischen Kontext. 1997. ISBN 90 04 10864 5

41. Winden, J.C.M. van. *Archè*. A Collection of Patristic Studies by J.C.M. van Winden. Edited by J. den Boeft and D.T. Runia. 1997. ISBN 90 04 10834 3

42. Stewart-Sykes, A. *The Lamb's High Feast*. Melito, *Peri Pascha* and the Quartodeciman Paschal Liturgy at Sardis. 1998. ISBN 90 04 11236 7

43. Karavites, P. *Evil, Freedom and the Road to Perfection in Clement of Alexandria*. 1999. ISBN 90 04 11238 3

44. Boeft, J. den and M.L. van Poll-van de Lisdonk (eds.). *The Impact of Scripture in Early Christianity*. 1999. ISBN 90 04 11143 3

45. Brent, A. *The Imperial Cult and the Development of Church Order*. Concepts and Images of Authority in Paganism and Early Christianity before the Age of Cyprian. 1999. ISBN 90 04 11420 3

46. Zachhuber, J. *Human Nature in Gregory of Nyssa*. Philosophical Background and Theological Significance. 1999. ISBN 90 04 11530 7

47. Lechner, Th. *Ignatius adversus Valentinianos?* Chronologische und theologiegeschichtliche Studien zu den Briefen des Ignatius von Antiochien. 1999. ISBN 90 04 11505 6

48. Greschat, K. *Apelles und Hermogenes*. Zwei theologische Lehrer des zweiten Jahrhunderts. 1999. ISBN 90 04 11549 8

49. Drobner, H.R. *Augustinus von Hippo*: Sermones ad populum. Überlieferung und Bestand - Bibliographie - Indices. 1999. ISBN 90 04 11451 3

50. Hübner, R.M. *Der paradox Eine*. Antignostischer Monarchianismus im zweiten Jahrhundert. Mit einen Beitrag von Markus Vinzent. 1999. ISBN 90 04 11576 5